Fractal Design Painter 4 Complete

KAREN SPERLING

First Edition—1996

Printed in the United States of America.

Library of Congress Cataloging-in-Publication Data
Sperling, Karen.
    Fractal Design Painter 4 complete / by Karen Sperling.
        pm.   cm.
    Includes index.
    ISBN 1-55828-482-6
    1. Computer graphics. 2. Fractal design painter. I. Title.
   T385.S665   1996
   006.6'869--dc20   96-19481
        CIP

10 9 8 7 6 5 4 3 2 1

MIS:Press books are available at special discounts for bulk purchases for sales promotions, premiums, fund-raising, or educational use. Special editions or book excerpts can also be created to specification.

For details contact: Special Sales Director
                         MIS:Press
                         a subsidiary of Henry Holt and Company, Inc.
                         115 West 18th Street
                         New York, New York 10011

Associate Publisher: Paul Farrell   **Managing Editor:** Cary Sullivan

Editor &Copy Editor: Judy Brief   **Technical Editor:** Bud Daumen

Production Editor: Maya Riddick

Dedication

To Herbert Katzin,
Thank you

Acknowledgments

I went to train someone to use Painter recently. The student, an Ancient Greek and Roman art scholar, is an art professor at a local college. He welcomed me into his studio, three of whose walls were lined with bookshelves containing thick volumes of art history. Covering the fourth wall were academic degrees and awards. We sat down at his computer, he opened a Painter file, and I was floored. There, looking back at me, was his name in three-dimensional hand-painted letters looking like my *Artistry* logo. This art scholar and professor had followed my tutorial and was using his new logo in a project.

Fractal Design Painter 4 Complete is my seventh Painter book, including the four Painter manuals I wrote, the *Companion* tutorial and *Painter 3 Complete*. And I've now written seven issues of *Artistry*, the newsletter.

I enjoy writing about Painter so much because of the artists who use it. I was thrilled to see that I was able to help this distinguished professor gain entry into the world of computer art. And I'm fascinated by the art that Painter pros create.

I'm especially proud to see this time around that artists featured in *Painter 4 Complete* used techniques that they discovered in *Painter 3 Complete*!

So the first thank you goes to Mark Zimmer for inventing Painter and giving everyone this amazing tool for creating art on the computer. And I appreciate Mark's always being available to answer my questions and show me cool Painter tricks, which also goes for John Derry, Fractal's Vice President, Creative Design.

Thanks, too, to Daryl Wise for keeping those beta copies flowing my way.

Thanks also go to the tech folks at Fractal who also are always there for me including Bud Daumen, who is this book's tech editor; Shawn Grunberger; Laurie Hemnes; Steve Rathmann; Michael Cinque; and Priscilla Shih. And thanks to Kim Hinrichsen, who helps me get through to everybody!

At the publishing end, thanks go to the MIS: Press gang, including Managing Editor, Cary Sullivan, for taking on the book; Editor Judy Brief, who copy edited and cheerfully kept the project moving forward; Production Editor, Maya Riddick, for laying out the book; Assistant Danielle DeLucia, for making initial artist contacts for me; and Marketer Erika Putre, for keeping the book's name in front of booksellers.

I'd also like to thank the Graybills and the Soibelmans for being a great family—I'm so glad I moved to California!

Finally, and most importantly, thanks go to the artists who contributed their images and know-how to this book. We did this book in record time, and it wouldn't have happened without everyone's cooperation. All of the artists are available for assignments, and you may contact them though MIS: Press. What follows is a list of the artists and the chapters in which you can view their work. Some of the images listed below can also be found in the color insert in this book's midsection. All the images are on the *Fractal Design Painter 4 Complete* CD in the corresponding chapter folder. The images are listed on the CD by figure number within the chapter.

Chapter 8, "Using Painter's Advanced Drawing Tools"

Chapter 9, "Introducing Painter's Paintbrushes"

Chapter 14, "Using Painter's Advanced Painting Tools"

Chapter 15, "Using Paths, Floaters and Shapes"

Chapter 16, "Working with Paper"

Chapter 18. "Working with the Image Hose"

Chapter 19, "Realistic Photo Retouching"

Chapter 20, "Colorizing Photographs"

Contents

Part I: Setup and Output

1 What is Fractal Design Painter? 9

Part II: Drawing

$\mathcal{C}$ONTENTS

6 Drawing Gadgets 67

Part III: Painting

9 Introducing Painter's Paintbrushes 117

10 Basic Painting in Painter .123

Part IV: Drawing and Painting Accessories

Part V: Photo Retouching and Compositing

26 Type Special Effects 347

27 Special Effects Backgrounds 361

Part VII: Cartooning and Animation

28 Cartoons 369

Foreword

Over the years, my dear friend Karen Sperling has been a primary storyteller for Painter. The 1.0 through X2 manuals and the Painter 2 *Companion* were Karen's work. She wrote *Painter 3 Complete* and currently, with the Artistry newsletter, she continues to tell the artists' stories as well as Painter's story. With *Painter 4 Complete*, Karen continues her tradition of unveiling the rich texture of technology in Painter in such a way as to make sense to you, the user. It's remarkable that Karen was the original author of the Shapes manual (which originally came with ColorStudio), so it makes sense that she would have a unique grasp of Shapes' capabilities. Also, editing and producing *Artistry* gives her a special understanding of how the professional artists create their work.

As much as I have enjoyed creating Painter, along with the crew here at Fractal Design, Karen has also enjoyed being an expert at Painter, and a professional navigator of Painter's interface and features. So it's no great wonder that Karen has often run users groups for Painter, and that she also offers professional training to Painter users. In fact, when we release a new version of Painter, we always make sure that Karen has a beta copy, and I always look forward to taking her on a guided tour of the new features and changes. This is particularly true with version 4.

One tale of version 4 needs to be told. When we released Painter 4, I was uncertain about whether the mosaic feature would be a hit. I programmed it while at the tip of Jutland in Denmark on a PowerBook 540c during vacation last summer and spent quite a bit of time (after arriving back at Aptos) making it useful. I even spent some days creating a mosaic for the poster, to demonstrate to the users that mosaics would be a cool feature. In house, mosaics gained popularity when John Derry created some really cool art, including the mosaic paint can which is on the front of the Painter 4 package. But it was not until I got the thumbs-up from Karen that I considered the mosaics feature to be a success.

We all strive to create great work. To do that requires a good working knowledge of the tools we use to accomplish these tasks. That's why it's good to see what other artists have done, in a step-by-step manner. Each artist has a story to tell in hir or her artwork. As time marches on, Painter's story also needs to be told. And you'll find those stories right here on these pages.

Mark Zimmer
Aptos, California

Introduction

Welcome to *Fractal Design Painter 4 Complete*!

Fractal Design Painter 4 is one of the most innovative, powerful, whimsical, useful, and yet elusive graphics software packages available for the Macintosh and Windows today. *Fractal Design Painter 4 Complete* is a reference source that thoroughly explains how to master Painter's abundant collection of painting, drawing, and special effects tools.

Arriving in its paint can, Painter announces its whimsical side right away. Take a whiff inside the can—it smells like paint! Load the software, open it, start to use it, and Painter's elusiveness soon becomes all too apparent. What's with all those palettes and dialog boxes? The adventurous will figure out how to use the program, but whether it's a lack of fortitude, shortness of time, or preference for other software, many users shrug their shoulders and close the program. As the months go by, they sometimes notice the paint can sitting patiently on the shelf and promise themselves to learn Painter, then another project hits and Painter falls lower on the things-to-do list.

Enter *Fractal Design Painter 4 Complete*. This book will show you how innovative, powerful, and useful Painter really is, whether you have actually used Painter or you don't know much about the program.

Throughout *Fractal Design Painter 4 Complete* are illustrations by more than 30 working artists, illustrators, photographers, photo retouchers, multimedia creators, cartoonists, animators, and Web artists. These images are accompanied by complete step-by-step instructions detailing how the artists used Painter's tools to create their images. I wrote these instructions based on what the artists told me; on my own in-depth knowledge of Painter gained from writing the Painter manuals, teaching Painter, and putting together my Painter how-to newsletter, *Artistry*; and on advice and hints from many Fractal Design Corporation executives. Lending this expertise were President and Painter inventor, Mark Zimmer; Vice President, Creative Design, John Derry; Technical Support Manager, Laurie Hemnes; Tech Support crew members Bud Daumen, Steve Rathmann, and Shawn Grunberger; and Quality Assurance Manager Michael Cinque.

Much of what you see in this book is information that I have taught in either one-on-one training situations or group seminars at animation studios, publishing companies, advertising agencies, colleges, greeting card companies, and design firms. The difference is in the way the information is presented. You may not have the benefit of asking me questions as you would in training seminars. But by reading *Fractal Design Painter 4 Complete*, you get something that no one instructor could ever offer, and that is a broad range of images and styles from artists working in various disciplines, along with insights from Fractal Design

Corporation staffers. Instead of just seeing one person's way of doing things or hearing one person's voice, you get help from artists working in all kinds of media and using different combinations of Painter's tools. Reading *Fractal Design Painter 4 Complete* is like attending sessions at a Painter symposium taught by more than 30 artists, instructors, and experts.

Using the exercises in this book you'll find out:

❖   How to use Painter's tools.

❖   How to combine these tools to create and edit images.

❖   What effects you can accomplish in Painter, from three-dimensional type to turning photographs into thick oil paintings.

What makes Painter seem so complex at first glance? Maybe it's that it doesn't act the way you wish it would. When you launch the program, you want it to be like starting a trip. You want to use the software in a progression, like driving along a highway, with the features lining the road like gas stations. You want to go along your merry way, and as you create an image, you want to pull over, get a paper texture, get back on the road a little later, pull over again, get a type effect, and so on.

But using Painter is less like driving down a highway and more like walking through a forest. When you launch Painter you stand at the beginning of many trails that wind their way in many directions with twists and turns through lush, beautiful, complex terrain. Take one trail to find a paper texture, go up a different trail for the airbrush. The trails may seem to appear and disappear, stretching infinitely ahead of you. There are so many of them that it's easy to get lost. But the trails are very clearly marked and very accessible. And once you're familiar with these trails, that is, where to go to find Glass Distortion or the watercolor brushes, then Painter turns out not to be all that difficult to use after all. And in fact, following Painter's many trails can lead you to new and wondrous creative adventures that you never thought possible. *Fractal Design Painter 4 Complete* is your compass in this Painter forest, showing you what kinds of images you can create with Painter and how to create them.

Because so many diverse individuals use Painter, I decided to divide this book into four categories: drawing/painting; photography; multimedia special effects; and cartoons/animation. This way, Painter's features can be described as they relate to the specific kinds of images that each user wants to create. So you'll find various tools reappearing throughout the book. Take selecting tools, for example. You'll find out how to select a section of a painting to edit it, then later in the book there's information for selecting a piece of a photograph so that you can float it, and still later is information for selecting part of a cartoon to add a gradation to it.

As you go through the exercises in *Fractal Design Painter 4 Complete*, keep in mind that the book is a compass, serving as a guide to the program. A compass shows you which way is north, it doesn't tell you to go north. The images shown are just a sample of what you can do with Painter. Breaking the book down into four categories is an arbitrary way to classify Painter's tools to make them more accessible. Classifying the tools doesn't mean that you can't use a pencil with a multimedia special effect or a paintbrush with a photograph. You can use any tool as you wind your way through the forest, picking the features like exotic fruits and berries, collecting them not in a basket, but in your image.

HOW TO USE THIS BOOK

Fractal Design Painter 4 Complete is designed to provide you with as quick access to using Painter as is possible with such a deep program. You can start by turning to the section that applies to you, be it drawing/painting, photography, multimedia special effects, or cartoons/animation. Within each section are chapters containing images and step-by-step exercises explaining how they were created.

Many of the images are available on the CD-ROM that comes with this book, so you can open up the artwork when you do the adjoining step-by-step exercise for even deeper insight into how to use Painter's many tools. You'll find an image in its corresponding chapter folder on the CD.

Focus on the section that's important to you, but don't ignore the other sections of the book. By going over them, you'll probably find other beneficial pointers for getting the most out of Painter, even if the artwork is very different from what you yourself do.

Using the Exercises

Fractal Design Painter 4 Complete has two kinds of exercises: simple ones that show you how a particular Painter tool works and more complex ones, where you go step-by-step through the same process that the artist took to create the featured image. These more advanced exercises give you insight into not only how to use Painter's tools, but also the quickest way to achieve a specific goal. With all these tools, it comes as no surprise that there are many ways to achieve the same effects. *Fractal Design Painter 4 Complete* helps you, among other things, to work efficiently in Painter.

Fractal Design Painter 4 Complete is for everyone, regardless of how familiar you are with Painter. The book is for users who have upgraded to Painter 4 from earlier versions of the program and for those who are using Painter for the first time. The information is offered with the intent that everyone from occasional users to daily practitioners might discover something new about Painter.

Since Painter is practically identical on Windows and the Mac, *Fractal Design Painter 4 Complete* is for both Macintosh and Windows users. The only differences between the two platforms are the shortcuts and the libraries, and keys and file names are stated for both Macintosh and Windows throughout the book.

Selecting from the menus is listed as it is in the manual, that is, **Menu: Menu Item: Menu Item Subcategory**. If you are to select **Open** from the File menu, it will be listed like this: **File: Open**.

A Look at What This Book Covers

Fractal Design Painter 4 Complete is divided into seven parts based on the way users work with Painter.

Part I: Setup and Output

Part I introduces you to Fractal Design Painter 4, system setup, resolution, and printing. Chapter 1 explains what Fractal Design Painter 4 does and who uses it. Chapter 2 goes over system setup. Chapter 3 has information about resolution and printing.

Part II: Drawing

The drawing tools have their own section in *Fractal Design Painter 4 Complete*. The chapters in this section progress from what you need to know about accessing the drawing tools through the more complex issues of customizing these tools for your own needs. The section wraps up with images drawn in Painter and step-by-step instructions that explain how they were created.

Chapter 4 introduces you to Painter's drawing tools. Chapter 5 shows you how to work with each drawing tool. Chapter 6 covers the gadgets that you'll use right away as you draw in Painter. Chapter 7 shows you how to customize the drawing tools. Chapter 8 features drawings created in Painter and step-by-step information about how they were done.

Part III: Painting

Six chapters are devoted to using Painter's paintbrushes. As in the drawing section, the painting chapters range in scope from simple introductions to detailed step-by-step instructions about how featured artists used Painter to create their paintings.

Chapter 9 introduces Painter's paintbrushes. Chapter 10 shows you how to work with each paintbrush. Chapter 11 covers Painter's special effects brushes, including the Image Hose. Chapter 12 goes over the gadgets that you'll use to help you paint in Painter. Chapter 13 explains how to customize Painter's brushes using all the palettes and sliders. Chapter 14 features paintings created in Painter with step-by-step instructions about how they were executed.

Part IV: Drawing and Painting Accessories

It's important to know how to use the drawing and painting tools, but this knowledge is only part of the story when it comes to using Painter. Part IV covers the features that you'll use with the drawing and painting tools.

Chapter 15 explains how Painter's paths, floaters, and shapes were used to create an image. Chapter 16 has information for creating and using paper textures for paintings and drawings. Chapter 17 covers working with color in Painter. Chapter 18 reveals how to generate paintings with Painter's Image Hose.

Part V: Photo Retouching and Compositing

Painter does not pretend to be a photo retouching tool on its own, primarily because it does not offer CMYK (Cyan, Magenta, Yellow, Black) color correction capabilities. However, it contains useful features for retouching and compositing photographs, which can then be brought into other programs for finishing touches.

Chapter 19 covers "realistic" image editing, that is, it gives you directions for using Painter's tools to retouch a photograph so that the end result still looks like a photograph. Chapter 20 shows you some Painter features for colorizing photographs, along with examples of their use.

Chapter 21, which shows special effects image editing in Painter using the drawing and painting tools and the Effects menu, can be said to cover "unrealistic" image editing, where the final retouched image is nothing like the photograph you started out with.

Chapter 22 covers photo-compositing using floaters. Chapter 23 goes over special effects created using the background mask. Chapter 24 takes another look at the Image Hose, this time showing its effectiveness for photo compositing.

Part VI: Special Effects for 3D, Photography, Multimedia, Slide Presentations, Video, CD-ROMs, and Web Pages

Many multimedia, 3D, photo retouching specialists and Web graphics creators use Painter as a sidelight to their imaging software of choice, opening the image in Painter, picking up a paper texture here and a type effect there, then returning the image to its original source software. Part VI explains how to use the sections of Painter that you would use for these extra added attractions and includes examples of how they're used.

Chapter 25 covers how to create type shapes and how to edit them. Chapter 26 offers step-by-step instructions for producing type special effects in Painter. Chapter 27 shows you how to use Painter for special effects backgrounds.

Part VII: Cartooning, Animation, and Web Graphics

Painter 4 is the program of choice for many cartoonists and Web page designers. Part VII shows examples of how working cartoonists and Web graphics designers use Painter.

Chapter 28 has step-by-step instructions for cartooning with Painter. Chapter 29 covers how to use Painter's animation tools. Chapter 30 shows you examples of Web pages created using Painter and how they were done.

SUMMARY

Pack a lunch, bring a jacket. You're ready to start your adventures in the lush forest of art tools called Painter.

Part I

Setup and Output

1

What is Fractal Design Painter?

FRACTAL DESIGN PAINTER: AN OVERVIEW

Imagine that you just bought an airplane hangar. Picture yourself standing inside your new hangar looking around. Before you are not airplanes, but rows and rows of tables stretching out in every direction as far as the eye can see. Placed on these tables are paintbrushes in limitless sizes and variations of tips and bristles; every imaginable drawing tool from pencils to pastels in every texture and consistency; endless varieties of canvas, paper, and other drawing and painting surfaces; stacks of lights and gobos in all varieties of intensity and size; piles of strange and wonderful type fonts and effects; darkroom essentials for focusing, adjusting exposure, and compositing; and animation creation and editing tools.

Now envision that this seemingly limitless array of art, photographic, and animation supplies has been moved into a software program on your computer. That software program is Fractal Design Painter.

With Painter you will:

✤   Paint and draw (see Figure 1.1).

Figure 1.1 New Mosaic by Chelsea Sammel.

❖ Edit, colorize, and composite photographs (see Figure 1.2).

Figure 1.2 *Hanged Man* by Dorothy Simpson Krause.

❖ Add special effects, type, and paper to images from other software programs including 3D and multimedia packages (see Figure 1.3).

Figure 1.3 Logo by Karen Sperling.

❖ Create Web page graphics (see Figure 1.4).

Figure 1.4 Web page by Dennis Orlando.

WHO USES FRACTAL DESIGN PAINTER?

Many artists choose Painter to create digital artwork because of Painter's lush stock of realistic drawing and painting tools, including pencils, chalk, felt pens, charcoal, bristle brushes, and other-worldly tools like mosaics and the Image Hose.

Photographers, photo retouchers, and multimedia digital imagers rely on other software programs as their mainstay and choose Painter for special-effects accents like paper textures, type, or lighting. Here's a closer look at who is using Fractal Design Painter 4.

Fine Artists

Painters with an art background use Painter's watercolors, bristle brushes, and airbrush tools to re-create the kinds of artwork that they created traditionally before they started using computers. Many of these artists output the artwork they create in Painter to watercolor paper and canvas and exhibit it in galleries, where it is sold to private collectors (see Figure 1.5).

Figure 1.5 *Night Owls* by Chet Phillips.

Illustrators

Artists use Painter to produce editorial illustrations for newspapers, magazines, and print ads (see Figure 1.6).

Figure 1.6 *Fat Cat* by Gregg Scott.

Cartoonists

Cartoonists use Painter to create people who are able to leap tall buildings in a single bound (see Figure 1.7).

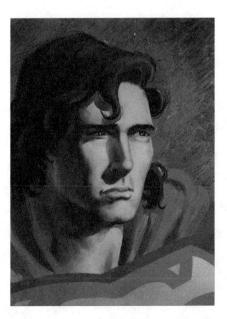

Figure 1.7 *Superman* ©1996 DC Comics painted by Jose Marzan.

Animators

Electronic storyboard artists use Painter for preliminary client presentations.

Commercial Artists

Chances are good that the next movie poster you see was created in Painter.

Children's Books Illustrators

Artists use Painter's drawing and painting tools to illustrate children's books.

Dabblers

You don't have to be an artist or a professional to use Painter. Another kind of user who turns to Painter exclusively is the hobbyist. Painter has opened up new creative vistas for doctors, dentists, retirees, and other nonartists who always wanted to paint or draw but never quite got around to it.

Photographers and Photo Retouchers

Photo manipulators will turn to other software for color correction and sometimes compositing, but they use Painter's drawing, painting, and cloning tools in addition to its floaters, background mask, and special effects including paper texture (see Figures 1.8 and 1.9).

Figure 1.8 Photograph by David Scott Leibowitz.

Figure 1.9 *Girl & Bike* by David Scott Leibowitz.

SUMMARY

Whether you originate images in Painter or use it to edit images from other software programs, whether you are a hobbyist or a professional, whether you plan to learn every minute detail about Painter or use it only once in a while, you're bound to have many creative adventures with this unusual software program; and *Fractal Design Painter 4 Complete* will show you the way.

2

Setting Up Your System

CHAPTER HIGHLIGHTS

- ❖ System requirements
- ❖ Optimize your system's memory resources

This chapter has some pointers about system requirements for running Painter on both the Macintosh and Windows. Also, check the manual and the tips sheet that Fractal Design tech support put together and included on the CD-ROM that ships with Painter. I got help with this chapter from artist Michael Savas, who wrote all the Windows information. Michael uses Painter on a PC and you can see examples of his art throughout this book. Also helping with this chapter were Shawn Grunberger and Bud Daumen at Fractal Design Corporation.

This chapter is mostly about Windows because using Painter in Windows brings with it more considerations than using Painter on the Macintosh. However, this chapter can't cover every single situation that you might encounter, especially in Windows. If you're experiencing difficulty running Painter, then your best bet is to call tech support at 408-688-8800. They can walk you through your system configuration and find out where the problem might be. Also, at press time, Fractal Design was maintaining its online presence on America Online at keyword: **Fractal** in the Mac and Tech support folders, and on the Internet through its web page at http://www.fractal.com. Fractal no longer logs onto CompuServe, but **Go: GUGRPA** (Graphic User Group A) is alive and well with participation by Painter users from around the world.

REQUIREMENTS

I wanted to find out what was important to tell readers about Painter 4 system requirements that isn't in the manuals. The folks at Fractal say that even though this book will have a quick turnaround, it's likely that whatever quirks the update has will be corrected in an interim bug fix by the time you read about them here.

So the following information is pretty much the same as it was for Painter 3, with a few additions.

System Requirements—Macintosh

Get the biggest, fastest Mac you can find and Painter will run well. The slower the machine, the groggier Painter will seem. If you can swing it, get a PowerMac. Even if you're a hobbyist you're going to get frustrated using Painter on that Mac IIsi.

You need at least 12 MB of RAM to run Painter version 4 at a decent speed, and the more the better. Don't forget, this is in addition to the RAM taken up by your system software. It's easy to find out how much RAM your system is using. When you're in the Finder, click and hold on the **Apple menu** in the upper-left-hand corner of your screen and select the first item, **About This Macintosh**. In the dialog box are listed any open applications and how many kilobytes (K) of RAM they're using (there are 1024 K in 1 meg of RAM, figure 1000 rounded off).

Let's say you have a total of 16 megs of RAM installed, approximately 16,000 K. In the About This Macintosh box you'd find that the System software uses anywhere from around 2900 K to 4500 K if you're running System 7. That means you have 16,000 minus 4500, or 11,500 K left over to run another program like Painter. But don't give every last drop of RAM to Painter or any other software. Fractal tech support recommends leaving at least a 500 K cushion.

After you figure out how much RAM you have available, the next step is to allocate RAM to Painter. Click on the **Painter** application icon in the Painter folder in the Finder and press **Command+I** (**Get Info**). The Get Info dialog box appears. It shows how much RAM is suggested and the minimum and preferred amounts. Click and drag to highlight over the preferred number and type in the number of K you're allocating to Painter, which is the total that you have minus the amount used by the System software, minus 500 K. Then close the window. Note that you can't change this amount if Painter is running. Quit the program first, then adjust the Get Info box.

In addition, get a decent-sized internal hard drive, and don't run off of SyQuests or floppies. Painter *virtualizes* to the hard disk, meaning that it turns to the hard disk for more RAM when it is working on big files. If you have 4 megs of left-over storage space on the hard disk, then you're going to have trouble working on images in Painter. Beware of things like Disk Doubler—it has caused conflicts with Painter in the past.

Painter features, including Apply Surface Texture, Apply Lighting, and Blobs, require a *Floating Point Unit* (FPU) to run. If these features are dimmed out in the menu, it's because you don't have an FPU.

If possible, get a pressure-sensitive stylus. Painter is all about painting and drawing and using a pressure-sensitive stylus allows you to take the most advantage of Painter's drawing and painting features. Check the tech support tips sheet on the Fractal CD for additional system-configuration advice.

System Requirements—Windows

Painter 4 requires a 486 minimum, or Pentium IBM-compatible computer. A minimum of 8 megabytes of RAM is required; 12 megs for Windows 95, and at least 16 megs are recommended. A hard drive, monitor, and Microsoft Windows 3.1 or later are also required. A super VGA color monitor is recommended, but Painter will run on a grayscale monitor as well. No matter what type of monitor you have, Painter requires a video display driver that supports at least 256 colors (8-bit).

For a full range of color (16 million), a 24-bit video card is recommended. A video card is a piece of hardware that is also referred to as a *graphics accelerator* or *video adapter*. This device is a plug-in circuit board that speeds up your system's video draw time dramatically by holding data in a memory buffer, or quick access area called VRAM, and feeds image data to your monitor quickly.

Video cards are available with different *buses* (data lines that information passes through), generally 32 and 64 bits. The larger the bus, the faster the throughput of data. Many video cards are sold with theatrical names like Viper, Hercules, Monalisa, and so on.

When choosing a video card you should consider using the proper resolution for the size of your monitor. The larger the monitor, the higher the resolution that will be needed to display an image at its best. As a general rule, 14-inch monitors will run fine at a resolution of 640 x 480. Use 800 x 600 for 15- to 16-inch monitors; 17-inch monitors require 1024 x 768. Monitors that are 20 to 21 inches require the highest resolution. Make sure the video card that you choose is compatible with your computer (namely, VESA, EISA, ISA, or PCI motherboards). If you are purchasing a video card for the first time, it is a good idea to do your research before purchasing one to see which device will best serve your needs.

When creating artwork either for your own enjoyment or as a profession, it is a good idea to use some type of electrical power backup device. These devices offer an uninterrupted supply of power in the event of an electrical blackout. They allow enough time for you to save your images and properly close down your computer system until the power is restored. They also have surge protection and line conditioning built in to protect the electrical supply to your computer. Backup systems (or UPS*es*) are relatively inexpensive compared to your computer investment; a 250 watt unit costs as little as $100 for approximately ten minutes of backup time. There are many different brands on the market to choose from; American Power and Tripp Light are among the most common. A pressure-sensitive graphics tablet is also highly recommended.

Painter features, including Apply Surface Texture, Apply Lighting, and Blobs, require a math co-processor to run in Windows. If these features are dimmed out in the menu, it's because you don't have a math co-processor.

PUTTING PAINTER ON A DIET—MAC AND WINDOWS

Painter seems to get fatter the more you work with it, that is, it hogs more storage space as time goes on.

Sometimes I find that doing housekeeping frees up a surprising amount of storage space. You may find that the 5 meg experiment with Apply Lighting isn't as great as it seemed at the time and can get tossed.

Another memory waster is the Painter Portfolio. This is where your floaters live when you save them in the Window: Objects: F. List: Floaters palette. As you save floaters into your Floaters palette, the portfolio grows in size. It would follow that if you delete floaters the portfolio would contract. Unfortunately, it doesn't.

Shrinking the portfolio is very simple. You do it by creating a new portfolio, copying the floaters you want to keep into the new portfolio, and deleting the old one.

If you haven't cracked Painter open yet and don't know what a floater is, skip this section and come back after you've worked with floaters for a while. But if you've saved a lot of floaters into your Floaters palette, read on.

The following steps show how to create a smaller portfolio.

1. Select **Objects: F. List: Floater Mover**. The Floater Mover dialog box appears.
2. Click the **New** button on the dialog's right-hand side. A dialog box appears asking you to name the New Floater Library. This can be a little confusing, because you're really creating a new portfolio.
3. Type in the name **Painter Portfolio 2** or an 8 character DOS name if you're in Windows 3.X (longer if you're using Windows 95), and click **Save**. You now have a new portfolio on the Floater Mover's right-hand side, ready to be filled.

Depending on whether you've been using floaters, you may have either all the default floaters on the left-hand side of this dialog box, or new ones that you may have created. Since you'll be deleting the file on the left-hand side, save all the floaters you want to keep. Those that you don't save will be deleted from your system and lost forever.

To save a floater into your new portfolio, do the following:

1. Click on a floater name in the left-hand column.
2. Click **Copy**. The floater now appears in the right-hand column, indicating is has been copied to the new portfolio.
3. Continue to click and copy floaters until you have the desired total in the right-hand portfolio.
4. When you're done copying floaters, click **Quit**.

Next you'll set up Painter to launch using the new portfolio.

1. Choose **Edit: Preferences: General**. The General Preferences dialog box appears.
2. Under Libraries and next to Floaters, type a **2** next to Painter Portfolio (or type the 8 character name from the previous step 3 if you are in Windows 3.X) so that it looks exactly like the name you gave your new portfolio, including spacing (Mac).
3. Click **OK**.
4. Choose **File: Quit** (**Exit** in Windows) to exit Painter.

Look in the Finder/File Manager. You'll see that the new portfolio is smaller than the old one, if you had saved additional floaters in the old one.

Now relaunch Painter, and it uses the new portfolio. You can delete the old portfolio from your system.

An alternative way to replace the fat portfolio with a streamlined one is to give the new portfolio a name in the Floater mover, quit Painter, delete the default Painter Portfolio, and rename the new one Painter Portfolio. Many Windows users of past versions of Painter had to replace their Painter settings file (painter.set) to launch Painter, in which case the General Preferences dialog box would default back to the Painter Portfolio and wouldn't be able to find a newly named portfolio. Fractal representatives say that having to reload the settings file should be less of an issue in Painter 4.

Either method for creating a new portfolio works.

Using the portfolio mover is a great way to organize your files by project, category, or however you want. Set up a portfolio for flower floaters and another for leaf floaters, for example. Access these various portfolios by clicking the **Library** button within the Floaters palette drawer.

Other areas of Painter have movers, like brushes, for example, under Brushes palette: Brushes: Brush Mover, and if you add a lot of variants (brush subcategories), you can reduce your Painter Brushes file with the Brush mover.

OPTIMIZING SYSTEM RESOURCES—WINDOWS

Regardless of how much RAM is installed in your system, there are ways to make the memory that you have more available to your applications and thus to have them run noticeably better.

Running Fewer Applications Concurrently—Windows

Every application that you run must be swapped out to your system or virtual memory when it is not in the foreground. This consumes memory resources. It is a good idea to avoid running more than a few applications at the same time. Minimize as many Windows Groups as possible in Program Manager. This will allow more system and virtual memory to be available to Painter.

Change Physical Memory Usage within Painter to Maximum—Windows

You can allocate all available memory to Painter. Just remember that you can't run other programs in the background if you choose this option. Follow these steps to change the memory usage inside of Painter.

1. Select **Edit: Preferences: Windows**. The Windows dialog box appears.
2. Under Physical Memory Usage, click on **Maximum Memory for Painter**. Click **OK**.

Acquire a Hard-Disk Drive with a Fast Access Rating— Windows

Hard drives come with different access ratings. A 9.50 millisecond rating is considered good. This may seem to be a little amount of difference from some of the slower rated drives, but on larger images time adds up quickly and the difference is very noticeable.

Regardless of the access rating of your hard drive, make sure that you have properly invoked Smartdrive (SMARTDRV.EXE) in your AUTOEXEC.BAT file. This will greatly improve hard drive access performance. If you are uncertain of how to configure your AUTOEXEC.BAT file, consult a computer technician. If you have good knowledge of computers and would like to accomplish this yourself, consult your Microsoft Windows User's Guide under Smartdrive. If you're running Windows 3.11, you can use 32-bit File Access (in the Windows Control Panel) in place of Smartdrive.

Painter's Virtualizing System—Windows

Many of Painter's operations are accomplished in what is called *virtual memory*. This is when Painter reads from and writes to a temporary file that it creates on your hard drive named PAINTER.TMP. You can specify in Painter's General Preference dialog box the drive to which this temporary file will be written. Make sure this drive is the fastest uncompressed drive you have available, preferably with a large amount of free space. Here is where Painter will perform various functions. Many of these operations occur regardless of how much RAM you have available. This repeated activity is normal for Painter but can slow down performance, especially on larger images.

Whether you are configuring your system for the first time or adding Painter 4 to your existing workstation, you can take certain measures to optimize Painter's performance. If only one large drive is available for Painter's temp file, partition or break up the existing drive to create another. Check your Windows or DOS manuals to find out how, or consult your dealer or a professional computer technician. Dedicated space can be assigned on your hard disk drive as temporary storage areas for Painter and other applications' temporary files. Reserving these storage areas is beneficial because it keeps data from fragmenting into other parts of the drive, and it helps keep data contiguous for faster access and fewer memory conflicts. Another benefit is having to defragment only this partition, which is much faster than having to defragment the entire drive.

Change the Windows Temporary/Permanent Swap File

The following steps apply only to Windows 3.X. In Windows 95 use the default settings, allowing Windows to manage the virtual memory.

1. Double-click on the **Main** icon in Program Manager. The Main program group appears.
2. Double-click on the **Control Panel** icon. The Control Panel window appears.
3. Double-click on the **386 Enhanced** icon. The 386 Enhanced window appears.

4. Click on the **Virtual Memory** button. The Virtual Memory dialog box appears.

5. Ideally, your virtual memory swap file settings should be half your RAM amount. So if you have 16 megs of RAM, your virtual memory should be about 8 megs. A swap file type of "permanent" is preferred over "temporary." However, this may have an adverse effect on how your other applications run because some programs need more virtual memory. If you have plenty of hard disk space and memory, you can use the default settings.

6. If the current settings need to be changed, click the **Change** button and make the necessary adjustments to the Type and New Size sections. Also, make sure the Drive setting is pointing to your fastest uncompressed hard drive or partition. Click **OK**.

7. Restart Windows by choosing the **Restart** button. Do *not* use **Ctrl+Alt+Del**.

OPTIMIZING SYSTEM RESOURCES—MAC AND WINDOWS

Limit the Number of Opened Images—Mac and Windows

The more opened image files you have running at the same time, the fewer memory resources you will have for the main image on which you are working.

Clear Painter's Copy and Cut Image Storage Area—Mac and Windows

If you have cut or copied a large image under Painter's Edit menu, clear the image from temporary storage by quitting and then reopening Painter. A large image can remain in this area until you restart Painter, and it will consume resources. This improvement will be subtle but noticeable if you have a limited amount of RAM. Another way to clear is to select a tiny part of the image with the rectangle in the Tools palette and then select **Edit: Copy**.

SUMMARY

Now that you've seen some of the ways to set up your system to run Painter smoothly, the next chapter will get you thinking about setting up images in Painter.

3

Printing

CHAPTER HIGHLIGHTS

- ❖ Resolution
- ❖ RGB versus CMYK
- ❖ Painter's EPS files
- ❖ Painter Service Bureaus

Since I wrote *Painter 3 Complete* I published six issues of my Painter newsletter, *Artistry*, and I now have experience with what it's like to print Painter images. This chapter, then, will first take a look at printing issues in general, followed by some personal experience about outputting Painter files. The chapter wraps up with a list of the three Service Bureaus known for printing out Painter files.

Printing seems mysterious when you're first learning to use bitmapped software like Painter, and it can be a very complex topic if you really master it. The scope of this book is not to offer in-depth printing information, but, with help from artist Michael Savas and Fractal tech support gurus Shawn Grunberger and Laurie Hemnes, to give you a few tips to help get you started.

Two issues are involved when you talk about printing, namely *resolution* and *color format*.

RESOLUTION

When you start a new Painter image using **File: New**, you type a number next to Resolution in the New Picture dialog box. Logic tells you that this number should match your printer resolution. Unfortunately, logic is wrong.

The number you type next to Resolution in the New Picture dialog box is the *image's resolution*, and though it's related to the output resolution, it isn't the same. To set an image resolution, you have to know what your eventual output will be.

Generally speaking, if the image is headed to a computer or video destination like a slide presentation, a CD-ROM, or a multimedia format, then you would set Resolution at **72** pixels per inch (ppi), which is a standard resolution for monitors.

If you will print the file, things get a bit more complex. First you have to consider the alternatives. If your piece will be printed in a magazine, brochure, or other print medium, then you will generally have it offset-printed. In this case, you will generally have it output at a service bureau on a high-resolution printer.

When determining what to set the resolution at for a file that will be output, it is a good idea to contact the service bureau you plan to use *before* you create your image. Generally speaking, you would set image resolution at twice the output resolution, generally described as lpi (*lines per inch*). Typically, lpi is either 133 or 150, therefore, the common image resolution for output is 300 ppi. The same rule of thumb generally applies to inkjet and dye sublimation printers such as Iris and 3M rainbow printers.

Meanwhile, don't confuse output resolution with lines per inch. Some desktop printers have a resolution as high as 720, but that isn't the same as lines per inch. For example, a desktop printer with a resolution of 300 ppi probably prints about 60 lpi, so setting image resolution at 120 ppi would probably produce good results from this desktop printer. A printer with a resolution of 720 ppi probably prints at 100 lpi, which means you would set image resolution at 200 ppi.

Default Settings

The width and height default settings of 640 x 480 pixels per inch represent a standard screen resolution of 72 ppi. If you keep the width and height set to pixels, changing the resolution or pixels per inch will affect the width and height of the image when printed.

However, if you change the width and height measurements to inches, centimeters, points, picas, or columns and you have the image resolution set to ppi, it will not affect the dimensions of the image when printed. This is beneficial because it allows you to alter the resolution of the image without affecting the output size.

Transparency Output

A whole new set of rules applies when determining resolution for transparency output. Film recorders that produce transparencies are RGB devices that use set resolutions referred to as RES 20, RES 24, RES 30, and RES 40. Each of these set resolutions requires a specified count of pixels per inch.

Calculations for the preceding set resolutions are as follows: RES 20 = 508.0 pixels per inch; RES 24 = 609.6 pixels per inch; RES 30 = 762.0 pixels per inch; and, RES 40 = 1016.0 pixels per inch.

RES 20 is barely adequate for sharp reproduction. Fine detail will be lost and "jaggies" will be visible. RES 24 and RES 30 are good average working resolutions, offering manageable file sizes and acceptable image quality, depending on subject matter and ultimate use. RES 40 is excellent quality, but file sizes may be prohibitively large for some systems. A standard 35mm slide 1 inch x 1 inch at RES 40 will require 1016 x 1524 pixels. A standard 4 inch x 5 inch transparency at RES 40 will require 4064 x 5080 pixels.

Calculating File Sizes for Transparency Output

As you might imagine, file sizes can quickly get out of hand at such high pixel resolutions. Following is a formula for calculating RGB file size: Horizontal pixel width times vertical pixel height times 3 (RGB) = file size.

For example, to determine the file size of a standard 35mm 1 inch by 1 inch slide at RES 40, the formula will be as follows:

1016 pixels x 1 inch = 1016; 1016 pixels x 1.50 inch = 1524; 1016 pixels x 1524 pixels = 1548 x 3 (RGB) = a file size of 4.6 megabytes.

The same calculation applies for determining CMYK file sizes, except you have to multiply the total pixel count by four (CMYK) instead of three (RGB). File sizes will vary depending on which program and format you used to create the image. For example, an image saved in a Photoshop format may differ greatly from an image saved in Painter. Even the same format may vary from program to program. This is because of the different ways a particular format version writes data.

CMYK VERSUS RGB

Now that you understand resolution, the next thing to consider is color. Most service bureaus require cyan, yellow, magenta, and black (CMYK) image files to produce film and proofs for color printing. Painter does not allow you to convert RGB images to CMYK and perform manual color corrections. You must do so in another program capable of making this conversion, such as Adobe Photoshop, or Aldus Photostyler.

What you see on your monitor is not necessarily what you will see in print. When converting an RGB image to CMYK there are several factors to consider, such as determining ink limits and making careful color corrections from hue shifts that may occur in the conversion process. Acquiring these useful prepress skills enables computer artists to produce printed artwork that more accurately conveys their original creative intentions. When dealing with image resolution it is important to note that a CMYK image file is about 33% larger in CMYK mode than in RGB mode because of the additional color information needed to produce magenta, cyan, yellow, and black negative film for printing.

Predicting Output Color

Becoming adept at converting RGB files to CMYK is a skill in itself, and one that you may or may not have time to master. There are a few ways, though, that you can get your RGB files to more closely resemble their output CMYK counterparts short of becoming a CMYK expert.

Jon Cone of Cone Editions Press, a well-regarded Iris printmaker, highly recommends working on a Painter image with **Printable Colors Only** selected in the Art Materials: Color palette. Printable Colors Only constrains RGB colors to CMYK equivalents based on ColorStudio color correction tables. Most people at this point have never heard of ColorStudio, but it was a program that actually preceded Photoshop for color image-editing on the Mac and was written by Mark Zimmer and Tom Hedges, Painter's inventors. Painter 4 has some other ColorStudio features, namely Shapes and Effects: Tonal Control: Correct Colors. Jon notes that when he takes the Painter RGB files and does the final CMYK color conversion through his own Photoshop customized printing inks tables, the files more closely resemble what they looked like in Painter.

Laurie at Fractal Design adds that if you create your images with Printable Colors Only and save your images as EPS files, then the screen colors have a better chance of resembling the output colors. This is because Painter uses the ColorStudio CMYK to RGB conversion tables for both viewing and converting files.

Laurie suggests that another ingredient to getting monitor and output colors to be similar is to calibrate your monitor. Programs like Photoshop and ColorStudio offer a way to calibrate your monitor through software. Hardware for calibrating your monitor is also available. Your output service can probably suggest what monitor calibration device to get.

In the meantime, Laurie adds that if you receive output that is too dark, you might turn down your monitor's brightness and contrast knobs. Then when you work on-screen you'll be aware of how dark the image will look when you print it out. Now your output matches your monitor so that future creations, when output, will look more like they did on screen.

FINE ART TRANSPARENCIES

Michael points out that you may choose to create your images for slide and transparency output, thus avoiding the conversion to CMYK altogether. Another benefit of creating RGB images for transparency output is that since your monitor displays true RGB transmitted light, what you see on your monitor (assuming your monitor is well-calibrated) should be a reasonable representation of how the final transparency will look.

SOME PERSONAL OBSERVATIONS

I create my newsletter, *Artistry*, in Quark XPress on an 8100 PowerMac.

Each month, artists send me images created in Painter and saved in various formats including Painter TIFF, RIFF, Photoshop TIFF, and Photoshop 3.0.

Regardless of the format, I'll open the image in Painter just to have a look at it, then I'll save it as a TIFF. I'll then open it in Photoshop and save it as a TIFF again because I can compress it in Photoshop using LZW and because Quark seems to read Photoshop TIFF files better. Mary Mathis-Meltzer at Fractal told me that if you uncheck **Save Mask Layer** in the Painter Save As dialog box you can place the Painter images in Quark.

I then open my Quark layout and bring in the image for position only. After writing the articles and fixing the layouts, it's time to do the color work.

I go into Painter and open each image. I choose **Effects: Tonal Control: Enforce Printable Colors** and see how things look in the Preview window. Like the Color palette's previously mentioned Printable Colors Only, the menu item Enforce Printable Colors translates the RGB colors into the CMYK equivalents based on ColorStudio tables.

Enforce Printable Colors always makes the image darker, and I'll usually cancel out of the dialog box and go into **Effects: Tonal Control: Brightness/ Contrast** and turn up the lower slider to brighten things up a bit and "fool" the enforcer. Then I go back into **Effects: Tonal Control: Enforce Printable Colors** and click **OK**.

Many of the colors on screen at this point have little to do with what the colors will look like when they are output. Blues, yellows, and greens look pretty much the same before and after Enforce Printable Colors, but reds go purple or brick, depending on how much orange they have in them. However, when they print out they are bright red.

After doing Enforce Printable Colors I save the file as a RIFF or TIFF to be able to edit later. Then I save the file as EPS, which creates the four CMYK plates. Painter doesn't read EPS files, which is why I save an image in another format first and then in EPS. I check next to **HEX (ASCII)** picture data because it makes things go faster. Also checked by default in Painter 4 are **Save PostScript data into preview file**, which creates a fifth low-resolution (72 ppi) plate for placement purposes and **Preview Options: Color preview**, which makes the low-resolution file appear in color.

Artistry is offset printed, so the next step is to send the Quark file (with all the Painter files) on disk to a service bureau. Up until the sixth issue I was getting color Canon proofs of the Quark files. For the particular service bureau I was using, the Canons, which are pre-separation proofs, and the Matchprints, which are made after the files are separated and output to film, were color-matched, so that I could make corrections after seeing the Canons. That's where the Painter TIFF/RIFF files came in. If I saw a green was too saturated in the Canon print, for example, I would go into the TIFF image, use **Effects: Tonal Control: Adjust Colors** and turn down the Saturation slider, bearing in mind that the Canon print will always look "juicier" or more saturated than the final output. Then I would resave the file as TIFF and then EPS, replacing the former EPS plates.

For the Dec./Jan. issue of Artistry I went straight to film and didn't even see the Matchprints, and everything came out fine because at that point I knew how to tell how the screen colors would print out! Pretty amazing.

If you do go the Canon proofing route, be forewarned. Most service bureaus are not used to Painter files, and because the Canons don't do color separations, they print out the low-resolution preview files. The bureau can get error codes while printing and the results are blurry 72 ppi images. Not to worry. You can tell how the colors will look from the Canon prints (if your service bureau has good color-matching among its machines). When you do the final film and separations, the EPS files print out fine.

Service Bureaus

A question I get all the time is about high-end Iris prints that artists can use, for example, for printing out Painter files on watercolor paper. I've heard varying reports about how long these prints will last without fading.

I do know that there continue to be three service bureaus that are considered to be the experts at oversized, high-end output of fine art images. They are:

Cone Editions

East Topsham, VT, and New York City

802-439-5751

Nash Editions

Manhattan Beach, CA

310-546-9380

Digital Pond

San Francisco, CA

415-495-7663

SUMMARY

Although you can't be a printing expert from reading a chapter in a book, at least you now have an idea about the kinds of issues that you should be aware of when printing out your Painter images. Really, the best way to learn how to print is trial and error. The longer you work on printing, the better you will get at it.

Now it's time to create those great Painter images that you will be printing out, and the next few chapters take you through Painter's fine art tools.

Part II

Drawing

4

Drawing Basics

CHAPTER HIGHLIGHTS

- ✤ Select a drawing tool
- ✤ Pick a color
- ✤ Select a paper texture
- ✤ Adjust opacity and paper grain
- ✤ Change line width
- ✤ Save variants

If you like to draw, you're going to love doing it in Painter. The traditional drawing tools are all here—pastels, charcoals, crayons, pencils, felt pens, and ink pens. So are erasers and stumps for smudging (in the form of the Water tool).

Unlike real-life drawing, however, you can erase without tearing the paper or leaving eraser droppings. You can have any number of paper textures within the same drawing, and you can quickly accomplish traditional drawing techniques, like adding ink washes, since you don't have to wait for colors to dry.

This chapter is like a beginner's class. It shows you the basics for using Painter's drawing tools; subsequent chapters cover Painter's more advanced drawing concepts.

THE DRAWING TOOLS—AN OVERVIEW

For many years, traditional artists stayed away from the computer because they disliked the high-tech look of the images it produced. Also, they saw drawing in vector-based programs using Bézier curves as unnatural and too different from what they were used to.

Then Painter came along. From its debut in 1991, Painter has offered more real-life drawing tools than any other program on either the Mac or Windows platform, including pens, pencils, chalks, charcoals, crayons, and felt pens. Indeed, it's easy to be intimidated by the seemingly infinite number of features Painter offers. But in many ways, Painter is very simple to use, as you're about to see.

First, you need an image to draw in. Start one by selecting **File: New**. The New Picture dialog box appears. Use the default settings for now, and click **OK**. A new image appears.

Next you'll select the chalk, change its color, adjust how it interacts with paper grain, fix its opacity, and finally, change its width.

CHOOSING A DRAWING TOOL

All of Painter's drawing and painting tools are stored in the Brushes palette, which you should see on-screen. If you don't, select **Window: Brushes** to reveal it.

Several tools appear on the Brushes palette front panel, and many more reside inside the palette's drawer. You open and close this drawer by clicking on its *pushbar*, which is the area containing the black arrow right below the tool icons. When you open the drawer, this arrow turns green (see Figure 4.1).

Figure 4.1 Click on the pushbar on the Brushes palette to reveal more icons and the pop-up menu. Drawing by Karen Sperling.

You select a tool in one of two ways: either click on its icon, or, until you learn what the icons represent, choose the tool from the pop-up menu within the Brushes palette drawer. The following exercise shows how to choose the Chalk and draw with it (see Figure 4.2).

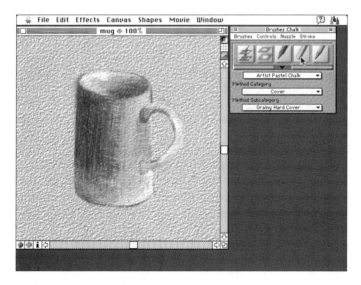

Figure 4.2 The Chalk.

Choosing the Chalk Tool

1. Click on the **Chalk** icon on the Brushes palette front panel. If you don't see the Chalk icon, open the Brushes palette drawer by clicking on the **pushbar**. Then, either click on the **Chalk** icon or click and hold on the pop-up menu within the Brushes palette drawer, drag to the word **Chalk**, and let go. The Chalk icon then appears on the Brushes palette front panel.

2. Click and drag in the image window. Chalk lines appear. If you have a pressure-sensitive stylus, alternate how heavily you press as you draw. You'll see different degrees of paper texture and opacity in your strokes—a useful feature for shading.

USING THE DRAWING VARIANTS

Within each drawing (and painting) tool are further choices, or *variants*, of the particular tool. The Chalk variants, for example, give you different chalk stroke widths. The next exercise shows you how to choose a variant (see Figure 4.3).

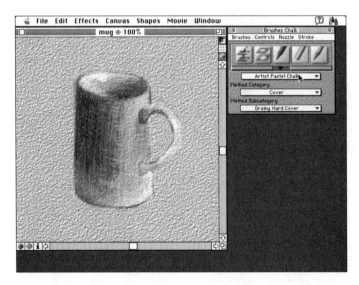

Figure 4.3 The Chalk Variants pop-up menu.

Selecting a Variant

1. Close the Brushes palette drawer by clicking on its pushbar.
2. Click and hold on the pop-up menu directly below the pushbar. This list shows you the chosen tool's variants.
3. Select **Large Chalk** and drag in the image. You still have a chalk line, but now it's thicker.
4. Select the other Chalk variants and draw in the image. Different-width strokes appear.

CHOOSING ADDITIONAL DRAWING TOOLS

Now that you've used the Chalk and its variants, you can choose other drawing tools. Save the painting tools for when you go through the painting chapters that follow these drawing chapters.

Choose the drawing tools from the pop-up menu within the Brushes palette drawer. The drawing tools include Pencils, Chalk, Charcoal, Pens, Felt Pens, and Crayons. Notice that there's an Eraser tool to erase strokes. The Water tool is great for smudging lines.

As you select various drawing tools, the tools may appear to fly around. What's really happening is that a selected tool's icon dims within the drawer and appears on the Brushes palette front panel, which displays the five most recently selected tools. Notice that after you choose a tool from within the drawer, the next time that you want to select it, you retrieve it from the front of the drawer. To reduce confusion, close the drawer after you select a tool.

Controlling Tool Placement

You can place tools where you want them on the Brushes palette front panel. To do so, click and drag a tool's icon from within the drawer and position it in the desired spot on the drawer's front panel, placing it on top of a current tool's icon. The "replaced" tool is "put back" inside the drawer, that is, its icon within the drawer becomes active.

You can lock up to four tools in place on the front panel. Click and hold on the tool's icon on the drawer's front panel. After a moment, a tiny green light appears, indicating that the tool will remain in this location. If you want to replace this tool, unlock it by clicking and holding on its icon until the green light goes off. Now a newly chosen tool can take its place.

CHOOSING A COLOR

When you draw traditionally, which tool you use isn't your only concern. You also make color and paper choices. The next sections discuss how to select color and paper in Painter.

Select **Window: Art Materials** to access the Art Materials palette if it isn't already showing. This is where you'll choose colors and paper textures.

The Color palette is the first icon on the Art Materials palette, and Paper is the second icon. With the **Artist Pastel Chalk** selected, click on the first icon on the Art Materials palette to reveal the Color palette if it isn't already showing (see Figure 4.4).

You select hues in the color ring. You can either single-click in the ring to pick a color or click and drag in the color ring to fine-tune your hue choice.

The chosen color family appears in the triangle within the color ring. The current color within the family appears in the front rectangle in the lower-left portion of the palette. You use the rear rectangle when you create gradations (see Chapter 18, "Working with the Image Hose") or two-toned brush strokes (see Chapter 7, "Advanced Drawing Tools").

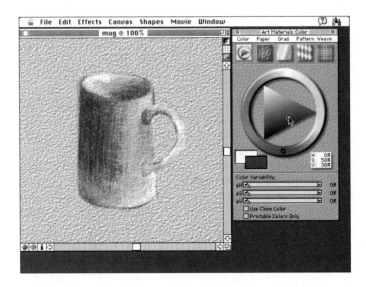

Figure 4.4 The Color palette.

To adjust the color's saturation and value, either click or click and drag in the triangle. The left-most portion of the triangle represents the least saturation (gray), and the right-hand corner is the highest saturation. The top of the triangle has the color's highest value (white) and the bottom of the triangle represents the lowest value (black). The rest of the triangle has all the colors in between.

The white box on the right-hand side of the palette shows the Hue, Saturation, and Value (H,S,V) percentages of the currently selected color in the triangle. The Hue percentage is just a point of reference. Click on **blue** on the color ring and drag until the H percentage is **0**. Now drag clockwise, and you'll see the percentage goes up to 99 and then hits 0 again.

The Saturation and Value percentages have more relevance. When you click on the left-hand side of the triangle, the S percentage is 0, and when you click on the right-hand side the percentage is 100. Value (V) is the luminance of the color, so when you click on **black**, the percentage in the box is 0, and when you click on **white**, it is 100.

Painter remembers the most recently chosen color, unless you quit the program. When you relaunch Painter, the color defaults back to black.

One way in which you can see the sophistication of Painter's tools is when you mix colors on-screen. Try the next exercise to see color mixing in action.

Choosing and Mixing Colors

1. Choose the **Chalk** if it isn't already selected.
2. Click on the **Color** icon to reveal the Colors palette if it isn't already showing.
3. Choose **yellow** with the following settings in the white box in the Color palette: H: **50%**; S: **100%**; V: **50%**.
4. Click and drag a yellow stroke in the image window.
5. Choose **blue** with the following settings: H: **84%**; S: **100%**; V: **50%**.
6. Click and drag a blue stroke next to and touching the yellow stroke.
7. Select **Water** from the pop-up menu within the Brushes palette drawer. The Water tool appears on the Brushes palette front panel.
8. Click and drag over the two strokes, smudging the colors together. You now have green!

SELECTING A PAPER TEXTURE

You select a paper texture in the Paper palette. To display it, click on the **Paper** icon in the Art Materials palette. The Paper palette appears (see Figure 4.5).

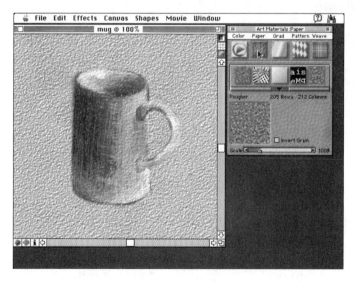

Figure 4.5 The Paper palette.

Selecting a paper texture in Painter is fairly straightforward, although at first it might not be clear what's happening in the image. You might think that when you select a paper grain, you're selecting it for the whole image. However, this is not the case. The designated paper texture interacts with just the brush stroke. Therefore, you can have many different paper textures within the same image.

To see how the papers work, with the **Chalk** selected, click on one of the textures in the Paper palette and draw in the image. Click on another grain and draw again. You can see that the Chalk picks up the currently selected paper grain.

You can edit paper grain easily by adjusting the Scale slider on the Paper palette front panel. The Preview window shows you the effect of Scale slider changes. Checking **Invert Grain** is another paper-editing feature. When using larger-grain textures, draw with one color. Then check **Invert Grain**, pick a different color, and draw over the same area in the image. You will get a duotone effect.

As with the Brushes palette, the Paper palette contains additional paper grains within its drawer. You open the drawer by pressing the Paper palette's pushbar. You can choose a texture by either clicking on its icon or selecting its name from the pop-up menu within the Paper palette drawer.

Click the **Library** button within the Paper palette drawer and you can access additional paper libraries. Painter comes with more than 100 different textures. You can also create your own paper textures, and you can buy more through Fractal Design Corporation and *Artistry*, the newsletter.

Tear-Off Palettes

You might want the Color and Paper palettes to be visible at the same time. For this to be the case, tear one away from the Art Materials palette. An icon must be deselected before it can be torn off. Therefore, click on the **Paper** icon. Then click and hold on the **Color** icon and drag it away from the Art Materials palette. The Color palette tears off into its own independent palette (see Figure 4.6).

ADJUSTING OPACITY AND TEXTURE

Two more sliders that you can use right away are Opacity and Grain. They are located in the Window: Controls palette.

Opacity controls how solid or transparent a line is. You can choose from 100% opacity, which means the line is solid, to 0% opacity, which produces no line. Try the next exercise to see how Opacity operates.

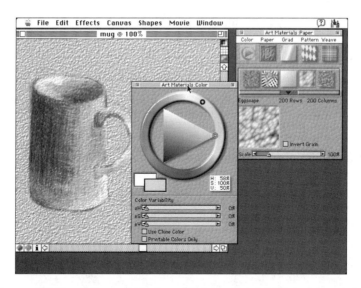

Figure 4.6 The Color palette torn off from the Art Materials palette.

ADJUSTING OPACITY

1. Choose **Window: Controls** to reveal the Controls palette if it isn't already showing.
2. Draw a line with the Chalk.
3. Drag the Opacity slider to around **30%** and draw another line. The second line is transparent.

Adjusting Paper Texture Level

The Grain slider determines how much paper shows through strokes that interact with paper grain. Move the slider to the right and you hide more paper texture, making the stroke appear more solid. Move the slider to the left and you reveal more paper texture, making the stroke appear grainier.

If you are using a mouse, the Opacity and Grain sliders are handy tools for shading. Changing their positions varies the intensity of a stroke, allowing you to approximate the variations that pressure-sensitive stylus users get from altering stylus pressure.

Changing Line Width

As you draw, you'll want to vary the width of the lines you create. You'll do this using the Size slider in the Size palette, accessed by choosing **Brushes palette: Controls: Size** (see Figure 4.7).

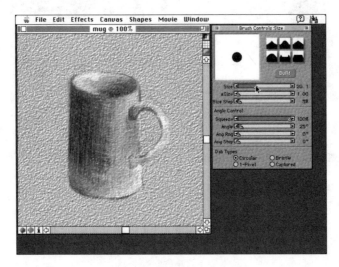

Figure 4.7 The Size palette.

Moving the Size slider to the left thins out lines; moving it to the right makes them wider. The circle in the Size palette Preview window represents line width. Whenever you change the size of your stroke, the change is reflected in the circle. Adjust the Size slider and drag a stroke in the image. You'll see how the slider, the circle, and the stroke interrelate. Depending on the computer that you are using, the wider you make the stroke, the longer you have to wait for the change to take effect.

Saving Variants

Changes to the Size, Opacity, and Grain sliders are temporary. When you switch to another tool, the changes disappear and the previously selected tool reverts to its default settings. You can, however, save Size, Opacity, and Grain slider changes by creating a new variant.

After you've made your adjustments, choose **Brushes palette: Brushes: Variants: Save Variant**. The Save Variant dialog box appears. Type your new variant's name in the text field and click **OK**. The new variant's name appears in the Variants pop-up menu in the Brushes palette.

SUMMARY

Congratulations! You now know how to pick up a chalk in Painter, change it's color, width, texture and opacity, and how to save the changes as a variant. The next chapter shows you Painter's vast stock of drawing tools and examples of the way they draw.

5
Drawing Tools

CHAPTER HIGHLIGHTS

- ❖ Pencils
- ❖ Chalk
- ❖ Pens
- ❖ Felt Tip Pens
- ❖ Crayons
- ❖ Charcoals

Painter has just about every kind of drawing tool that you can imagine. As you saw in Chapter 4, "Drawing Basics," each tool has several variants that give you additional choices for the kind of stroke the tool produces.

This chapter shows you each tool and variant and what they do. Chapter 7, "Advanced Drawing Tools," explains why the tools act the way they do and how you can adjust them to suit your own working style.

This chapter refers to several palettes that were introduced in Chapter 4, including the Brushes palette: Controls: Size palette, the Controls palette, and the Color and Paper palettes in the Art Materials palette. You should have these palettes open as you go through this chapter. Select them from the Window menu if they aren't already visible.

Also, this chapter assumes that you read Chapter 4's instructions for choosing tools and variants.

I drew all the thumbnail sketches in this chapter. They're based on a mug sketch I drew freehand with the Pencils 2B Pencil using a coffee cup on my desk for reference (see Figure 5.1).

Figure 5.1 First "mug shot."

I did each thumbnail by selecting **File: Clone**, then **Edit: Select All**, pressing **Delete**, Mac; **Backspace**, Windows; then choosing **Canvas: Tracing Paper** and sketching the shape of the mug in the clone.

PENCILS

Painter provides several different kinds of pencils with which you can draw. All the pencils share certain characteristics. For example, they all pick up the selected paper texture from the Papers palette. Also, if you're using a pressure-sensitive stylus, in most cases, pressing lightly reveals more paper grain, while pressing heavily hides more.

Another way to alter the amount of paper grain in a pencil stroke in most cases is to adjust the Grain slider in the Controls palette. Moving the slider to the right removes paper by adding color, moving the slider to the left reveals more paper.

Meanwhile, the harder you press on your pressure-sensitive stylus, the darker your line is, while pressing more gently gives you a fainter stroke.

Additionally, you can adjust color by moving the Opacity slider in the Controls palette. Drag it to the right for a darker line, move it to the left for a lighter one.

You can change line width by adjusting the Size palette's Size slider. Move the Size slider to the right for a wider line, to the left for a thinner one.

By the way, you won't be able to draw a light-colored pencil line on a dark one; for now, use the Chalk. Chapter 7, "Advanced Drawing Tools," explains why.

The following sections note variant characteristics if they differ from the above descriptions.

2B Pencil

This variant is the one chosen by many artists for creating pencil drawings in Painter; the 2B refers to the hardness of the lead. Artists' B pencils have softer and therefore darker-colored leads, and H pencils have harder and therefore lighter-colored ones. You can get the look of different-weight leads by choosing **black** in the Colors palette and adjusting the Opacity slider. You could also choose different shades of gray along the left edge of the triangle in the Colors palette. Another possibility is to use the Gray Range or Grayscale Color Sets that come with Painter. To access them, choose **Window: Color Set** to see the Color Set palette, then choose **Art Materials palette: Color: Adjust Color set** and then click **Library**, and choose from within the Colors, Weaves and Grads folder within your Painter 4 folder on Mac. In Windows, look in the Goodies folder on the Fractal Design CD. It is also in the sub-colors directory within Painter 4 on the PC (gray.pcs and grayscal.pcs).

You'll see a lot of texture when you draw with this variant, regardless of stylus pressure, whereas with the other variants, pressing heavily on a stylus hides paper texture. Also, adjusting the Grain slider has no effect on this variant.

500 lb. Pencil

This variant is great for tonal drawing and for filling in large areas.

Colored Pencils

Use the Colored Pencils with different colors chosen in the Colors palette. The Colored Pencils strokes mix together to produce a third color the way you smudged the Chalk Strokes with the Water in Chapter 4.

Sharp Pencil

The Sharp Pencil is like the 2B Pencil except that it reveals paper texture based on stylus pressure. Pressing heavily hides paper grain, and pressing lightly reveals it. Choose a large grain texture and draw first with the 2B Pencil and then the Sharp Pencil, altering stylus pressure with both, and you'll see the difference. And the Sharp Pencil is, well, sharper.

Single Pixel Scribbler

This variant draws a line that's one-pixel wide. You'll see a lot of texture when you draw with this variant, regardless of stylus pressure. Also, adjusting the Grain slider has no effect on this variant.

Thick & Thin Pencils

This variant is nice because you can get thin and thick strokes based on the direction in which you drag your stylus or mouse.

CHALK

The chalk variants are the computer equivalent of traditional artists' pastels. As you saw in Chapter 4, the main difference between the variants is the width of the line they draw.

Chalk strokes are paper-sensitive. Choosing different grains in the Paper palette varies the look of the chalk strokes. All chalk variants are sensitive to stylus pressure. Pressing lightly on a pressure-sensitive stylus allows more paper to show in each stroke; pressing heavily causes the color to cover the paper grain more.

You can also adjust the amount of paper grain in chalk strokes by moving the Grain slider in the Controls palette. Dragging the slider to the right removes paper by adding color; moving the slider to the left reveals more paper.

Drag the Opacity slider in the Controls palette to the right for a darker line or to the left for a lighter one.

Artist Pastel Chalk

This variant draws a medium-width chalk line.

Large Chalk

The Large Chalk draws a wider line.

Oil Pastel

This variant draws lines similar to an oil pastel stick, which is gooey, where a plain pastel is powdery.

Sharp Chalk

The Sharp Chalk draws a narrower chalk line.

Square Chalk

This variant has a square tip and is a captured brush. Chapter 12, "Painting Gadgets," explains how to capture a brush tip.

PENS

The Pens category has many different tools to keep your creative drawing juices, or inks, flowing.

All the pens produce ultra-smooth lines (especially when you use black) that look so much like they came directly from an inkwell that it's surprising they don't drip down your computer screen. That's because most of them—except the Scratchboard variants—don't react to stylus pressure in terms of opacity. You get a solid-color line throughout the stroke.

With many of the variants, pressing heavily on a stylus will give you a wider line, while pressing more lightly will give you a narrower one, as if you were drawing with a nib and stylus.

Most of the pens are oblivious to paper texture; the exceptions are noted in the individual variant sections that follow.

And finally, lines drawn by most of the variants, except as noted below, hide underlying lines and become more intense as you repeat them, rather than turning black.

Calligraphy

If you like to do hand-lettering, this is a good tool to do it with.

The calligraphic strokes are produced by varying the direction in which you drag your mouse or stylus and changing the pressure levels on your pressure-sensitive stylus.

Fine Point

This variant interacts with the designated texture in the Papers palette. However, unlike the Chalk variants, the Fine Point pen doesn't react to the Grain slider in the Controls palette or to pressure-sensitive stylus pressure. All Fine Point strokes contain the same level of grain sensitivity.

Sometimes the Fine Point pen can look like it's skipping. Usually the culprit is a big-grain paper texture. Pick a small grain to smooth out the lines.

The Fine Point's strokes build to black as you layer them—a useful characteristic for shading. Use the Opacity slider in the Controls palette to determine how quickly they turn black. Move it to the left to keep the strokes lighter; move it to the right to make strokes turn black more quickly.

Also, because lines build up the color of underlying ones, some colors will mix on-screen. Moving the Opacity slider to the left sometimes improves results.

Flat Color

This variant is useful when you want to fill in large areas quickly. I also discovered that this is a great tool to do three-dimensional hand-lettering, which is how I created the *Artistry* logo. Chapter 27, "Type Special Effects," has the steps I did to create it.

Leaky Pen

Would somebody get the cap to this pen? It's leaking all over the place! Don't drag it so slowly—the ink spots are getting bigger! Many artists find this tool useful for creating background textures. I've also played around with the same three-dimensional effects as I used with Flat Color to get some interesting blobs.

Pen and Ink

With the Pen and Ink variant, the width of the stroke is determined by how fast you drag your stylus or mouse. The faster you go, the thinner the lines will be; the slower you drag, the thicker the lines will be.

Pixel Dust

The Pixel Dust can be used as a fine spray in a drawing or painting, but you can also get an interesting tonal drawing from it.

Scratchboard Rake

This variant produces a multibristled stroke that is ideal for creating cross-hatch shading. When you press lightly on a pressure-sensitive stylus, you'll get fewer bristles in the stroke, when you press heavily you'll get more.

Scratchboard Tool

With its smooth, tapered stroke, this variant is great for both regular drawing and white-on-black scratchboard-style renderings.

Single Pixel

Draw one-pixel-wide lines with this variant.

Smooth Ink Pen

Smooth Ink Pen gives you "unsmooth" ink since it interacts with the designated texture in the Papers palette. Smooth Ink Pen is a larger version of the Fine Point variant, and as such is impervious to changes in the Grain slider in the Controls palette and to pressure-sensitive stylus changes. Also, overlapping strokes' colors will mix on-screen.

FELT PENS

Felt Pens strokes muddy to black as you repeat them and will mix on-screen, depending on the variant, as you'll see in the following descriptions.

For colors that turn black, pressing heavily on a pressure-sensitive stylus muddies the color sooner, while pressing lightly keeps the color truer to the one you chose in the Colors palette.

Adjusting the Opacity slider affects how soon the color muddies to black. Moving the slider to the right makes the line turn black sooner, while moving the slider to the left keeps the line closer to the color you chose in the Colors palette.

You can mix two colors to produce a third color with the Felt Pens. Colors mix best when you press more lightly on the stylus and when the Opacity slider is moved to the left.

Meanwhile, if you try to draw a light color, including white, on a dark one, nothing will happen. The explanation for this is in Chapter 7, "Advanced Drawing Tools." For now, switch to Chalk to draw light lines on dark.

The Felt Pens don't pick up paper grain. Choosing paper textures and moving the Grain slider will have no effect on them.

Fine Tip Felt Pens

Fine Tip Felt Pens generate narrow felt pen lines.

Medium Tip Felt Pens

This variant gives you medium felt pen lines. You can vary the line width by changing how fast you drag your stylus or mouse. Dragging quickly gives you thin strokes, dragging slowly gives you wide ones. Colors will mix and bleed together. Move the Opacity slider to the left to get the best results.

Felt Marker

Produces a softer line than the other Felt Pens variants. Colors will mix but will not bleed with this variant. Vary the line width by dragging your mouse or stylus in different directions.

Dirty Marker

As with the Felt Marker variant, the line width varies based on the direction in which you drag your mouse or stylus. Also, mix different color strokes and notice how they bleed and mix together.

The following exercise illustrates the differences among the Felt Pens variants (see Figure 5.2).

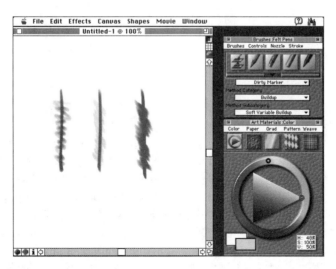

Figure 5.2 Lines drawn by (left to right) the Medium Tip Felt Pens, the Felt Marker, and the Dirty Marker.

Using the Felt Pens Variants

1. Draw three vertical red lines, one each with the Medium Tip Felt Pens, the Felt Marker, and the Dirty Marker. Notice that they look pretty much the same.

2. Next, with yellow, draw a zigzag line on top of each red line with the corresponding variant, so that you have a red zigzag Medium Tip Felt Pens line on top of the first straight red line, and so on.

3. The result is that the first, Medium Tip Felt Pens lines, show some bleed and some color mixing; the second, Felt Marker lines, produce some mixing with no bleed; and the third, Dirty Marker lines, mix and bleed together like crazy.

Single Pixel Marker

This variant draws a one-pixel-wide line.

CRAYONS

Who says drawing has to be serious all the time? Why not sit down and color something? Here are the crayons with which to do it.

The Crayons react to the selected grain in the Paper palette. Moving the Grain slider to the left will cause your lines to reveal more paper texture; moving it to the right will make them denser, allowing less of the paper grain to show.

Using a pressure-sensitive stylus can also control how much paper texture crayon strokes have. Pressing lightly allows more of the paper texture to show through; pressing heavily reveals less grain.

Another quality the Crayons share is that they produce strokes that muddy to black as you repeat them; this comes in handy for shading. The Crayons' nature also means that you can mix colors on-screen with them. As you work with the Crayons you may find that strokes turn black too quickly to suit your illustration. Move the Opacity slider to the left for the strokes to stay lighter longer. Move it to the right to make them turn black more quickly.

The Crayons are also pressure-sensitive in terms of opacity, that is, in general, the harder you press on the stylus, the blacker your strokes will be, and the lighter you press, the lighter in color your strokes will be.

Because most Crayon strokes muddy to black, you won't be able to add a light Crayon stroke to a dark one. If you try, the stroke will darken or not change at all, depending on how dark the underlying line is. For now, switch to the Chalk to get a light color to appear on a dark one. Chapter 7 tells you other remedies.

Default

This is your basic crayon.

Waxy Crayons

Waxy Crayons give you the effect of melted crayons because of the way colors bleed together. Sometimes when you put colors together all you'll see is black. Just move the Opacity slider to the left for better results.

CHARCOAL

The Charcoal variants are great for roughing out preliminary sketches, or you can use them for the final drawing, too.

Stylus pressure affects opacity. Heavy pressure makes the stroke more opaque, light pressure makes it more transparent. Also, moving the Opacity slider in the Controls palette to the left makes the stroke more transparent, moving it to the right makes it more opaque.

Default

Draw with this variant and it's like you're holding a stick of charcoal. It exposes lots of paper texture through its rich strokes. Default variant lines pick up the paper textures chosen in the Papers palette. How hard you bear down on a pressure-sensitive stylus will affect the amount of texture in Default strokes. Pressing lightly makes strokes more grainy; pressing heavily cloaks paper.

Adjusting the Grain slider in the Controls palette also affects paper sensitivity. To show more paper, move the slider to the left, to intensify the color hiding the grain, move it to the right.

Gritty Charcoal

Drawing with the Gritty Charcoal gives you lines with a certain hardness to them. You can get interesting edges and different widths based on the direction in which you drag your stylus or mouse and how heavily you bear down on a pressure-sensitive stylus. This variant reacts to paper texture in the same way as the Default variant.

Soft Charcoal

This variant's lines have an ethereal quality. Soft Charcoal strokes are unaffected by changes in the Grain slider.

SUMMARY

You have just learned which drawing tools are available in Painter and how they work. At this point you could create wonderful drawings in Painter. However, Painter goes a lot deeper than just offering the computer equivalents of natural media. The next chapter shows you what I call "drawing gadgets," that is, features within Painter that you will use along with the drawing tools to create your artwork.

6

Drawing Gadgets

CHAPTER HIGHLIGHTS

- ❖ Multiple undos
- ❖ Getting around on-screen
- ❖ Drawing straight lines
- ❖ Playing back strokes and scripts
- ❖ Setting up tracing paper

A drawing gadget is something that helps you draw along with a drawing tool like a pen or pencil. Painter has many such drawing gadgets, as you'll see in this chapter.

MULTIPLE UNDOS

Painter 4 provides multiple undos, allowing you to go backwards through your most recent maneuvers to return to an earlier version of your image. To do so, select **Edit: Undo** (whatever your most recent action was).

The default number of undos is five. To change the default, choose **Edit: Preferences: Undo**. The Undo Preferences dialog box appears. Type in the desired number of levels. As the dialog box notes, you can set up to 32 levels of undo. However, be forewarned that the more levels you set, the more memory will be allocated to saving all of those steps, and the slower things might get. Click **OK**. You can now undo the number of times that you designated.

EMPTYING THE IMAGE WINDOW

One of the best Painter gadgets is selecting the whole image and deleting. This is useful if you are experimenting and want to eliminate everything you've just done so that you can start over; it is like starting a fresh page in your sketch pad. The following exercise shows how to empty your screen.

Deleting the Entire Image

1. Choose **Edit: Select All** or press **Command+A** on the Mac or **Ctrl+A** in Windows.
2. Press **Delete** on the Mac or **Backspace** in Windows. The image and selection marquee disappear.

GETTING AROUND ON-SCREEN

When you draw in real life you move closer to your paper to get a detail just right. Then you move back to see how the change looks and how the overall composition is turning out. In Painter, use *image zooming* and the Grabber Tool to focus in on the finer points and to view the overall scheme of things.

Image Zooming

All images in Painter open at 100% magnification. When you zoom in on an image, you increase the magnification, making it easier to see specific image pieces. You zoom out, or decrease the magnification, to see more of the image (see Figures 6.1 and 6.2).

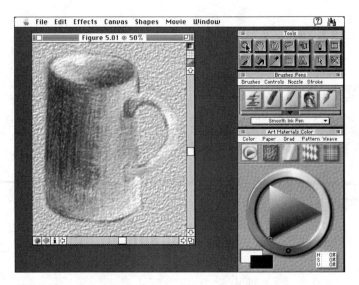

Figure 6.1 Image at 50% magnification.

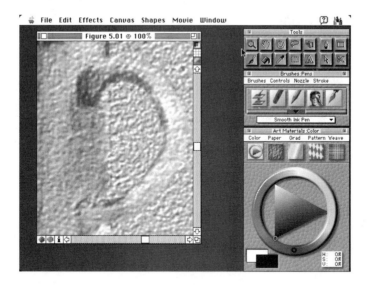

Figure 6.2 The same image at 100% magnification.

The current magnification level appears in the title bar next to the document's name. As you zoom in and out of the image, the percentage in the title bar updates to reflect the change. Zooming applies just to the image's on-screen appearance and not to the final output.

The fastest way to zoom in and out of an image one magnification notch at a time is to use the shortcut keys. You have a choice. You can press **Command+Spacebar** and click on the Mac or **Ctrl+Spacebar** and click in Windows. Doing so zooms in on the area at which you point. Or, you can press **Command+Plus Sign** on the Mac or **Ctrl+Plus Sign** in Windows, which will simply increase magnification. To zoom down, press **Option+Command+Spacebar** on the Mac or **Alt+Ctrl+Spacebar** in Windows and click in the image. Or, you can press **Command+ −** on the Mac or **Ctrl+ −** in Windows.

The fastest way to zoom to a specific magnification level is to use the Zoom Level pop-up menu in the Controls palette. Click on the **Magnifier Tool** or the **Grabber Tool** (covered in the next section) in the Tools palette and you'll see the Zoom Level pop-up menu in the Controls palette. Then you can select the desired magnification level in this pop-up.

To return to 100% magnification, double-click on the **Magnifier Tool** in the Tools palette. To fit the image in the image window, choose **Window: Zoom To Fit Screen**, which also centers an image.

Grabbing the Image

When the image is zoomed up, it can be inconvenient to move to another part of the image because you have to either zoom down first or use the scroll bars on the side and bottom of the image window.

It's much easier to grab the image and move it around; instead of clicking on the **Grabber Tool**, it's easier to press the **Spacebar** and click and drag in the image to "travel" to the desired spot. To center the image quickly, click once in the image with the Grabber Tool.

MAKING ROOM ON-SCREEN

Painter's numerous palettes can eat up screen real estate in no time. Following are some of the gadgets to help you clear things up quickly.

Hide Palettes

Choose **Window: Hide Palettes** to hide all open palettes simultaneously. Choose **Window: Show Palettes** to bring them back. Choose **Window: Clean Up Palettes** to bring up the default palettes and line them up.

Screen Mode Toggle

Choose **Window: Screen Mode Toggle** (**Command+M** on the Mac; **Ctrl+M** in Windows) to hide image window elements like scroll bars (see Figure 6.3). Choose **Window: Screen Mode Toggle** again to bring them back. While you're in Screen Mode Toggle, you can use the shortcuts for zooming in and out and grabbing the image.

TURNING THE PAPER

Most artists draw with their pad or paper at an angle. Painter 4 lets you angle your image in a similar way (see Figure 6.4). You can rotate the image either clockwise or counterclockwise and position it at any angle. Angling the image is a nonprinting change. The image will print out upright. To rotate an image for real, choose **Effects: Orientation: Rotate**.

Figure 6.3 Image with Screen Mode Toggle activated.

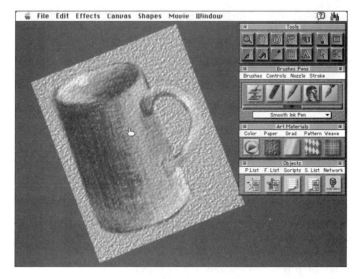

Figure 6.4 Image angled.

71

The following exercise shows how to angle your image.

Setting Image Angle

1. Click on the **Rotate Page Tool**, the third icon from the left in the top row of the Tools palette.

2. Move the cursor over the image. The cursor becomes an upward-pointing hand.

3. Click and drag on the image window. You see a rectangle with an arrow in it.

4. Drag on the image until the page is at the desired angle, then let go. The image is now positioned at an angle and the Controls palette designates the new angle. The Magnifier, the Grabber, and the Screen Mode Toggle work when the image is angled.

If you press the **Shift** key before you click and drag with the Rotate Page Tool, the amount you can rotate the page is constrained to 90° angles, an interesting way to edit reflections—turn the paper upside down! Angling the page is a temporary change for the session. The next time you open the image it will be back at 0°.

If you don't like the angle, you can continue to click and drag and change it as long as the **Rotate Page Tool** is selected. To get the image upright again, click once on it with the Rotate Page Tool.

SMUDGING

A common drawing technique is to smudge pencil, chalk, and charcoal lines to produce shading. The Water category in the Brushes palette provides many choices for *smudging* and diluting drawn lines.

Draw some lines with the chalk and then smear them with one of the Water variants and you'll see the effect.

It's a good idea to turn down the Opacity slider if you want to leave some paper grain behind as you smudge. Also, the harder you bear down on a pressure-sensitive stylus, the more smeary the lines will get.

What distinguishes the Water variants is how they interact with the paper grain (see Figure 6.5).

The *Just Add Water* variant completely removes the paper grain. The *Grainy Water* variant reacts to the chosen paper grain in the Papers palette and is ideal for smearing existing textured strokes, because it helps them maintain their graininess. Grainy Water can also be used to add some texture to smooth strokes. The *Frosty Water* variant smears with a sticky kind of stroke. Try choosing different textures in the Papers Palette for some interesting results.

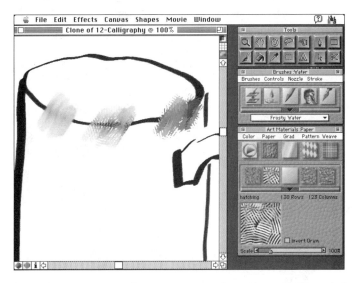

Figure 6.5 Various amounts of paper texture show through (from left to right) Just Add Water, Grainy Water, and Frosty Water.

FADE

Regular Painter users rave about **Edit: Fade**. You can *fade*, or partially undo, any recent maneuver, whether it's a drawn stroke or a special effect.

You can also use fade as a shortcut to draw something that's symmetrical. The next exercise shows how I use fade to draw a heart (see Figure 6.6).

Drawing a Heart

1. Select the Pens' **Scratchboard Tool** variant.
2. Draw the left side of the heart.
3. Click on the middle **rectangle** in the Tools palette. Click and drag a selection marquee surrounding the heart. The idea is to have the left side of

the heart in the rectangle's left side because you're about to flip it to the right (see Figure 6.7).

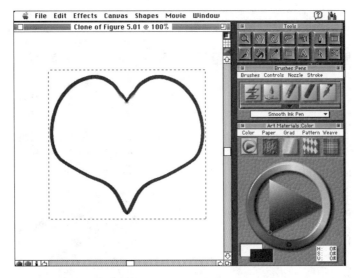

Figure 6.6 Heart created using Fade.

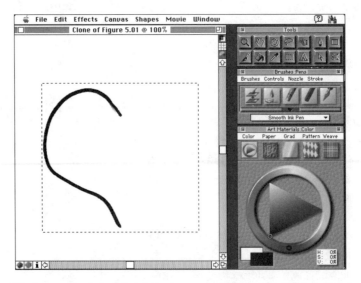

Figure 6.7 Select the left side of the heart so that it's in the left-hand portion of the rectangle.

4. Select **Effects: Orientation: Flip Horizontal**. Now you have the right side of the heart.

5. Choose **Edit: Fade**. Click **OK**. You now have a heart.

6. To darken it, select **Effects: Tonal Control: Adjust Colors**. The Adjust Color dialog box appears. Move the Value slider to the left. Click **OK**. By the way, click **Reset** in the Adjust Color dialog box to return the sliders to their default positions.

SETTING STYLUS AND MOUSE SENSITIVITY

Painter, whenever possible, uses as its metaphor real-life artists' supplies and actions. In real life, drawing tools respond to such hand movements as the amount of pressure that the artist applies or how quickly he or she drags a tool along the drawing surface. Artists use these hand movements to control such line attributes as width and interaction with paper texture. Also, each artist's touch is unique. Applying a "normal" amount of pressure can produce as many different results as there are artists. Painter is designed to pay attention to these individual hand signals. Using the Brush Tracking dialog box (see Figure 6.8), you can adjust Painter to respond to how hard you press a pressure-sensitive stylus and to how fast you drag a stylus or mouse.

If you're using a pressure sensitive stylus, you will not be able to draw freehand with the mouse and Brush Tracking with the mouse is also diabled.

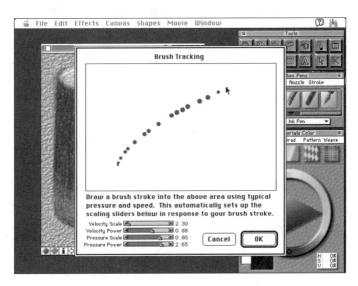

Figure 6.8 The Brush Tracking dialog box.

The next exercise shows you how brush tracking sets up stylus and mouse sensitivity for opacity. Brush tracking can also control stroke width, grain sensitivity, and other characteristics, depending on an individual brush's settings. These settings are discussed in Chapter 7, "Advanced Drawing Tools."

Note that as the number of pressure-sensitive stylus manufacturers proliferates, so do the specifications for styluses. Refer to your stylus manual if the following Brush Tracking recommendations don't work for you.

Adjusting Brush Tracking

1. Select **Edit: Preferences: Brush Tracking**. The Brush Tracking dialog box appears.

2. If you have a pressure-sensitive stylus, drag your stylus across the Scratch Pad area at a normal speed and with a normal amount of pressure. Varying the amount of pressure that you apply in the Scratch Pad area adjusts how your stylus performs in the image window. A stroke appears in the Scratch Pad area and the sliders at the bottom of the dialog box automatically update. You won't ever adjust these sliders manually because the way they operate is so esoteric that it's easier to drag on the Scratch Pad than to learn how the sliders function. Fractal Design Corporation has never explained these sliders in any manual for any version of Painter. Non-pressure-sensitive stylus and mouse users: drag at a normal rate of speed in the Scratch Pad area. Brush tracking adjusts pressure- and velocity-sensitivity for styluses, it controls velocity-sensitivity for mouse users. If you're using a pressure-sensitive stylus, you will obviously not be able to draw freehand with the mouse. In this case, Brush Tracking with the mouse is also disabled.

3. Click **OK**.

4. If you have a pressure-sensitive stylus, select the **Felt Marker** variant of the Felt Pens, although you could use any tool that is set up to react to stylus pressure. Chapter 7 explains how to tell which tools in the Brushes palette are pressure-sensitive. Draw in the image with a "medium" amount of pressure and speed. The stroke appears in a medium stream. Non-pressure-sensitive stylus and mouse users, drag at a medium velocity, and the stroke also appears to be medium.

Brush Tracking is useful when you want to make your mouse or stylus ultra-sensitive to pressure or dragging speed.

Pressure-sensitive stylus users, try the next exercise to see how to set up the stylus for delicate strokes.

Adjusting Opacity with Brush Tracking

1. With the Felt Marker variant of the Felt Pens, draw a line in the image window, pressing very lightly on your stylus. Not much color appears in the stroke.

2. Select **Edit: Preferences: Brush Tracking**. Drag lightly in the Scratch Pad area. A series of dots appears if you drag quickly; a line appears if you drag slowly. Click **OK**.

3. Draw lightly in the image. Color flows with less effort and the stylus is more sensitive to your light touch.

4. Drag heavily in the image. Color now gushes from the stylus. Pressing more lightly doesn't produce much of a variation. This is a useful stylus setting if you want a lush line.

5. Open the Brush Tracking dialog box again. This time, drag heavily in the Scratch Pad area and click **OK**.

6. Drag lightly and heavily in the image window. You now get more opacity variations.

Mouse and non-pressure-sensitive stylus users can use varying dragging speeds to alter stroke attributes such as opacity, line width and paper-grain sensitivity. By adjusting the Brush Tracking dialog box to react to different dragging speeds, the user can get results similar to those available to pressure-sensitive stylus users. The next exercise shows an example of setting up brush tracking to make a mouse or stylus sensitive to dragging speed.

You will use the Medium Tip Felt Pens variant because it was set up to react to velocity. See Chapter 7 to find out how to tell which other variants were set up this way.

Adjusting Mouse Reaction to Velocity

1. Select the **Medium Tip Felt Pens** variant of the Felt Pens.

2. Draw a line quickly in the image window, then draw a line slowly next to it. You will see only a slight difference in the width of the two strokes.

3. Select **Edit: Preferences: Brush Tracking**. Drag quickly—actually, scribble—in the Scratch Pad area. A series of dots appears. Click **OK**.

4. Draw a line quickly in the image, and then draw one slowly next to it. The first quick line is just about the same as before, but now the second, slower line is much wider. Try drawing a continuous line with different dragging speeds. You get some pretty interesting line-width

variations. Drag slowly in the Brush Tracking dialog box to tone down the effect.

Just as your signature varies, so does the way you work with the stylus at any given time, so Fractal Design Corporation intended for you to set up brush tracking each time you launch Painter. When you quit Painter, the brush tracking gauges return to their default settings.

DRAWING STRAIGHT LINES

You can draw straight lines in Painter very easily by using the **Straight Lines** option in the Controls palette. The following exercise shows how.

Using the Straight Lines Tool

1.   Choose a drawing tool in the Brushes palette.
2.   In the Controls palette, choose **Draw Style: Straight Lines**.
3.   Click the stylus or mouse where you'd like your stroke to start. An origin point marker appears.
4.   Click and hold where you want your stroke to finish. A line connects the two points. Before you let go, move the stylus or mouse around until it's where you want the other end of the line to be. To constrain your line to a 45° or 90° angle, hold down the **Shift** key on the Mac or **Shift+Ctrl** in Windows before making the second mark. Let go of the mouse or stylus. A stroke now connects the two points.
5.   Click elsewhere. A stroke appears connected to the first.

You can continue to click in the image. When you are done, choose **Draw Style: Freehand** in the Controls palette. This completes the last line drawn. Now you can draw freehand strokes again. You can also click back on **Straight Lines** and start a straight line that's unconnected to the ones you drew earlier. If you just want one line, click next to **Straight Lines**, click at the beginning and end of the line, and then click next to **Freehand**.

If you want your group of lines to finish off into an irregular polygon, do one of two things. Either click the last point on the first one, and then click on **Freehand**, or press **Return** or **Enter** on the Mac or **Enter** in Windows; this will connect the first and last points if there's space between them.

AUTOMATED DRAWING

Painter has two features for saving strokes and playing them back. The following sections describe these features.

Automating Brush Strokes

Sometimes your artwork calls for repeated lines. One example is hair (see Figure 6.9).

Figure 6.9 Hair created with **Record** and **Playback Stroke**.

You can record and play back strokes to get these repeating lines. The following exercise shows how I used repeating strokes to create the hair in Figure 6.9.

Recording and Playing Back Brush Strokes

1. Draw someone's face with the Scratchboard Tool.
2. Select **Brushes palette: Stroke: Record Stroke**.
3. Next, draw one hair strand. The stroke is now recorded.
4. Select **Brushes palette: Stroke: Playback Stroke**.
5. Click once where you want the strand to appear. The stroke is played back each time you click.

6. The stroke will play back with any of the drawing or painting tools regardless of which brush you recorded it with. Choose the **Artist Pastel Chalk** variant of the Chalk.

7. Click in the image. The strand is now drawn with the chalk.

8. Also, the stroke will be whatever color you select in the Colors palette. Choose **orange**. Click in the image. The hair is now orange.

To resume normal drawing, choose **Brushes palette: Stroke: Playback Stroke** to deselect it.

Don't forget about the **Straight Lines** option. It works with auto playback. Activate **Straight Lines**, choose **Record Stroke**, click the start and end of the line, finish off the line by clicking next to **Freehand** in the Controls palette, then choose **Playback Stroke** and click in the image. You get repeating straight lines. Click in the middle of where you want the line to be.

Recording Scripts

In Painter, you can record your work and play it back at another time. Doing so has several advantages.

For one, you can record your script with one tool and play it back with another. For example, you might do a pencil sketch, but you want to see how it would look as a felt pen drawing. Using scripts, Painter reconstructs your pencil strokes as felt pen lines. The secret lies in **Objects: Scripts: Script Options: Record Initial State**. With **Record Initial State** checked, Painter saves your script as is, including the tool, color, and paper texture you used when you recorded the script. By unchecking **Record Initial State**, Painter just remembers the strokes. Then, when you play back the script, Painter will use the current tool, color, and other settings.

Another reason to record scripts is to work at a lower resolution and play back at a higher one. The bigger your document is in terms of both dimensions and resolution, the longer things take to accomplish, so it's quicker to work at a low resolution and let Painter play back your art at a higher resolution. Playing back at a higher resolution is preferable to resizing using **Canvas: Resize**. When bit-mapped programs resize an image up, they guess where pixels should be added. The result can be a blurry image. You can get a larger image that's truer to your original by playing back a script at a higher resolution.

The next exercise shows you how to record a script at a low resolution and play back at a high one.

Recording a Script

1. Start a new document. Select **inches** in the pop-up menus next to Width and Height. Type **4** next to Width and Height. Type **100** next to Resolution. Click **OK**. A new image window appears.

2. Choose **Edit: Select All** (**Command+A** on the Mac or **Ctrl+A** on a PC) to select the whole image.

3. Click the red **Record** button on the Objects: Scripts palette.

4. Draw your artwork.

5. When you're done, click the black **Stop** button on the Objects: Scripts palette. The Name the Script dialog box appears. Type a name and click **OK**. The script is now saved.

Now you'll play back the image at a higher resolution.

1. Start a new document. Keep the width and height the same as before, but type **300** next to Resolution. The dimensions can also be higher, but to avoid distorting the image, make sure the height and width are proportional to the original. Click **OK**.

2. Choose **Edit: Select All** (**Command+A** on the Mac or **Ctrl+A** on a PC) to select the whole image. If you don't see the selection rectangle it's because the image appears large at 300 pixels per inch (ppi). Zoom down the image and you'll see the Selection rectangle.

3. Click the Scripts palette's **pushbar** and select the script you just created from the pop-up menu within the Scripts palette drawer.

4. Click the right-pointing **Play** arrow on the Objects: Scripts palette. Painter plays back the recorded strokes at the new resolution.

There are some cautions to consider when playing back a script at a higher resolution.

The following information is from John Derry, Vice President, Creative Design, and Laurie Hemnes, Manager, Tech Support, at Fractal Design Corporation.

You won't be able to play back scalable items higher than they can go. For example, the maximum stroke width that you can set in the Size slider is 1500 pixels. Suppose you create a drawing at 72 ppi with your brush set at 500 pixels. If you playback the script at four times the resolution, or about 300 ppi (288 to be exact), the brush will only go up to 1500 pixels, not 2000 pixels.

Many of Painter's features, such as Scale in the Paper palette, have an upper limit. Paper scale goes up to 400%. Therefore, if you set your paper texture at 200% and play back your image at four times the resolution, Painter will only be able to play back paper at the maximum, 400%, not 800%. Playback is also limited in terms of data. While playback at a higher resolution produces better results than resizing an image up, it is still limited by the amount of data captured in the original image. If you draw a circle, for example, and play it back at too high a resolution, straight lines would connect the points, making it look faceted like a stop sign. Painter can't guess what points should go between the original ones. John recommends that you play back your image at a resolution that's three or four times higher than the original, but not more than that.

He also suggests that instead of automatically recording the script at 72 ppi—a common choice because the image appears at its normal size at this resolution on most monitors—you choose a resolution that's just below when your brush strokes start to slow down. If you find that things slow down at 300 ppi, but they're not so bad at 200 ppi, record your script at 200 ppi and play back at 300 ppi. You'll be able to work faster and get good results.

Laurie suggests having a plan for your work so that you're not spending a lot of time undoing strokes and building brushes, all of which get recorded along with the drawn strokes.

Users of America Online and CompuServe also report some quirkiness in playing back some features and some filters like Kai's Power Tools. It's always a good idea to test-drive a tool in a miniscript before using it in an elaborate script.

Also, it's unwise to record a script for six hours and then try to play it back. In this case, it's best to record scripts in chunks. You can then play back these multiple scripts in one image.

CHOOSING A PAPER COLOR

When you start a new document, you can select your image's background color using the Paper Color rectangle in the New Picture dialog box (see Figure 6.10).

Designating paper color in the New Picture dialog box is terrific in many ways. For example, when you use the Eraser variants, you erase back to the image color. So if you make your image green, when you erase, you erase back to green, not white. If, however, you fill the image with green using either **Effects: Fill** or the **Paint Bucket**, you erase back to white. You can, however, erase back to white after you set the color in the New Picture dialog by using the bleach variants of the Eraser.

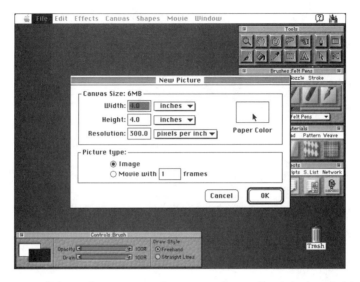

Figure 6.10 Click on the **Paper Color** rectangle on the right-hand side of the New Picture dialog box to choose a colored background.

The color you choose in the New Picture dialog box also fills areas that you **Edit: Cut**, **Edit: Clear**, or delete with **Delete** on the Mac or **Backspace** in Windows.

The next exercise shows how to set paper color.

Setting Paper Color

1. Choose **File: New**. The New Picture dialog box appears.
2. Click the **rectangle** above Paper Color. A color picker appears. Choose the desired color and click **OK**. You return to the New Picture dialog box.
3. Click **OK** again. A new image appears filled with the chosen color.

SUMMARY

Now that you've seen Painter's drawing tools and gadgets, you could stop here and still create drawings using Painter. But within Painter are some pretty amazing settings for honing your drawing (and painting) tools to create the exact strokes you're looking for. You'll learn about these in the next chapter.

7

Advanced Drawing Tools

CHAPTER HIGHLIGHTS

- ✤ Controlling color intensity
- ✤ Adjusting paper grain interaction
- ✤ Setting stroke contour
- ✤ Working with brush dab angles

Here they are, all those Painter palettes, menus, and sliders that make some people faint, but make others cheer because of the tremendous power and control they offer for making the drawing and painting tools do just what you want them to do.

You've already test-driven some of these customizing features in Chapters 4 and 5, namely, the Size slider in the Size palette and the Opacity and Grain sliders in the Controls palette. This chapter shows you how to use some of the more esoteric controls. Chapter 8, "Using Painter's Advanced Drawing Tools," has step-by-step examples of how artists take advantage of these features to create their artwork.

You can skip this chapter if you want to. All of Painter's tools are ready to use straight out of the Brushes palette. The features covered in this chapter are available to fine-tune brushes, but if you don't use them, you can still use Painter.

The version 4 manual contains brush-customizing information. Rather than repeat it here, I'd like to try to show you some of the actual uses that artists have found for the sliders. For example, I've yet to talk to anyone who uses the Clone Location: Variability and How Often sliders located in Brushes palette: Controls: Random palette. They're for randomizing strokes in a clone. But many people are changing Methods, for example, and it's a good idea for you to know how to change them, too.

Any of the following adjustments can be saved in the particular tool's Variants pop-up menu by following the steps listed at the end of Chapter 4.

COLOR INTENSITY

Painter provides you with many features to control color intensity of drawn lines in terms of opacity levels and color interaction. This section goes over some of these controls.

Opacity and Method

As you saw in Chapter 5, Painter's drawing tools behave differently. Some, like the Chalk and Charcoal, get more opaque the more you repeat or layer strokes. Others, like the Felt Pens, muddy to black.

The way to tell how a tool acts is to check its method in the Method Category and Method Subcategory pop-up menus in the Brushes palette (see Figure 7.1). If you don't see these menus, then your Brushes palette is collapsed. Expand it by clicking in the palette's upper-right-hand corner.

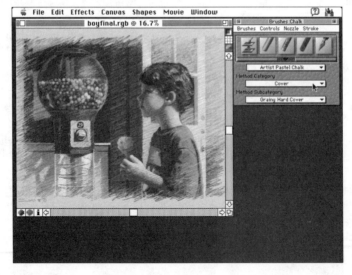

Figure 7.1 Click in the Brushes palette's upper right-hand corner to reveal the Method Category and Method Subcategory pop-up menus, which determine whether drawing tools' layered lines get blacker or more opaque. *Boy* by Michael Savas.

The Method Category menu shows each tool's method. The Method Subcategory lists the tool's other attributes within the main method.

Click and hold on the **Method Category** pop-up menu. The first method, **Buildup**, is what makes strokes build to black, and it is the default method for the Felt Pens. The next one, **Cover**, makes strokes intensify in color, and it is the default method for the Chalk.

You can change a tool's method to solve a design problem and then switch back to its default method. For example, the Felt Pens build to black because that's what they do in real life, giving them a natural feel. But, as mentioned in Chapter 5, you can't draw light-colored Felt Pen lines on top of dark ones. In Chapter 5 you were instructed to choose **Chalk** for the light lines. You can still do that, but another alternative is to change the Felt Pens method from Buildup to Cover by selecting **Cover** in the Method Category menu. Then you can draw light-colored lines on top of dark ones.

Methods and the Opacity Slider in the Controls Palette

You've already seen how the Opacity slider in the Controls palette operates. Adjusting the Opacity slider has a different effect, depending on the tool's method.

In the case of Buildup tools like the Felt Pens, moving the Opacity slider to the left makes strokes more true to the color chosen in the Color palette, slowing down their tendency to muddy to black. Moving the slider to the right makes the lines turn black more quickly, which is great when you want to use the tool for shading. Turning down the Opacity slider helps when you want to mix colors from Buildup brushes.

As for Cover method tools like the Chalk, moving the Opacity slider to the left makes strokes more transparent; moving it to the right makes them more opaque.

Opacity and the Sliders Palette

You've now seen how to adjust Opacity and how method decides the adjustment's effect.

Another way to control opacity is with mouse and stylus actions. You set these actions in the Sliders palette (see Figure 7.2). Open the palette now by selecting **Brushes palette: Controls: Sliders**.

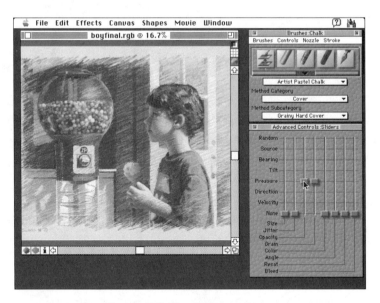

Figure 7.2 The Sliders palette.

The Opacity setting in the Sliders palette is set to **Pressure** for many of the drawing tools. This means that changes in stylus pressure will produce varying levels of opacity. Pressure-sensitive stylus users: try it and see—with the Sliders palette open, select variants of the Chalk or the Felt Pens. You can see that the Opacity setting is on **Pressure** in each case, and when you draw, light pressure produces pale lines, and heavy pressure results in dark ones.

Now choose the Pens' **Flat Color** variant. The slider moves to **None**, and when you draw with Flat Color, you see no difference when you vary stylus pressure.

This means that you can set the Opacity slider to **None** for any variant if you would prefer that the variant produce an even-colored stroke. Conversely, you can give a tool like Flat Color opacity levels by setting Opacity in the Sliders palette to **Pressure**.

Mouse and non-pressure-sensitive stylus users: the Sliders palette is especially useful for you. Choose a Chalk and set Opacity in the Sliders palette on **Direction**. Now, dragging in different directions produces different levels of opacity. This is a good workaround until you get a pressure-sensitive stylus.

I don't know anyone who uses choices other than Pressure, Direction, and None. I've played around with Source to create tonal drawings (see Figures 7.3 and 7.4).

Figure 7.3 Piece of Takeoff photograph ©1996 PhotoDisc.

Figure 7.4 Tonal drawing in clone with Opacity in Sliders palette set to **Source**.

In *Painter 3 Complete*, I showed this exercise using a photograph I took in Cold Spring, N.Y. It was a very high-contrast photograph so the effect was easy since the photograph already had specific light and dark areas. This time I used a photograph from the Painter 4 CD from Fractal called *Takeoff*. The next exercise shows how I used Opacity set to **Source** to turn *Takeoff* into a tonal drawing.

Using the Source Setting

You're going to prepare *Takeoff* so that it clones well. First you'll crop the photo to get rid of some of the sky.

1. Open the Takeoff photograph on the Fractal Design Painter 4 CD (it's in the Goodies: Photos: Urban folder).

2. Click on the rectangle in the middle of the Tools palette. Zoom out on the image as described in Chapter 6; click and drag a selection marquee around the plane.

3. Select **Edit: Copy** then **Edit: Paste: Into New Image**. The cropped area is now a new image.

Next you'll pump up the image's light and dark areas.

1. Select **Effects: Tonal Control: Equalize**. Use the default settings and click **OK**. The image's gray areas are pushed toward black or white.

2. Select **Effects: Tonal Control: Brightness/Contrast**. Move the top slider to the right until the image's contrast is heightened. Click **Apply**.

Next you'll set up the clone to draw in.

1. Select **File: Clone**; a clone of the original appears.

2. Choose a **light gray** in the Color palette, then choose **Canvas: Set Paper Color**.

3. Press **Command+A**, then **Delete** on the Mac or **Ctrl+A**, then **Backspace** in Windows. The image clears and turns light gray.

4. Press **Command+T** on the Mac or **Ctrl+T** in Windows. Tracing Paper comes on.xc

5. Choose a paper in the Papers palette and choose **Effects: Surface Control: Apply Surface Texture**. The Apply Surface Texture dialog box appears. Use the default settings for now, including Paper Grain in the Using menu, and click **OK**. Paper now covers your image.

Now you'll set up the Chalk.

1. Choose the Chalk's **Artist Pastel Chalk** variant.

2. Choose **black** in the Color palette.

3. Choose **Brushes palette: Controls: Sliders palette**. Set Opacity in the Sliders palette to **Source**.

4. Draw in the image, dragging the stylus or mouse back and forth as if you were doing a rubbing as opposed to drawing the elements in the image. Painter reads the light and dark areas of the original to determine where to alter opacity in the clone. I created the frame just by not filling in the area at the image edges. Toggle Tracing Paper on and off (**Command+T**

on the Mac, **Ctrl+T** in Windows) to see how you're doing. When finished, turn off Tracing Paper.

5. Select **Effects: Tonal Control: Negative**. The image reverses and you now have a tonal drawing. Try using colors other than black when you draw in the clone and then choose **Negative** for an unusual effect.

Color Intensity and the Well Palette

The Well palette (see Figure 7.5) contains three great sliders that together can give you drippy, bleeding strokes or strokes that fade out into wispy mists. To show the Well palette select **Brushes palette: Controls: Well**.

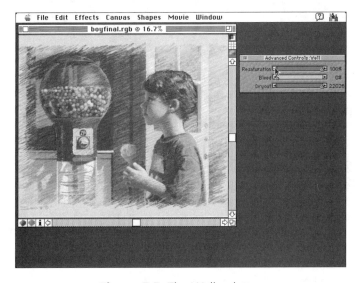

Figure 7.5 The Well palette.

The Well palette's three sliders work together and with the Controls palette: Opacity slider. Adjusting one slider has an effect on the others. You've already seen how these sliders determine brush strokes. The Felt Pens variants' different bleed levels, illustrated in Chapter 5 in Figure 5.2, were created with these sliders set in different positions.

Dryout adjusts drawn lines to run out of color at the end. I've found that Dryout is useful for shading. Try choosing the **Chalk** and moving the Bleed slider to **20%** and the Dryout slider to **4.4**. Then draw short strokes. The strokes start out with a dark color and fade out. Also, going over existing strokes blends them (see Figure 7.6).

91

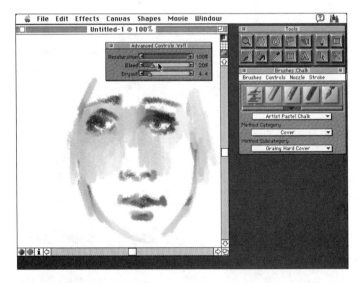

Figure 7.6 Chalk sketch by Karen Sperling with Well palette: Bleed set at **20%** and Dryout on **4.4**.

Color and the Sliders Palette

You can draw two-color strokes by setting Color in the Sliders palette to anything but None. The two colors that make up a stroke are chosen in the Overlapping Rectangles in the Color palette. The next exercise shows how to set up a two-color chalk that you can use to create tonal drawings without having to change colors.

Drawing with Two-Color Strokes

First, start a new image with a paper color that will serve as your midtones.

1. Select **File: New**. The New Picture dialog box appears. Click on the **Paper Color** rectangle, select a **medium gray**, and click **OK**. Click **OK** again. You now have a gray image. Now you'll select the **Chalk** and choose its two colors in the Color palette.

2. Choose the Chalk's **Artist Pastel Chalk** variant. If you made the Dryout slider changes in the previous section, clear them by clicking on another tool, then clicking back on the **Chalk**.

3. Select a dark color in the Color palette to use for shadows. The front rectangle in the palette's lower-left-hand corner turns this color.

4. Click on the rear rectangle in the Color palette to select it. Choose a light color that you will use for highlights. The rear rectangle reflects this color. Click back on the front rectangle.

Now set up the Sliders palette and draw.

1. Choose **Brushes palette: Controls: Sliders** if the Sliders palette isn't already showing.

2. Set Color to **Pressure** in the Sliders palette if you have a pressure-sensitive stylus or to **Direction** if you have a mouse or a non-pressure-sensitive stylus.

3. Draw in the image. With pressure-sensitive styluses, pressing lightly gives you the light color, pressing heavily gives you the dark one, and medium pressure gives you something in between. Setting Color on **Direction** in the Sliders palette means that dragging the mouse or stylus one way will produce one shade, dragging in another will produce another, and dragging in a third direction will give you a color in between.

As you saw earlier in this chapter, the **Source** setting in the Sliders palette sets up the tool to draw in a clone based on the light and dark areas of a clone source. Set the Color slider to **Source** and when you draw in a clone, the colors from the overlapping rectangles are chosen based on the lights and darks in the source image. Finish up by choosing **Effects: Tonal Control: Negative**, and you get an other-worldly image.

CONTROLLING PAPER TEXTURES

As you've seen, some of Painter's drawing tools interact with paper grain and others don't. You can guess which do and which don't because the tools act like their real-life counterparts. It should come as no surprise that the Chalk, Charcoal, and Pencils produce lines with paper grain in them and the Felt Pens do not.

You can control whether a tool interacts with paper grain, how it does it, and how much.

Paper Texture and Method

You saw earlier in this chapter that the Brushes palette: Method Category and Method Subcategory pop-up menus tell you how a tool's overlapping brush strokes interact. The Method Subcategory tells you another important characteristic of brush strokes: whether they interact with paper grain. If you see the word *Grainy* in this menu, then the particular tool's strokes will reflect the paper grain that's selected in the Paper palette. If the word Grainy isn't showing, then the tool's strokes will be smooth.

A question I always get is how to turn off paper grain. The way to do this is to change the Method Subcategory. If you have **Chalk** selected, for example, change the Method Subcategory from the default **Grainy Hard Cover** to **Soft Cover** (there is no plain Hard Cover). Likewise, you can make a "smooth" tool like Felt Pens interact with paper grain by changing the Method Subcategory to one that has the word Grainy in it.

The words Soft, Hard and Flat in the Method Subcategory have to do with the strokes' anti-aliasing or edge smoothness. Soft has the smoothest transition with the area around the stroke, Hard means the strokes will be semi-anti-aliased and Flat gives you jagged-edge strokes.

I added paper-sensitivity to the Felt Pens to create hair in a quick sketch (see Figure 7.7). The next exercise shows how to add texture to Felt Pens strokes.

Figure 7.7 A sketch with paper sensitivity added to the Felt Pens.

Adding Texture to Felt Pens Lines

1. Select **File: New**. The New Picture dialog box appears. Click on **Set Paper color** and choose **white** if it isn't already chosen. Click **OK**, then click **OK** again. A white image appears.
2. Choose the **Medium Tip Felt Pens** variant of the Felt Pens.
3. Draw a face.

You could switch to a chalk to get the graininess in the hair, but you'd lose the feel of the felt pens. Instead, you'll give the Felt Pens paper sensitivity.

1. In the Brushes palette: Method Subcategory choose **Grainy Soft Buildup**.
2. Select **Window: Art Materials: Paper palette** if the Paper palette isn't already showing. Choose **Rougher** from the pop-up menu within the Paper palette's drawer. Draw in the hair. Your lines now interact with the paper grain in the Paper palette.

Grain in the Sliders Palette

You now know how to control whether a tool is paper-sensitive. Earlier in this chapter you saw how to control opacity using the Sliders palette. Likewise, you can control graininess with mouse and stylus actions by adjusting Grain in the Sliders palette.

Grain in the Sliders palette is set to **Pressure** for many of the paper-sensitive drawing tools. This means that changes in stylus pressure will produce varying levels of paper grain.

If you change the Felt Pens to react to grain by changing their Method Subcategory to **Grainy**, and if you have a pressure-sensitive stylus, then you might want to set the Grain slider in the Sliders palette to **Pressure** to control the amount of texture in a stroke.

Mouse and non-pressure-sensitive stylus users can set Grain in the Sliders palette to **Direction** to approximate this effect. Then the direction in which you drag in the image determines the amount of paper texture in the stroke.

Select **None** for Grain in the Sliders palette and an even amount of texture shows throughout the stroke.

You saw previously that you can draw in a clone with Opacity or Color (or both) in the Sliders palette set to **Source**. You can also set Grain in the Sliders palette to **Source** and the light and dark areas in the source image determine texture levels in the clone (see Figure 7.8).

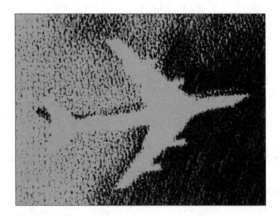

Figure 7.8 Clone of *Takeoff* image drawn using Chalk with Grain set to **Source** in the Sliders palette.

STROKE CONTOUR

You saw how to adjust stroke width in Chapter 4 using the Size Palette: Size slider. Width is just one characteristic of stroke contour that you can adjust in Painter; this section shows you the others.

Stroke Tapering

Painter has controls in the Size palette and in the Sliders palette for tapering strokes. Select **Brushes palette: Controls: Size and Sliders** if these palettes aren't already showing.

Squeeze and Angle

One way to taper strokes is to adjust the Size palette: Squeeze and Angle sliders (see Figure 7.9). Move the Squeeze slider to the left, and the circle in the Preview window becomes an ellipse. Now stroke width will vary based on the direction in which you drag in relation to the direction of the ellipse. Notice in Figure 7.9 that the strokes are narrow when drawn along the ellipse and wide when they go against the ellipse. You change the direction of the ellipse by dragging on the Angle slider.

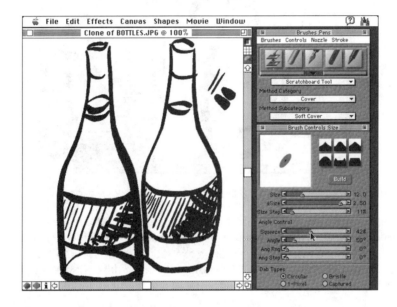

Figure 7.9 Bottles drawn with the Squeeze slider turned down.

±Size Slider and the Sliders Palette

Another way to taper lines is to move the ±Size slider to the right and set Size in the Sliders palette on anything but None.

When you move the ±Size slider to the right, the circle in the Preview window splits in two. The inner black circle shows the stroke's narrow end. The outer gray circle shows the stroke's widest area. The further you drag the slider to the right, the more vast the difference is between the thinnest portion of your stroke and its widest point (see Figure 7.10). Be advised—the more you move this slider to the right, the longer it takes to build, especially on slow or older machines. If the ±Size slider is all the way to the left, you don't have to click **Build** when you move the Size slider.

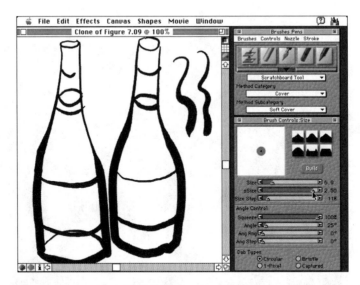

Figure 7.10 Move the ±Size slider to the right to draw tapered strokes.

Meanwhile, you have to adjust Size in the Sliders palette for changes to the ±Size slider to take effect. When you set Size to **Pressure** in the Sliders palette, stylus pressure will produce varying levels of stroke tapering. Mouse and non-pressure-sensitive stylus users: set Size on **Direction** and drag in different directions to produce different amounts of stroke tapering.

Also, when Size is on anything but None, adjustments in the Edit: Preferences: Brush Tracking dialog box will affect the degree to which the stylus or mouse will respond to changes in stylus pressure and dragging speed. See Chapter 6, "Drawing Gadgets," for information about setting up brush tracking.

Size Step Slider

The Size palette: Size Step slider decides whether your line goes smoothly or abruptly from thin to fat. The further the slider is to the left, the smoother the transition is. The further it is to the right, the more abrupt the transition appears (see Figure 7.11).

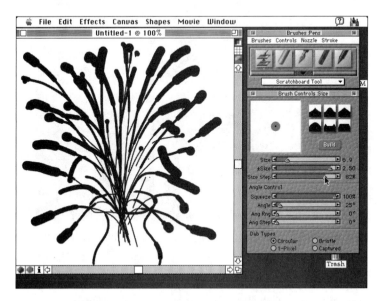

Figure 7.11 Strokes drawn with the Size Step slider turned up have an abrupt transition from narrow to wide.

DABS WITHIN STROKES

The strokes made by the drawing and painting tools are really a series of closely spaced dabs of color. You can control the amount of spacing between the dabs, their shapes, and their angles. By playing around with these brush dabs, I was able to set up the chalk to put a little fuzz on a peach (see Figure 7.12). The following exercise shows how I set up the Chalk to draw the peach fuzz.

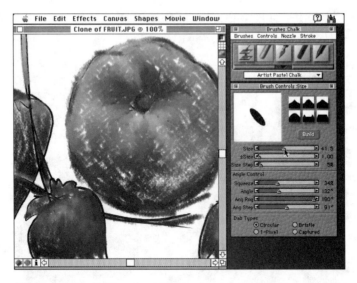

Figure 7.12 A fuzzy peach drawn with continuous strokes
with varying brush-dab angles.

The manual explains all of the brush dab settings, but this exercise shows them in action. For further information about how these controls work, check the manual.

Drawing with Angled Brush Dabs

1. Select **File: New**, use the defaults, and click **OK**. A new image appears. Of course, you can use a photograph as your original and turn on cloning as described in the other exercises in this chapter. I used the Goodies: Photos: Objects: Fruit photo on the Fractal Design Corporation Painter 4 CD as my starting point.

2. Draw in the outline with the Pens' **Scratchboard Tool** variant.

3. Select the Chalk's **Artist Pastel Chalk** variant. Select the following settings:

Brushes palette: Controls: Size palette:

Size	**41.5**
±Size	**1.00**
Size Step	**5%**
Squeeze	**34%**
Angle	**132°**
Ang Rng	**180°**
Ang Step	**91°**

Click **Build**.

Brushes palette: Controls: Spacing palette:

Spacing/Size	**71%**
Min Spacing	**7.4**

Brushes palette: Controls: Sliders palette:

Angle	**Random**

Window: Art Materials: Color palette:

±H,S,V sliders	Move to the right. If you don't see these sliders, click in the palette's upper-right corner to reveal them.

Draw the peach's fuzz.

That wasn't so bad, was it? You can see how adjusting Painter's customizing features can help you achieve the desired effect in your artwork.

Stay tuned, in Chapter 8 are examples of how working artists use these Painter controls.

8

Using Painter's Advanced Drawing Tools

CHAPTER HIGHLIGHTS

- ❖ Drawing with the Chalk
- ❖ Using the Scratchboard Tool
- ❖ Creating an ink wash

In previous chapters you saw the kinds of drawing tools Painter offers, how to custom-tailor them, and some gadgets to use with them. Now it's time to look at how working artists use Painter's drawing tools for actual projects.

California-based Chelsea Sammel is a traditional artist. Her illustrations have appeared in children's books, magazines, and corporate projects.

SKETCHING WITH PAINTER'S COLORED PENCILS

Figure 8.1 *Electric Apples* by Chelsea Sammel.

Chelsea is Fractal Design's Painter demo artist extraordinaire. She drew *Electric Apples* (see Figure 8.1) using Colored Pencils in one sitting as a quick demo of Painter at Macworld. To begin, she sketched with the Colored Pencils default Buildup method, then switched to the Cover method for areas of bright color so they wouldn't darken down. To get a "denser deposit of color," Chelsea moved the Controls palette: Grain slider to the right, which increases the color and lessens the paper texture in the stroke.

Chelsea rotated her paper frequently using **Spacebar+Option+Click and drag in image**, Mac; **Spacebar+Alt+Click and drag in image**, Windows to get the various brush stroke angles in the apples. She also used the keyboard shortcuts for zooming in and out frequently (zoom in is **Spacebar+Command+Click in image**, Mac; **Spacebar+Ctrl+Click in image**, Windows; zoom out is **Spacebar+Command+Option+Click in image**, Mac; **Spacebar+Ctrl+Alt+Click in image**, Windows).

Take a look at this image on the *Fractal Design Painter 4 Complete* CD to see the colors Chelsea used in the image. "I find myself reaching for brighter colors in a demo for eye candy," says Chelsea.

DRAWING WITH THE SCRATCHBOARD TOOL

Steve Rathmann, a tech support specialist at Fractal Design Corporation, gave long-time freelance artist Chet Phillips an amazing way to create color scratchboard drawings. *Wired* is a great example of the technique (see Figure 8.2). Take a look at *Wired* on the *Fractal Design Painter 4 Complete* CD to see the way Chet used colors in the image.

Based in Dallas, Chet is an experienced traditional illustrator who now produces computer artwork for advertising agencies, corporations, newspapers, magazines, book publishers, and occasional gallery shows. The following exercise shows how Chet created *Wired*.

Figure 8.2 *Wired* by Chet Phillips.

Scratchboard Drawing

Traditional scratchboard drawings are made by using a tool to scratch through black ink or other pigment to expose the white surface beneath. Chet uses a similar approach in Painter, scratching white into black. The first step, then, is to set up the black image.

1. Select **File: New**. Click **OK**. A new image appears.
2. Choose **black** in the Color palette. Choose **Effects: Fill**. The Fill dialog box appears. Choose **Current Color** and click **OK**. The image is now black.

3. Choose **Edit: Select All** (**Command+A** on the Mac; **Ctrl+A** in Windows).

4. Choose **Tools palette: Floater** tool (the left-pointing hand).

5. Click on the image. The whole image is now a floater.

You're now going to draw white scratchboard lines in the floater with the Scratchboard Tool (see Figure 8.3).

Figure 8.3 The black and white scratchboard version of *Wired*.

1. Choose the Pens' **Scratchboard Tool** variant.

2. Choose **white** in the Color palette.

3. Draw your artwork. You can choose **black** and draw to fix mistakes.

The next step is to set up the floater so that you can fill the white lines with color without affecting the black areas. The way this works is to paint in the area behind the floater.

1. Choose **Window: Controls palette** if it isn't already showing. Choose **Tools palette: Floaters** tool (the left-pointing hand). The Controls palette updates to reflect options related to the Floaters tool.

2. Choose **Gel** from the Controls palette's Composite Method pop-up menu. Now when you paint in the image behind the floater, the color will show through the white lines.

3. Choose **Edit: Deselect** to deselect the floater. Now when you paint, the color will go into the image area behind the floater. It's OK if this is difficult to grasp. It's not an easy concept. Continue to follow the steps, and eventually it will make sense.

4. Choose the Pens' **Flat Color** variant and a color in the Color palette. Draw where you want the color to appear. The white lines fill with the selected color, while the black areas are not harmed. Pretty cool, huh? Chet painted in the colors in the dog's hair, the coffee cup, and the table.

Next, Chet filled in the background. At this point, there was color in the image behind the floater. But the black hairs that frame the dog's shape were in the floater. Chet drew a path around the dog's shape (the paths always go in the image layer, not on a floater), up the image's right side, across the image's top, and down the image's left side. The next few steps show how to then apply the paper texture.

1. Choose **Art Materials: Paper palette: Library** button. A dialog box appears.

2. Open the **More Wild Textures** library, Mac; **MOREWILD.PAP**, Windows.

3. Choose **Wriggle** in the pop-up menu within the Paper palette drawer.

4. Close the Paper palette drawer and move up the Scale slider on the Paper palette's front panel. Choose a color in the Art Materials: Color palette.

5. Choose **Effects: Surface Control: Color Overlay**. The Color Overlay dialog box appears. Choose **Paper Grain** in the Using menu and click next to **Hiding Power**. Click **OK**. The selection in the image fills with the chosen color and paper grain.

6. Check **Invert Grain** on the Paper palette front panel. Choose another color. Repeat **Color Overlay**. The grain inverts and the colorless areas within the selection fill with the current color.

When the colors and background were done, Chet clicked on the floater with the Floater tool and chose **Edit: Drop**, incorporating the floater into the background image.

Lastly, Chet touched up the black areas with the Scratchboard Tool. Touching up the colors without having to worry about hurting the black is a little tricky. Here's what Chet did:

1. With the Airbrush's **Fat Stroke** variant selected, change the Brushes palette: Method Category to **Buildup** and the Method Subcategory to **Soft Buildup**.

2. Select a color in the Color palette and paint in the desired area. You can paint a dark color on a light one, but not the other way around. Because buildup methods muddy to black, the color will not affect the black areas.

3. To lighten colors, select **Dodge** from the pop-up menu within the Brushes palette's drawer and paint. To darken them, select **Burn** from the pop-up menu and paint. Reduce the width of both in the Brushes palette: Controls: Size palette before editing or you will paint in the black areas by mistake.

PEN AND INK WASH DRAWINGS IN PAINTER

A traditional way to shade black-and-white pen and ink drawings is to paint in them with watercolors or inks diluted with water. Washington-based illustrator Gregg Scott uses Painter's watercolors to get the same effect (see Figure 8.4).

Figure 8.4 *Fat Cat* by Gregg Scott.

Gregg specializes in editorial illustrations for newspapers, magazines, and books. He did the illustrations for my Artistry coupon (there's one in the back of this book).

A conventional technique that illustrators have used for years is to render the line art on an overlay (acetate) and then do a wash under-drawing (mixing water and ink to produce gray values) on a separate piece of illustration board. "With this technique a camera person has to take these two pieces and marry them with a double burn," Gregg says. "This gives you a finished piece with crisp black lines and half-toned values of gray. But you can achieve this same technique faster in Painter and eliminate the costly extra camera work."

The following exercise shows how Gregg uses Painter's watercolors to create ink washes.

Using Pen and Ink with a Wash

1. Draw your artwork off-screen. Gregg uses a felt tip pen. He notes that you can draw the line work directly in Painter, but he feels more comfortable starting out with a traditional line drawing.

2. Scan in this line art (see Figure 8.5). Gregg scans in his art through Photoshop, where he converts it to a bitmap (black-and-white drawing). Then he brings it into Painter.

Figure 8.5 Line art scanned in.

Next, Gregg sets up a custom Color Set with levels of gray. "Since I'm working in black and white most of the time, I create a palette made up of gray values in 5%

increments, which is very hard to do when mixing water and ink. It's a really cool feature to be able to just grab a perfect 45%, 10%, or 85% gray and just paint away," notes Gregg. Using the H,S,V box in the Color palette as his guide, Gregg sets up grays with V settings in 5% increments. The following steps show how.

1. Select **Art Materials: Color: Adjust Color Set.** The Color Set palette appears. Click **New Set**. A tiny empty Color Set appears and the word **Untitled** is listed under Current Color Set.

2. Using the H,S,V box in the Color palette as your guide, click and drag along the triangle's left edge until V (Value) is **80%** and S (Saturation) is **0%**. It doesn't matter what H (Hue) is if S is 0%.

3. Click **Color Set palette: Add Color**. The color is added to the untitled Color Set. Continue to add grays in 5% increments, including a 50% gray.

4. To save this Color Set, click **Color Set palette: Library**. A dialog box appears. Click **Save**. Another dialog box appears. Type in a name for the new Color Set and click **Save**. Another dialog box appears. Click on the Color Set you just created and click **Open**. The new set is listed under Current Color Set in the Color Set palette.

After opening the original line art scan in Painter, select **Water Color** from the Brushes palette drawer. Then select the **Simple Water** variant and a 15–20% gray in your new Color Set. In the Brushes palette: Controls: Size, set the Size slider at around **25** or **30**. Also in the Controls palette select an Opacity of **60** to **70%** and a Grain setting of **0**.

Wet into Wet

Start with the cat himself leaving the Water Color brush in Canvas: Wet Paint mode until he's almost done. Lay in a wash with your 15–20% gray all around. You can leave light areas or highlights (eyes, areas close to light source) don't worry about everything being covered with a flat gray. Remember, watercolor is supposed to have variation and happy accidents, so have fun! (See Figure 8.6.)

Don't dry your canvas. Stay in the Wet Paint mode and select a darker value—say 40–50% gray—and start to define your dark or shadow areas. Once you lay in these darker areas you'll want to soften the edges where different values meet. This can be achieved a couple of ways, from varying the pressure as you paint (using a stylus) to picking a value somewhere in between (in this case a 25 or 30% gray) and going back in and blending the edges. It takes a little experimenting to get a method down and the results you want, but the big advantage you have with

Painter over traditional watercolor is that your wet paint stays wet until you want it to dry. So you can take your time.

Figure 8.6 Wash painted with light areas left open.

Lifting out Color

In traditional watercolor, while your paint is still wet you can go back with a clean brush or tissue and lift color out of your artwork. You can do that in Painter's Wet Paint mode too (see Figure 8.7).

Figure 8.7 Color "lifted" in Wet Paint layer from eye and beard.

I make sure a 0% gray is defined in the color set or use the **Wet Eraser** (only works in the Wet Paint mode), and I can go into areas like the cat's eyes, which may have been overpainted, or an area that just got a little too dark, and lift the color out," Gregg says. "Notice that this does not affect your original line art scan. Experiment with different Opacities in the Controls Palette and/or vary the pressure of your stylus."

After the cat and keyboard are nearly done, except for some minor details, go ahead and dry your paint under the Canvas menu. Next you'll paint the mousepad using another method.

Wet into Dry

With the Simple Water brush and the same settings as you used previously, choose a 30**% gray** and paint the entire mousepad in. You'll notice that nothing gets darker than 30% gray while you are in the Wet Paint mode. Now check to see if there are any areas (like the wire) where you may want to lift out color, then go ahead and **Canvas: Dry** to dry the paint. Now with the same brush and 30% color, go back to the mousepad and add color areas. Notice how the value darkens even though you have not changed the color, just like real watercolors (see Figure 8.8).

Figure 8.8 Mousepad painted, "dried," then painted again for darkening effect.

Working wet into dry produces different effects, textures, and harder edges than painting wet into wet. Again you can experiment with different Opacities and pressure to get different effects.

Adding the Shadows with Diffusion

In the last step you'll add the shadows on the ground (see Figure 8.9).

Figure 8.9 Shadows on ground added with Diffusion.

With Simple Water brush set to a little smaller size (**10–15**) in the Brushes palette: Controls: Size slider you will also set the Diffusion Slider to **5** in the Brushes palette: Controls: Water palette. Select a **50% gray** and paint a short stroke under the cat's tail.

You can see the stroke as you paint, but stop for a split second and watch as your stroke diffuses as if you were applying color to a very wet area. This is a great way to get soft edges and those "happy accidents." Experiment with different diffusion amounts and values to build the shadows.

Works Great in Color Too

Although you created a grayscale illustration, this watercolor technique works great for full-color artwork as well. Working wet into wet and wet into dry with different colors produces some very interesting effects. The options you have with the Water Color brush in Painter seem endless.

SUMMARY

The artists in this chapter use Painter to not just create natural media-type images on the computer, but to streamline time-consuming traditional drawing techniques. It's nice to know you can do both.

This completes the drawing section of this book. Next are the painting chapters, which go in progression from simple things like choosing a painting tool through the more complex steps that show how working artists use Painter's painting tools to create their artwork.

Part III

Painting

9

Introducing Painter's Paintbrushes

Chapter Highlights

- ✤ Accessing a paintbrush
- ✤ Adding colors to bristle brushes
- ✤ Creating instant oil paintings

Painter's brushes let you re-create the look of oils, watercolors, acrylics, and gouache; and you can use all the brushes to invent other-worldly artistic phenomena. You can even draw or paint a stroke in an image and make that stroke into a new paintbrush using **Brushes palette: Brushes: Capture Brush**.

This chapter provides an introduction to using Painter's paintbrushes. Subsequent chapters get under Painter's hood and show you how to tinker with the brushes for various effects. Chapter 14, "Using Painter's Advanced Painting Tools," rounds out the painting section with step-by-step examples of how working artists use the brushes to create their artwork in Painter.

Accessing Painter's Painting Tools

Did you go through the drawing chapters? If you did, then you have a pretty good idea about how to find Painter's paintbrushes.

In several cases, such as the Brush and the Airbrush, you choose a painting tool from the Brushes palette the same way that you chose the drawing tools. However, with others like the Image Hose, a certain amount of setup is required before you can paint with the tool. These other painting tools are covered in depth in subsequent chapters.

For now, you'll learn how to select a brush and a variant and how to add colors to bristle brush strokes. Lastly, you'll see a quick way to make painted strokes look like thick oils.

Choosing a Paintbrush

Painter has many paintbrush categories. Within each category are several more choices or variants.

Most of the bristle brushes are variants of the Brush (see Figure 9.1). The following exercise shows how to choose the Brush.

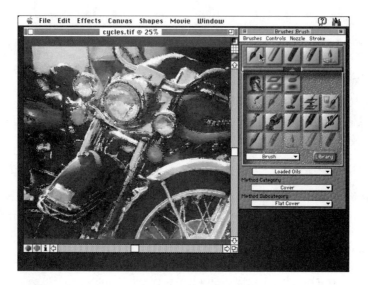

Figure 9.1 The Brush category contains most of Painter's bristle brushes.
Cycles by Michael Savas.

Choosing the Brush

1. Select **File: New**. Click **OK**. A new image appears.
2. Select **Window: Brushes** if the Brushes palette isn't already showing.
3. Click on the palette's pushbar to open its drawer. The drawer opens.
4. Select **Brush** from the pop-up menu within the Brushes palette drawer.
5. Close the drawer by clicking on the pushbar.

Drag in the image window. A brush stroke appears. What it looks like depends on what's listed in the Variants pop-up menu, covered next.

118

Using the Painting Variants

Within each paintbrush are further choices, or *variants*, of the particular tool. The variants differ from one another in terms of brush width or number of bristles, for example (see Figure 9.2).

Figure 9.2 The Brush's Variants pop-up menu.

The next exercise shows how to select a Brush variant.

Choosing a Variant

1. Click and hold on the **Variants** pop-up menu on the Brushes palette front panel.

2. Continue to hold as you drag to a variant until it's highlighted. Let go. The variant's name now appears on the Brushes palette front panel.

3. Drag in the image.

ADDING COLORS TO BRUSH STROKES

Like the drawing tools, Painter's various paintbrushes and variants can be adjusted to suit your artwork.

One easy but useful adjustment that you can make right away is to increase the number of colors in each bristle of a brush stroke. You do so by adjusting the ±HSV sliders in the Color palette (see Figure 9.3). If you don't see these sliders, then the Color palette is collapsed. Click in the palette's upper-right-hand corner to expand the palette.

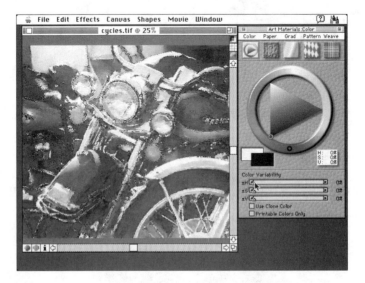

Figure 9.3 The ±HSV sliders are in the Color palette's bottom portion.

The next exercise shows how to adjust these sliders.

Adding Colors

1. Select **Brush** in the Brushes palette if it isn't already chosen. Select the **Digital Sumi** variant.

2. Choose a color in the Color palette and paint in the image. You see a very fine bristle-brush stroke.

3. Move the ±H slider to the right and paint in the image. The stroke has random multiple colors. The colors are the ones located on either side of the color in the Color palette's color ring. The further you move the ±H slider to the right, the further away the colors are chosen on the color ring, and the greater the number of colors there are in the stroke.

4. Move the ±H slider to the left and move the ±S slider to the right and paint. The stroke now contains varying levels of Saturation chosen randomly from

left to right in the triangle in the Color palette. Move the ±V slider to the right and paint, and the stroke has a range of values chosen randomly from top to bottom in the triangle.

ADJUSTING OPACITY

As you saw in the drawing chapters, another easy and useful change is to adjust brush-stroke opacity. You can do so by moving the **Window: Controls palette: Opacity** slider, or you can use keyboard shortcuts.

The keyboard keys **1** through **0** represent opacity in 10% increments. Try the following exercise to see how these keyboard commands work.

Using Painter's Opacity Keyboard Shortcuts

1. Paint a brush stroke.
2. Type **1** on your keyboard and paint another stroke. The second stroke is painted at 10% opacity.
3. Type **8** on your keyboard and paint another stroke. The new stroke is at 80% opacity.

QUICKIE OIL PAINTING EFFECT

You're going to find when you read the later chapters in this section that most traditional artists use Painter's brushes "straight" without applying effects to them. But if you want to do a quick oil effect, where the paint has a thick, built-up appearance, do the following exercise.

Painting Thick Oils

1. Select the Brush's **Small Loaded Oils** variant.
2. Paint some strokes in the image. It doesn't matter how elaborate a painting you make. You're just going to see the thick oil effect.
3. Select **Effects: Surface Control: Apply Surface Texture**. The Apply Surface Texture dialog box appears (see Figure 9.4).
4. Select **Image Luminance** in the Using menu.

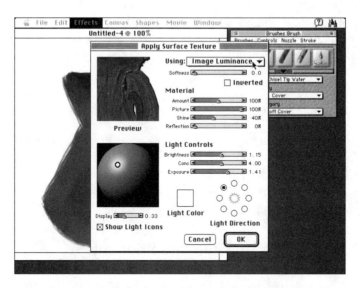

Figure 9.4 The Apply Surface Texture dialog box.

5. Experiment by clicking on the different buttons going around the sun in the lower-right-hand portion of the dialog box and by dragging on the light source on the sphere. The Preview window shows the results. I've also found some interesting shadows and highlights by clicking a second light source in the sphere and moving it in different positions in relation to the first light source. When the strokes have the desired thickness, click **OK**.

SUMMARY

Now that you know how to choose a brush, the next question is which one should you choose?

The next chapter provides thumbnails for quick reference to help your search for the right tool.

10

Basic Painting in Painter

CHAPTER HIGHLIGHTS

- ❖ New Painter 4 Brushes
- ❖ Brush
- ❖ Liquid
- ❖ Artists
- ❖ Airbrush
- ❖ Dodge
- ❖ Burn
- ❖ Water Color

Each new version of Painter includes new brushes usually as variants in existing brush categories. In version 4 Fractal includes the new brushes as separate libraries because they are large memory-wise. But they're a lot of fun, as you'll see in this chapter's first section. The rest of the chapter shows you the strokes made by the rest of Painter's paintbrushes.

Later chapters contain information about Painter's more esoteric paintbrushes like the Image Hose, in addition to the sliders and palettes you would use to edit all the brushes.

I did all the thumbnails in this chapter the same way I did the mugs in Chapter 5, that is, by painting a fish then using it as the basis for the others by turning on Tracing Paper (**File: Clone**; **Select All**; **Delete/Backspace**; **Canvas: Tracing Paper**). Then I selected **Use Clone Color** in the Color palette, and the brush picked up colors from the original image. All the fish, except Auto Van Gogh, are hand-painted, not filters. Take a look at them on the *Fractal Design Painter 4 Complete* CD to see colors and details.

PAINTER 4 BRUSHES

Painter 4 comes with three new brush libraries, located in the Painter 4 folder: Extra Brushes, Mac; Painter 4 subdirectory called Brushes, Windows. They are Fun

Brushes, Nature Brushes and String Brushes, Mac; Fun.brs, Nature.brs and String.brs, Windows 3.X; Open, Windows 95.

To load one of these brush categories, click the **Library** button within the Brushes palette's drawer, locate and click on the desired category, then click **Open**, Mac; **OK**, Windows 3.X; **Open**, Windows 95.

Each variant may seem to take a long time to load at first. That's because it has to be *unpacked* (my term—it's some kind of code compilation thing). Subsequently, when you load the variant it should open fairly quickly.

FUN BRUSHES

The Fun Brushes are fun or silly depending on your frame of mind, but I did find painting my fish that you can get some interesting tonal effects with them, as you'll see in the following thumbnails.

For each Fun variant, the amount of pressure that you apply to the stylus affects the size of each individual element within a brush stroke. Pressing lightly gives you smaller elements, pressing heavily produces bigger ones.

In many cases, you can point the individual stroke parts in a specific direction based on the direction in which you drag your mouse or stylus.

Stroky, Stroky Cloner

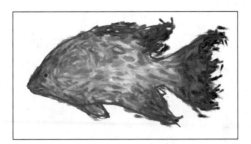

Stroky produces multicolored quick brush dabs. Stroky Cloner is Stroky with **Color palette: Use Clone Color** checked and saved as a variant (instructions for saving changes as a variant listed at end of Chapter 4). Use Stroky Cloner when painting in a cloned image.

Chalky

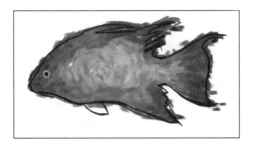

Paints like Stroky with Square Chalk-type marks.

Branchy

Has an out-on-a-limb feeling.

Catapillary

Produces furry strokes whose width you can adjust by varying stylus pressure.

Pentagonia

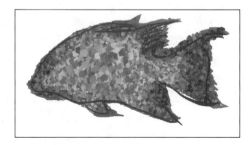

Paints with pentagons.

Fire

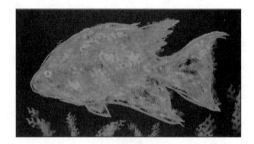

Paints with, well, do you smell something burning?

Watery

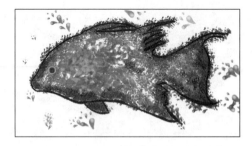

Uses splashes of color.

Diamondy

Paints with diamonds whose direction depends on which way you drag your stylus or mouse.

Leafy

Paints with vegetation.

Treey2

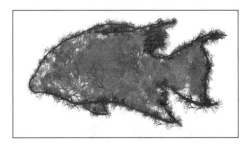

Paints with trees.

Treey

Paints branchier trees than Treey2.

Triangly

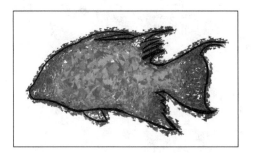

Paints with confetti-esque diamonds.

Diamondy2

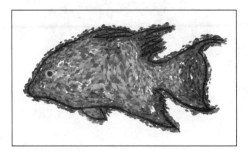

Produces confetti-like diamonds.

NATURE BRUSHES

The Nature Brushes are the third generation of Painter brushes created by John Derry, Vice President, Creative Design at Fractal, to reproduce nature, following Trees and Leaves and the Image Hose. The Nature Brushes are all *captured brushes*, where an image element is captured using **Brushes palette: Brushes: Capture Brush** and turned into the current brush's tip. Capture Brush was introduced in Painter 3 and was used to create the Chalk's Square Chalk variant. Choose the **Square Chalk** variant and click on the **Brushes palette: Controls: Size palette's Preview** window and you'll see the shape that John drew and captured to create the brush's tip.

"Originally we did Capture Brush mostly to capture the signature shape of different media," says John. "Square Chalk gives a better result in that it has a more realistic chalk look."

But squares aren't the only shape that you can capture.

"Once we did that, we realized the captured brush could be anything. It led me back to my Trees and Leaves stage. Growth patterns in nature are simply the repetition of the same element, which is what a captured brush does. It lets you paint repetitions of the same element. It was a perfect candidate to do some nature stuff. One thing I like about captured brushes versus Trees and Leaves and the Image Hose is that it's far less resource-intensive. Captured brushes allow you to have these different natural growth patterns follow a direction based on which way you drag the stylus or mouse. Also, growth patterns tend to change scale in a linear pattern. You can adjust element size by varying stylus pressure, giving you that same graphic visual bite of what makes a growth pattern."

John hopes you find these tools useful. "The whole reason for Trees and Leaves, Image Hose, and now the Nature Brushes is to give people tools to re-create reality. It's hard to delineate a frond of a fern, but here's a tool that accomplishes it for you. Maybe not in a totally realistic way, but in a fanciful way to create the complexity of nature without having to delineate every last detail."

Ivy Cluster

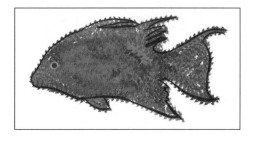

Paint the ivy on the garden wall with this variant.

Spiral

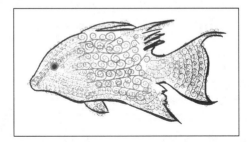

Add the trellis with this one.

Fern

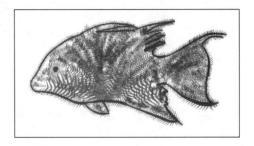

Brings back memories of the Upper East Side of the 1970s.

Ivy

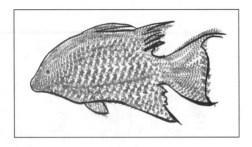

Strings of ivy as opposed to clusters of it.

Leaf Stencil

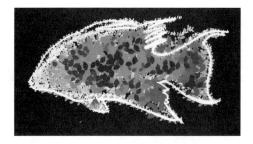

Paints with flat, stencil-like leaves.

Wavelet Wand

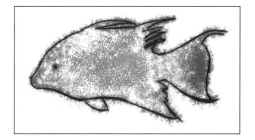

Paints multidirectional waves.

Leaves

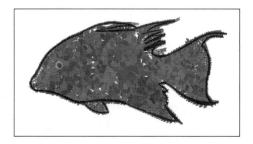

Paints enough leaves to fill a forest.

131

Uncle Wiggly

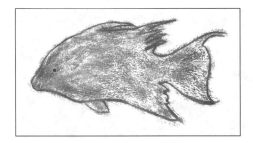

Similar to Wavelet Wand except that it paints strokes in one direction while Wavelet Wand strokes are more haphazard.

Complex Fern

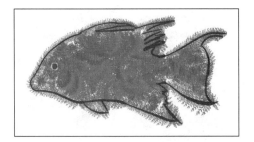

Get the garden shears—this thing is getting out of hand.

STRING BRUSHES

The third category of new Painter 4 brushes contains some great playtime brushes, especially the String Art Brush, which is my personal favorite.

Highly Variable Cloner

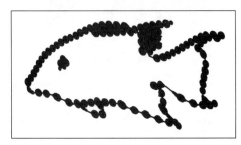

Brush width in the clone is based on light and dark areas in the source image and the result is a highly variable clone. I produced this fish by not having a source image open. Starting with version 4, when you use a cloner brush without an open source image, the cloner turns to the Art Materials: Pattern palette for its source information. I chose the **Industrial** pattern and turned the Scale slider on the Pattern palette's front panel way down to get the ragged look.

Really Nice Brush

Paints thick, rich strokes.

Pine Brush

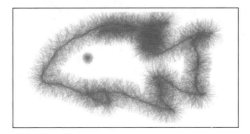

Like painting with pine needles.

String Art Brush

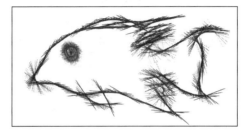

Like painting with pick-up sticks.

Variable Pattern Cloner

Similar to Highly Variable Cloner except that it also picks up clone source color, if you have an original image open. If not, it picks up the pattern in the Art Materials: Pattern palette, including the color. Once again I chose the **Industrial** pattern with the Scale slider lowered and got a Chinese lantern thing going.

Variable String Spray

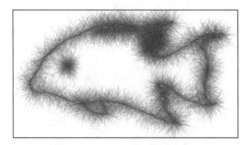

Less clustery than Pine Brush.

Cool Angled Cloner

The strokes are based on the light and dark areas of the source image. In my case, it gave me a furry fish.

BRUSH

As you saw in Chapter 9, "Introducing Painter's Paintbrushes," the Brush category in the Brushes palette contains most of the bristle brushes. The following sections give you an idea of the differences among the variants.

The new ones in Painter 4 are shown first with an asterisk.

Big Wet Ink*

Paints big, fat, fast colorful strokes great for quick painting.

Big Dry Ink*

Similar to Big Wet Ink with different bristles.

Brushy

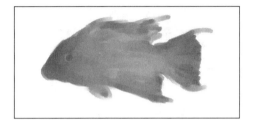

Paints big, smooth, bristly oil strokes that pick up underlying colors. Notice how the strokes run out of color at the end.

Hairy Brush

Paints smooth strokes. Drag a line and wait. The stroke appears a moment later. The faster your machine, the shorter the delay will be.

Graduated Brush

Decides on a hue from the Color palette's overlapping rectangles depending on how heavily you press on a pressure-sensitive stylus. Add a color to the rear rectangle by clicking on it and selecting a color. Click back on the front rectangle to prevent confusion later.

Penetration Brush

Gives bristly, hard-edged oil- or gouache-like strokes.

Camel Hair Brush

Produces smooth, bristly oil- or gouache-like strokes.

Oil Paint

Has multicolored, paper-sensitive oil- or gouache-like strokes.

Rough Out, Big Rough Out, Huge Rough Out

Creates quick, paper-sensitive, acrylic-like, or dry-brush-like strokes.

Cover Brush

Provides smooth, soft strokes.

Coarse Hairs

Paints big-bristle strokes.

Fine Brush

Provides smooth, minibristle strokes.

Sable Chisel Tip Water

Smears and mixes underlying strokes.

Ultrafine Wash Brush

Produces light, paper-sensitive strokes.

Smaller Wash Brush

Similar to the Ultrafine Wash Brush, but its strokes are more bristly.

Loaded Oils

Provides life-like bristly oil paint strokes.

Big Loaded Oils

Is a larger version of Loaded Oils.

Big Wet Oils

Paints oils diluted with a little linseed oil.

Small Loaded Oils

Is Loaded Oils concentrate.

Digital Sumi

Provides paint-dipped-comb-like strokes.

LIQUID BRUSHES

Everybody loves the Liquid variants. Click and drag on a painting or a photo, and smear away. Note that some variants like Distorto don't work on a blank image because the **Window: Controls palette: Opacity** slider is turned all the way down.

Smeary Bristles

Provides mushy smears with color and paper texture.

Total Oil Brush

Produces thicker smears than Smeary Bristles.

Tiny Smudge

Smears tiny bristly areas.

Smeary Mover

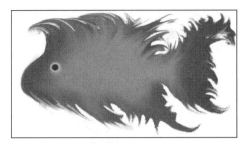

Gives colorless, paper-sensitive smears.

Coarse Smeary Mover

Provides hard-edged, paper-sensitive smears.

Distorto

Produces plain smears.

Coarse Smeary Bristles

Provides hard-edged smears with color and paper sensitivity.

Coarse Distorto

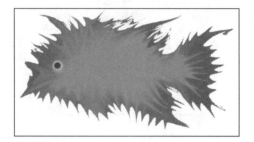

Paints edgy, colorless smears.

Thick Oil

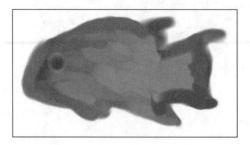

Provides big, fat, colorful smears.

ARTISTS

Here are Painter inventor's Mark Zimmer's tributes to the Impressionists.

Van Gogh

Paints multicolored brush strokes à la Impressionist artist Vincent Van Gogh. Try to paint short strokes as there is a delay while the stroke computes.

Van Gogh 2

Right this way, with this updated version of the Van Gogh variant, there is no waiting.

Seurat

Produces pointillist dots à la Georges Seurat.

145

Impressionist

Creates multicolored strokes based on the direction in which you drag your stylus or mouse.

Auto Van Gogh

Auto Van Gogh is just that: a way to produce an automatic Van Gogh painting. Purists scoff at the notion, but it's kind of fun. Try it and see what you think. The following exercise shows you how.

Creating an Auto Van Gogh

1. Open a color photograph.
2. Select **File: Clone**. A clone of the image appears. Choose **Edit: Select All** (**Command+A** on the Mac; **Ctrl+A** in Windows), then press **Delete** on the Mac or **Backspace** in Windows.
3. Select the Artists' **Auto Van Gogh** variant.
4. Select **Effects: Esoterica: Auto Van Gogh**. After a while you have a Van Gogh version of your original image.

Flemish Rub

Smears an existing image with an Impressionistic effect.

Piano Keys

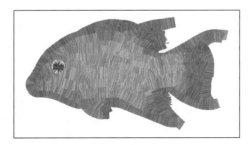

This is an Impressionist "what if" brush, as in, "What if there was an Impressionist who painted this way." Move the ±H,S,V sliders in the Colors palette to the right to see the "piano keys." The direction in which you drag determines the "keyboard" layout.

AIRBRUSH

Painter's Airbrush variants reproduce the look of the real thing. Use these variants with paths to get hard edges.

Fat Stroke

Paints large paint streams.

Thin Stroke

Produces thin, soft paint streams.

Feather Tip

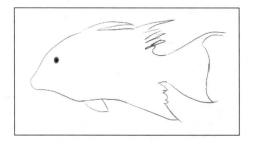

Provides narrow paint streams.

Spatter Airbrush

Produces paper-sensitive paint streams.

Single Pixel Air

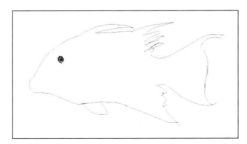

Paints one-pixel lines good for editing pixel by pixel.

Dodge

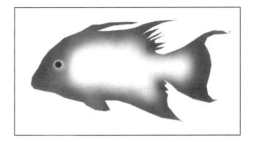

Access this variant in the pop-up menu within the Brushes palette drawer. It lightens an area.

Burn

Access this variant in the pop-up menu within the Brushes palette's drawer. It darkens an area.

WATER COLOR

Painter's watercolor brushes paint in a separate, Wet Paint layer that floats above the main image area. To incorporate these colors into the main image, select **Canvas: Dry**. When you switch to another brush category, select **Canvas: Wet Paint** to shut off the Wet Paint layer.

Simple Water

Paints blended watercolor strokes.

Spatter Water

Spatters puddles of color.

Pure Water Brush

Use this brush on existing strokes in the Wet Paint layer to dilute and mix them.

Broad Water Brush

Produces lush, paper-sensitive strokes.

Water Brush Stroke

Paint a line and wait; a smooth watercolor stroke appears a moment later.

Large Water

Produces big, wet strokes.

Diffuse Water

Paints strokes that "explode" after you paint them. They produce the effect of painting on dampened paper.

Wet Eraser

Erases strokes while they are still in the Wet Paint layer, that is, before you select **Canvas: Dry**.

Large Simple Water

Produces large watercolor strokes.

SUMMARY

There you have all of Painter 4's paintbrushes. In the next chapter you'll see what I call Painter's special effects brushes, that is, brushes that take a bit of setup to use or that produce other-worldly paint strokes, including Painter 4's new Mosaic feature.

11

Special Effects Brushes

CHAPTER HIGHLIGHTS

❖ Mosaics

❖ Image Hose

❖ Cloners

So far you've seen Painter's repertoire of conventional brushes, if anything in Painter can be termed conventional. This chapter discusses how to paint with Painter's more esoteric brushes. Like the preceding chapter, this one is just a sampling of these brushes. Later chapters discuss how to set them up the way you want.

MOSAICS

The hot news in Painter 4 is the mosaic feature. The manual covers mosaics thoroughly, so read it to get the lowdown on creating your own tile-istic images and fine-tuning the mosaic settings.

It's so thorough, in fact, that it's not easy to see at first glance from the manual what mosaics are. For a quick look at mosaics, try the following exercise, in which you will turn a guitar photograph into a mosaic, first by hand, and then by computer. First, though, reduce the guitar image's size so that your experiment can go quickly.

1. Open the Guitar.jpg file on the Painter 4 CD (it's in the Goodies:Photos: Objects folder).

2. Choose **Canvas: Resize**. The Resize dialog box appears. Uncheck **Constrain File Size** and choose **inches** in the pop-up menus next to Width and Height.

3. Type a **2** in the Width field and click **OK**. The guitar image is now smaller.

Next make sure the Color palette is set up properly.

1. Choose **Window: Art Materials: Color palette**, if it isn't already visible.

2. Check **Use Clone Color**. If you don't see Use Clone Color, expand the palette by clicking in its upper-right-hand corner.

Now you're ready to do a mosaic of the guitar. You'll do so in a clone.

1. Select **File: Clone**. A clone of the image appears.

2. Select **Canvas: Make Mosaic**. The Make Mosaic dialog box appears and the image turns black. This black is the grout that will fill the spaces between tiles.

3. Check **Use Tracing Paper**. The original guitar image shows through.

4. Paint in the image. The original comes through as a mosaic (see Figure 11.1).

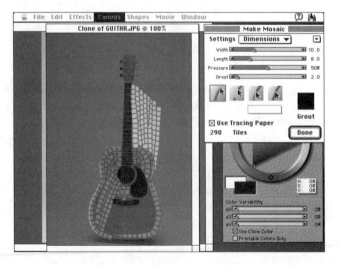

Figure 11.1 With **Use Tracing Paper** checked, you can paint mosaic tiles using the original image for reference. *Guitar ©1996 PhotoDisc*

Click in **Use Tracing Paper** to hide the original image and to see your mosaic's progress (see Figure 11.2).

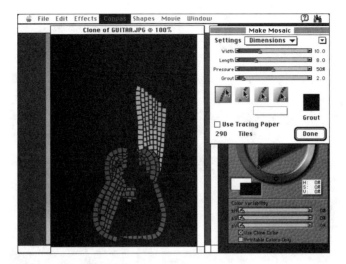

Figure 11.2 The same image with **Use Tracing Paper** unchecked.

Click in **Use Tracing Paper** again and proceed. Click **Done** to close the Make Mosaic dialog box.

That's how you create a mosaic in a clone by hand. You can of course start a new image, choose **Canvas: Make Mosaic**, and paint from scratch, as well.

As previously mentioned, you can also let the computer do the work. The following steps show you how. **Color palette: Use Clone Color** should still be checked.

1. Select **File: Close** to close the Guitar clone.

2. Select **File: Clone** to create a new clone.

3. Choose **Canvas: Make Tesselation**. The Tesselation dialog box appears.

4. Choose **Add 500 Clone-Spaced Points** from the pop-up menu on the dialog's right-hand side. After a moment, a network of spaces appears. These spaces will be the tiles in a moment.

5. Select **Add 500 Clone-Spaced Points** several more times, pausing in between to let Painter do its calculations.

   Each time, Painter applies spaces based on the lights and darks in the original image. The more you apply the effect, the better the pattern will get (see Figure 11.3).

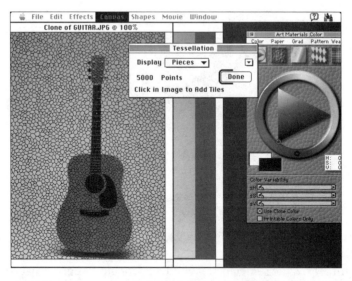

Figure 11.3 The image after **Add 500 Clone-Spaced Points** was applied
a handful of times.

Unfortunately, the better the pattern, the longer it will take to render into tiles.

6. Click **Done**. Painter fills the clone with tiles. At this point, the grout is white. Change it to black by choosing **Canvas: Make Mosaic**, clicking on the **Grout** square, choosing **black**, and clicking **OK**, then **Done** (see Figure 11.4).

For 3D tiles, first put the tiles in the mask and then use Surface Texture. It's OK if you don't know what this means. Masks and Surface Texture are discussed later in the book. For now, just follow the next steps.

1. Choose **Canvas: Make Mosaic**. The Make Mosaic dialog box appears.

2. Choose **Render Tiles into Mask** from the pop-up menu.

3. Wait awhile. Once the operation is complete, click **Done**.

4. Choose **Effects: Surface Control: Apply Surface Texture**. The Apply Surface Texture dialog box appears.

5.   Choose **Mask** in the Using menu.

6.   Move the Softness slider to adjust how tall the tiles look, visible in the Preview window. Click **OK**. Your tiles now appear to be raised.

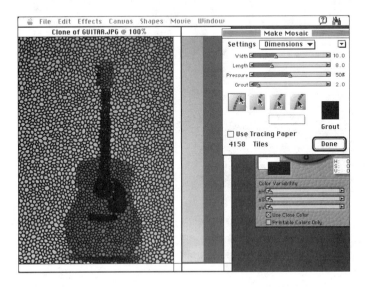

Figure 11.4 The guitar turned into tiles with black grout.

IMAGE HOSE

For those who have begun using Painter with version 4, the Image Hose lets you paint complex images in one simple stroke. You combine several images into one image, called a *nozzle*, and like a hose spraying a stream of water, the Image Hose then sprays the nozzle images in one stream onto your image. I painted the image in Figure 11.5 with nozzles from an amazing new add-on program called the Garden Hose, created by Dennis Berkla for Fractal Design and available through Fractal. Fractal Design President/C.E.O. Mark Zimmer and Vice President, Creative Design, John Derry, came up with the idea of the Image Hose after noticing repeating patterns in nature. They saw that even the most complex pattern is based on a few repeated objects.

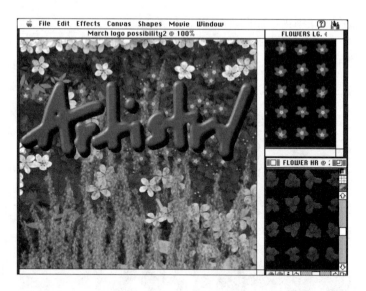

Figure 11.5 Paint repeating patterns (left) using an Image Hose nozzle (right). Fractal Design introduced the Image Hose in Painter version 3 and has enhanced its features in Painter 4.

"Look at a tree," says John. "It's made up of one thing. A leaf. It's the shape that's repeated. Anything in nature tends to be the same way. The original question was, 'Why do I have to paint individual leaves? Why can't I paint with leaves?'" Mark adds, "We would point at things and say, 'How can we paint with that texture?' The Image Hose is a way to fake patterns, like *trompe l'oeil* is a way to fake patterns in traditional art."

This chapter shows you how to use the Image Hose variants.

Chapter 18, "Working with the Image Hose," shows how to create your own Image Hose nozzles and variants.

Loading the Image Hose

Fractal simplified the Image Hose a bit in Painter 4. You can now choose a nozzle from a palette rather than having to go into a menu. Fractal also added new Image Hose editing features that let you resize image elements and adjust their color, as the next few exercises show.

First you'll see how to choose an Image Hose nozzle from the palette. Then you'll see how to choose a different library.

1. Select **File: New** and click **OK**. A new image appears.
2. Select the **Image Hose** from the pop-up menu within the Brushes palette drawer.
3. Select **Brushes palette: Nozzle: Nozzles**. The Nozzle palette appears.
4. Choose **Red Cubes** from the pop-up menu within the Nozzle palette's drawer.
5. Click and drag in the image.

You are painting with cubes that were saved in a document in Painter's native RIFF (on the Mac) or **.RIF** (in Windows) format. Another new Painter 4 feature lets you see this document easily. Choose **Brushes palette: Nozzle: Check Out Nozzle**. The image containing the cubes appears. The Image Hose sprays these cubes onto the image you're painting in.

Painter 4 lets you load additional libraries containing nozzles. You can create your own libraries, or buy them from Fractal. You'll find a sample of Fractal's first Image Hose collection, the Garden Hose, on the CD with Painter.

Here's how to load a library.

1. Click the **Library** button within the **Nozzle palette**. A dialog box appears.
2. Open the **Goodies: Nozzles** folder on the Painter 4 CD. Click on one of the **.NZL** names..
3. Click **Open** if you're on a Mac; **OK** in Windows 3.x; **Open** in Windows 95.
4. Either click on an icon or choose a nozzle from the pop-up menu within the Nozzle palette drawer and paint. (See Figure 11.6.)

Another couple of nice new Painter 4 features include the ability to resize the nozzle elements and to change their colors.

To resize nozzle elements, adjust the **Nozzle palette: Scale** slider (close the Nozzle palette drawer to see the slider).

Here's how to change nozzle element color:

1. Click on the rear rectangle in the Art Materials: Color palette.
2. Choose a color in the Color palette. The rear rectangle turns that color. Click back on the front rectangle to avoid confusion later.
3. Move the **Controls palette: Grain** slider to the left.
4. Paint in the image. The elements pick up the chosen color. The more you move the Grain slider to the left, the more the elements will reflect the color chosen in the Color palette.

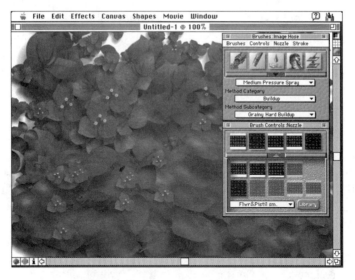

Figure 11.6 Image painted with
BOUGNVIL.NZL from the Garden Hose Collection

It's interesting to note that the Color palette color mixes with the nozzle element color. In the case of the red bougainvillea nozzle elements in Figure 11.6, if you choose **blue**, the various Grain slider positions will give you varying shades of purple (blue plus red); orange if you choose **yellow** in the Color palette, etc. You can also load nozzles individually, which is something you might do if you create your own nozzle.

The next exercise shows how to load an Image Hose nozzle.

Choosing a Nozzle

1. Select **Brushes palette: Nozzle: Load Nozzle**. A dialog box appears.
2. Click on the **Pressure plants** image, Mac; Pplants.rif, Windows within the Nozzle folder inside the Painter 4 folder. Click **Open**, Mac; **OK**, Windows 3.x; **Open,** Windows 95.

3.   Click and drag in your image. Instant fauna! Pressure-sensitive stylus users: Set the Rank 1 slider in the Nozzle palette on **Pressure**. Now you can control which nozzle element appears, based on how hard you press on the stylus.

As with the other Painter drawing and painting tools, the Image Hose has a set of variants containing different settings that affect the tool's appearance. The next several sections go over the Image Hose variants. In the case of the Image Hose, the variants determine which nozzle elements are sprayed, in what order, and how far apart.

The first two listings with an * are new in Painter 4. The following images show the sample bougainvillea nozzle included on the Painter 4 complete CD.

Medium Pressure Linear*

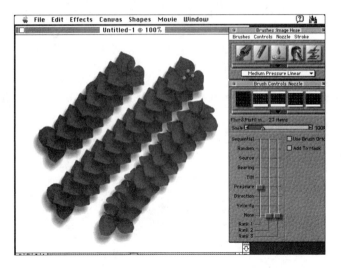

Chooses nozzle elements based on stylus pressure. Nozzle elements are separated by a medium amount of space and appear in rows.

Medium Pressure Spray*

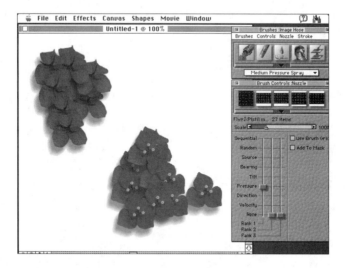

Also chooses nozzle elements based on stylus pressure. Nozzle elements are separated by a medium amount of space and appear in a nonlinear fashion.

Small Sequential Linear

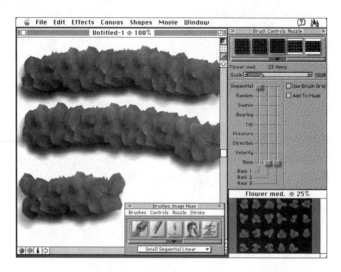

The Sequential Linear variants place the nozzle elements in the most orderly fashion of all the variants. Using this variant, the elements appear in a row in the same order in which they appear in the original file from left to right. *Small* means there is little space between elements as they are placed.

Medium Sequential Linear

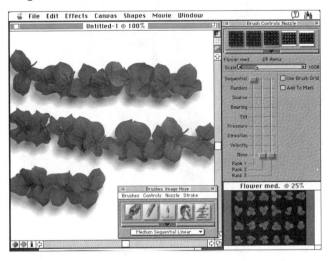

Nozzle elements have a medium amount of space between them.

Large Sequential Linear

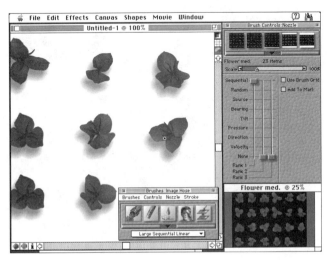

Nozzle elements have a large amount of space between them.

165

Small Directional

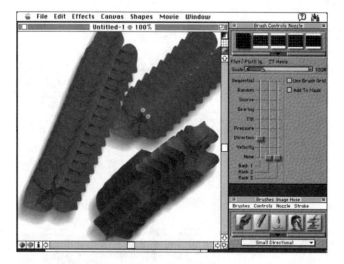

The Directional variants choose nozzle elements based on the direction in which you drag your stylus or mouse. The image elements appear in orderly lines. *Small* means there is little space between elements as they are placed.

Medium Directional

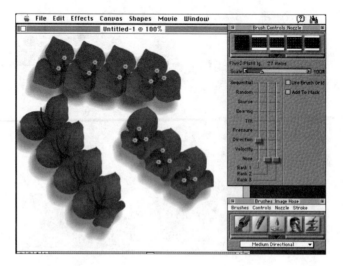

Elements are spaced a medium amount apart.

Large Directional

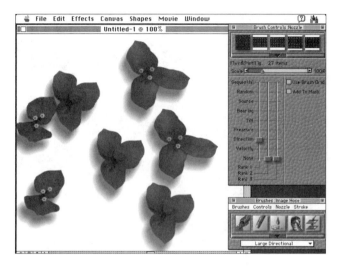

A large amount of space exists between elements.

Small Random Linear

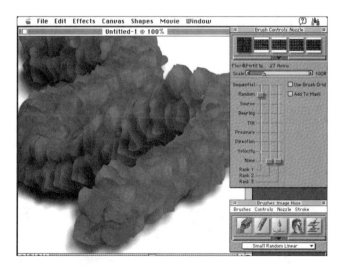

Nozzle elements are selected randomly. *Small* means there is little space between elements as they are placed.

Medium Random Linear

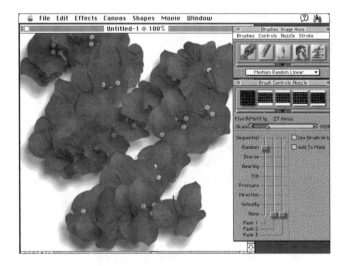

Nozzle elements have a medium amount of space between them.

Large Random Linear

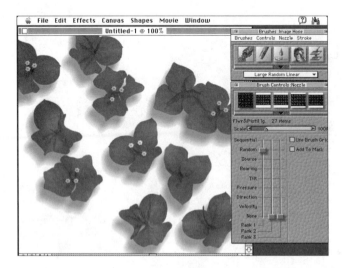

Nozzle elements have a large amount of space between them.

Small Random Spray

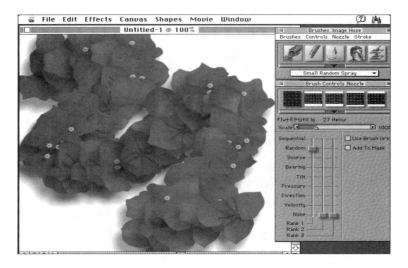

Random Spray elements are chosen at random and are placed in a nonlinear manner. *Small* means there is little space between elements as they are placed.

Medium Random Spray

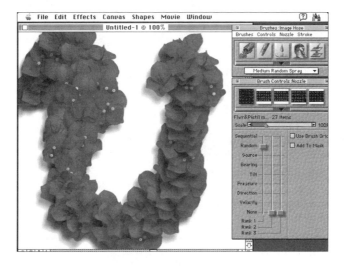

Nozzle elements have a medium amount of space between them.

Large Random Spray

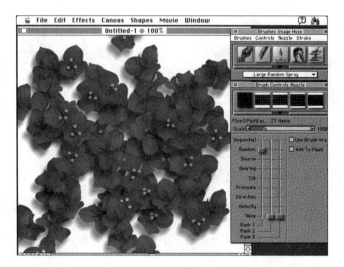

Nozzle elements have a large amount of space between them.

2 Rank R-P, 2 Rank P-D, 2 Rank P-R, 3 Rank R-P-D

See Chapter 18 for information about using these variants, which are 2- and 3-Rank Image Hoses.

Small Luminance Cloner

Throughout this book are examples of the effects you can get when using cloned images, and here's another one (see Figure 11.8).

In a few easy steps (see Figures 11.7 and 11.8) you can create an interesting sketch using the **Small Luminance Cloner** variant and some Effects menu items. The following exercise takes you through the steps. I cloned the Takeoff.jpg © 1996 PhotoDisc photograph with the BOUGNVIL.NZL nozzle from the Garden Hose. You can select any Image Hose file that you like.

Using the Small Luminance Cloner

1. Open the Takeoff.jpg image on the Fractal Design CD located in Goodies: Photos: Urban.

2. Since the Small Luminance Cloner reads the lights and darks in the original image, you'll want to boost both areas. To do so, first

choose **Effects: Tonal Control: Equalize**, use the defaults, and hit **OK**. Next, choose **Effects: Tonal Control: Brightness/Contrast** and move the top slider to the right a bit. Click **Apply**.

3. Select **File: Clone**. A clone of the image appears. Choose **Edit: Select All** (**Command+A** on the Mac; **Ctrl+A** in Windows) and press **Delete** on the Mac or **Backspace** in Windows.

4. Select the Image Hose's **Small Luminance Cloner** variant. You should have the Image Hose selected from previous exercises. I used the Flower&Pistil sm. from the Garden Hose CD. You can use the sample from the Painter 4 Complete CD.

5. Select **Effects: Esoterica: Auto Clone**. Dabs of flowers appear. For a really cool effect, choose a color like yellow in the rear overlapping triangle in the Color palette as described above. Then the flowers appear in colors ranging from the yellow through orange to the bougainvillea red based on the original image's luminance. Let Auto Clone run for a while. Once the area is filled in, click anywhere in the image to stop Auto Clone (see Figure 11.7).

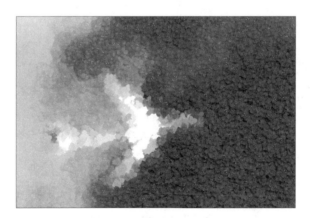

Figure 11.7 Image Hose applied in clone with **Small Luminance Cloner** variant.

Next you'll bring back the jet's outline.

1. Select **Effects: Surface Control: Apply Surface Texture**. The Apply Surface Texture dialog box appears.

2. Select **Original Luminance** in the Using menu. Click **OK**. Painter adds surface texture based on the light and dark areas of the original image (see Figure 11.8).

Figure 11.8 Cloned image with **Apply Surface Texture using Original Luminance** applied.

CLONERS

The Cloners in the Brushes palette are preprogrammed brushes that you can use to turn an original image into a new medium in a clone. To do so, open the image, which can be either a photograph or artwork, select **File: Clone**, select **Edit: Select All** (**Command+A** on the Mac; **Ctrl+A** in Windows), press **Delete** on the Mac or **Backspace** in Windows, and then choose **Canvas: Tracing Paper**. Select a Cloners variant and draw or paint in this cloned image. The original comes in as the selected variant's medium.

Now that you've seen all of Painter's drawing tools (Chapter 5) and painting tools (Chapter 10), most of the Cloner variants should be self-explanatory. For instance, the Cloners' Chalk Cloner variant re-creates the original as a chalk drawing in the clone. Try it and see. Others, however, are worth noting specifically, and the following sections tell you what they do.

You can turn any of Painter's brushes into a cloner by checking **Color palette: Use Clone Color**.

Painting with the Driving Rain Cloner

The way the individual brush dabs slant in this brush give the illusion that you're viewing your image through pouring rain (see Figure 11.9). There's a way to set up Painter to do this effect for you, as the following exercise illustrates.

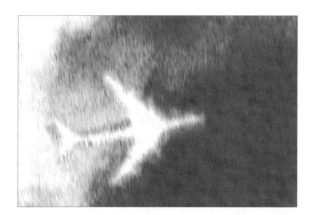

Figure 11.9 Image after applying **Driving Rain Cloner**.

Applying the Driving Rain Cloner

1. Select **File: Open**, choose an image, and click **OK**. Choose **File: Clone**. A clone of the image appears. Don't delete the image.

2. Select the Cloners' **Driving Rain Cloner** variant.

3. Select **Effects: Esoterica: Auto Clone**. Sit back with some cocoa and watch the rain.

4. Click anywhere in the image to stop Auto Clone.

Straight and Soft Cloners

Use the Straight and Soft Cloners to bring the original image back into the clone (see Figure 11.10). The Straight Cloner brings the original in at 100% while the Soft Cloner brings in a transparent version of the original. You can bring in other images with the Straight and Soft Cloners, or any Cloners variants, for that matter. Select **File: Open**, choose an image, and click **OK**. Select the image you just had open from the Window menu. Select **File: Clone Source** and choose the image you just opened. Now when you paint with a Cloners variant, this newly opened image is brought in.

Figure 11.10 The plane from the original Takeoff.jpg image restored with **Straight** and **Soft Cloners**.

SUMMARY

Now you have a general idea of what special effects brushes Painter holds in store for you. All the brushes are useful in solving design problems, or just to play around.

You now have at your fingertips enough Painter knowledge to create beautiful images. But if you really want to know every corner of the program, you should read the next couple of chapters that plumb Painter's more esoteric brush-customizing features. Following them is a look at how working artists use these tools to create their artwork.

12

Painting Gadgets

CHAPTER HIGHLIGHTS

- ❖ Creating a motion blur brush
- ❖ Dampening watercolor
- ❖ Creating a brush category
- ❖ Creating a captured brush

If you read Chapter 6, "Drawing Gadgets," then you already have some handy tools at your fingertips for creating and editing images. Features that were covered in that chapter can be used with the paintbrushes as well. This chapter has more Painter gadgets that are especially useful when painting.

MOTION BLUR BRUSH

Blurring an image element is a useful technique for making objects appear to be in motion (see Figure 12.1). In Painter 4 you can turn any Cloners brush variant with the word Cloning in its Method Category pop-up menu into a motion blur brush. The following exercise shows you how.

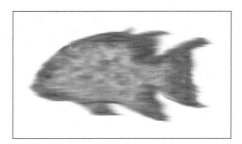

Figure 12.1 Fish blurred using the Motion Blur Brush.

Creating a Motion Blur Brush

1. Select **File: Open**, then select a fish from the Chapter 10 folder on the *Fractal Design Painter 4 Complete* CD. Click **Open.** A fish appears.

2. You're going to set up the image as its own clone source. Do so on the Mac by choosing **File: Clone Source** and then selecting the current document. In Windows, select **File: Clone** first, then select **File: Clone Source**: the current document. Bud Daumen in Fractal Design's tech support department notes that in Windows, if you set up an image as its own clone source without cloning the image first, motion blur is activated automatically and can't be turned off.

3. Select the Cloners' **Soft Cloner** variant.

4. Press **Esc**, then press **Shift+C**.

5. Paint on the image. The cloner is extracting a piece of the image and cloning itself. To shut off the motion blur brush, press **Esc**, then press **Shift+C** again, on the Mac, in Windows, press the key sequence twice.

You can also set up this motion blur brush to clone one image into another (see Figure 12.2).

Figure 12.2 Shore.jpg © 1996 PhotoDisc cloned into the fish image using Motion Blur brush.

1. Open the Goodies: Photo: Scenic: Shore.jpg image on the *Fractal Design Painter 4* CD.

2. Select **Window: fish** image.

3. Select **File: Clone Source:** the **Shore.jpg** image.

4. If you shut off Motion Blur at the end of the previous exercise, with the **Cloners' Soft Cloner** variant selected, press **Esc**, then **Shift+C**. I found I had to press the keys a few times for the effect to work. Paint in the fish image. The Shore.jpg image comes in as a motion blur.

You can bring any image into any other image using any of the Cloners' variants.

ADDING WATER TO WATERCOLOR STROKES

As you saw in Chapter 10, "Basic Painting in Painter," the Water Color's Diffuse Water variant's strokes appear to have been painted on dampened paper. You can add this dampened look to any Water Color strokes with a keyboard shortcut (see Figure 12.3).

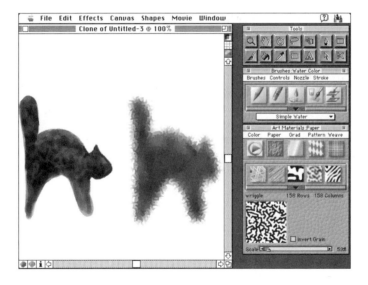

Figure 12.3 Water Color variants' strokes before (left)
and after (right) post-diffuse.

Paint some strokes with the Water Color's Large Simple Water variant. Press **Shift+D**. This does a post-diffuse, like adding water to the stroke edges after the fact. Note that the strokes diffuse with whatever grain is chosen in the Papers palette.

CREATING A NEW BRUSH CATEGORY

The brush categories in the Brushes palette were created with tools within Painter, and you can use these same tools to construct your own brushes and variants. Brush categories are arranged in libraries, or files, accessed by clicking the **Library** button, located within the Brushes palette drawer.

You can set up libraries based on any number of situations. For instance, create a new library for a realistic type of tool that isn't currently available, like rapidograph pens. Or create libraries organized by client or by project.

Setting up separate brush libraries also helps with some disk-storage and maintenance issues. In terms of disk storage, as you add variants to existing brushes, they get placed into the Painter Brushes library on the Mac or PAINTER.BRS in Windows. The more variants you create, the bigger the file gets and the more space it consumes on your disk. If you have space limitations (and who doesn't?), you can create new brushes files and store them on other disks. Also, as discussed in Chapter 2, just as adding floaters to the Floaters palette swells the Portfolio, so does adding variants to the Brushes Library. It's a good idea to create a new Brushes Library and delete the old one to free up disk space.

The other issue is that sometimes Painter gets corrupted, especially in Windows, and you have to reinstall it. If you do reinstall Painter, you start with a fresh default brushes file, losing the variants you created. Separating brushes into their own files ensures that you'll still have them after you've reinstalled Painter.

Another possibility is to set up a library for whimsical brushes like the new Painter 4 brush libraries Fun, Nature and String, illustrated in Chapter 10.

The easiest way to create a new brush category is to copy an existing one, change its icon, and edit or delete its variants. The following exercises show you how to create a brush library and a brush category. Following that are steps for creating a variant using Capture Brush.

Creating a New Brush Library

The first thing to do is to either create a new picture or open an existing one that will represent your new brush category in the Brushes palette. With Painter 4's new brushes as my inspiration, I decided to make a Wildlife library and a Birds brush category within it. I selected a piece of Gulls.jpg ©1996 PhotoDisc as my Birds brush image and then saved it as an icon in the Brushes palette (see Figure 12.4).

Figure 12.4 The selected image piece is the brush icon in the Brushes palette.
Gulls.jpg ©1996 PhotoDisc

1. Open the Goodies: Photos: Nature Gulls.jpg image on the Painter 4 CD.

2. Choose the **rectangle** in the middle of the Tools palette, and, holding down **Shift** click and drag a square selection marquee surrounding a bird. I chose the gull in the lower right-hand corner.

You'll get better results if you select a small piece of a picture. The more you select, the smaller the picture will appear in the Brushes palette. Next you'll create a new brushes library and copy a brush category into it using the Brush Mover (see Figure 12.5).

First create a new brush library.

1. Choose **Brushes palette: Brushes: Brush Mover**. The Brush Mover dialog box appears.

2. Click **New** on the right-hand side of the dialog box, creating a new brush library. A dialog box appears. Type in **Wildlife** on the Mac or **WILDLIFE.BRS** in Windows.

3. Click **Save**. The Wildlife library now appears on the Brush Mover dialog's right-hand side.

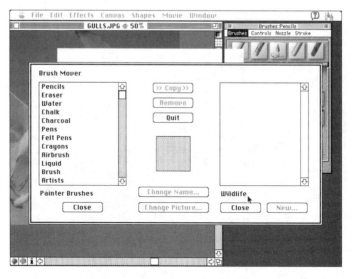

Figure 12.5 The Brush Mover.

Next you'll create a brush category within the Wildlife brush library.

1. Click **Airbrush** on the left-hand side of the dialog box.

2. Click **Copy**. A copy of the Airbrush category now appears in the new brush file on the right.

Now rename the copy.

1. Click **Airbrush** on the right-hand side of the dialog box to select it.

2. Click **Change Name** in the bottom of the dialog box. The Change Brush Name dialog box appears. Type in the name **Birds**. Click **OK**. Now the Birds brush category appears on the right-hand side of the dialog box.

Next you'll replace the Airbrush icon with the selected gull (see Figure 12.6).

1. Click **Birds** on the right-hand side of the dialog box.

2. Click **Change Picture**. The Change Brush Picture dialog box appears with your selection. Click **OK**. The selection now appears in the dialog box.

3. Click **Quit**.

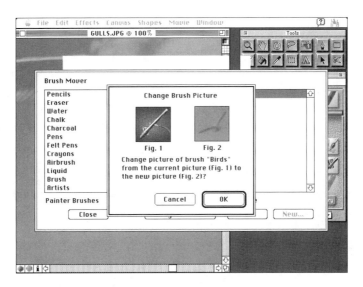

Figure 12.6 The Change Brush Picture dialog box.

You still have to load the Wildlife file into the Brushes palette.

1. Click **Library** within the Brushes palette drawer.

2. Locate Wildlife and click **Open**. The Wildlife library is now loaded into the Brushes palette (although you won't see the word Wildlife anywhere) and your Birds icon now appears on the Brushes palette's front panel and within its drawer. To get the Painter default Brushes palette back, click **Library** in the dialog box, locate Painter Brushes on the Mac; PAINTER.BRS in Windows, and click **Open**. The original Brushes palette brushes come back. For now, you should have the Wildlife category loaded in the Brushes palette.

3. Click and hold on the **Variants** pop-up menu. Notice that it contains all of the Airbrush category variants. That's because all you did was change the name of the file and transfer it over. Now you can use the variants from the Airbrush category as the foundation for new Birds variants.

If you wish to delete a variant, select it in the Variants pop-up menu, select **Brushes palette: Brushes: Variants: Delete Variant**. In the dialog box that appears, click **Yes**.

181

CAPTURED BRUSHES

The variants like Fire and Watery in the Fun brushes were created by capturing a piece of an image as the brush tip. You're going to create a couple of duck variants the same way using **Brushes palette: Brushes: Capture Brush**.

The first step is to create a duck to capture. I used as reference duck photos I took last summer on a vacation in Maine. I didn't scan them in though, I just looked at them. I used shapes to create the basic outlines then painted with the Airbrush.

1. Select **File: New** and click **OK**. A new image appears.
2. Create shapes for each of the duck's separate parts (see Figure 12.7).

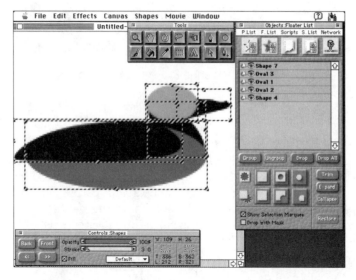

Figure 12.7 Duck made up of separate shapes.

I created each shape with either the pen or circle in the Tools palette. Then I rotated, resized and moved each shape with the floater tool (the left-pointing hand). The command keys from former versions work with the floater tool, so rotate by holding **Command**, Mac; **Ctrl**, Windows and clicking and dragging on a shape's corner. Resize by holding **Shift** and clicking and dragging on a corner. Hold **Command**, Mac; **Ctrl**, Windows and click and drag on a shape's top handle to skew. I tweaked each shape by selecting the hollow arrow in the Tools palette and clicking and dragging on a shape's corner. This calls up its Bézier handles and you can adjust them.

Next I combined the shapes into a floater and painted it.

1. With the left-pointing hand selected, click and drag a marquee around all the shapes to select them.

2. Click **Objects: F. List: Group**, which combines the individual shapes into one group.

3. Click **Objects: F. List: Collapse**, which turns the group into one floater.

4. Choose **black** in the Color palette and **Effects: Fill** to fill the duck with black.

5. Choose the Airbrush's **Fat Stroke** variant (which you have here in the Birds category) and **white** in the Color palette and paint in some light areas (see Figure 12.8).

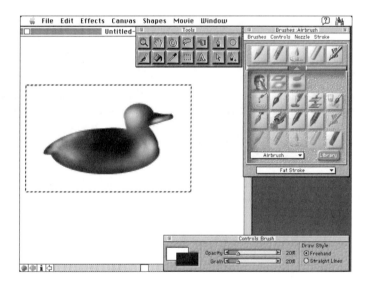

Figure 12.8 Duck with highlights.

Next you will capture the duck as a brush tip.

1. Save the image as a RIFF file to keep the floater. Select **File: Clone** to clone the image, which drops the floater.

2. Click on the **rectangle** in the middle of the Tools palette and click and drag a selection marquee around the duck.

3. Choose **Brushes palette: Brushes: Capture Brush**. The duck is now a brush tip (see Figure 12.9).

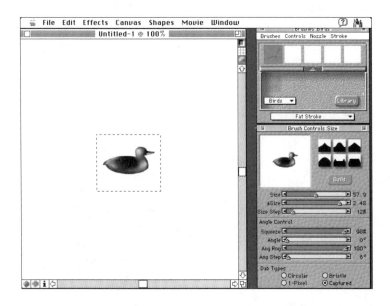

Figure 12.9 The duck as a captured brush tip.

Choose the following brush settings. Some of these settings were covered in Chapter 7 and some will be covered in Chapter 13.

Brushes palette: Controls: Size palette

Size	**57.9**
±Size	**2.48**
Size Step	**12%**
Squeeze	**98%**
Angle	**0°**
Ang Rng	**180°**
Ang Step	**6°**

Brushes palette: Controls: Sliders

Size:	Pressure
Angle:	Direction

Brushes palette: Controls: Spacing

Spacing/Size	**100%**
Min Spacing	**20.0**

Controls: Opacity   100%

Click **Brushes palette: Controls: Size palette: Build**.

Choose **black** in the Color palette and paint with the brush. Your ducks are in a row, going in the direction in which you drag. Also, pressing lightly on a pressure-sensitive stylus produces little ducks, pressing heavily gives you big ones (see Figure 12.10).

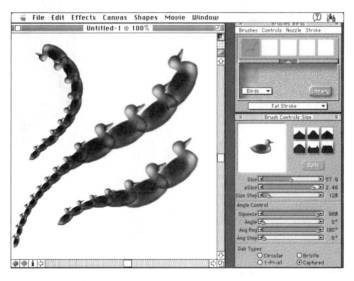

Figure 12.10 Ducks painted in a row.

Save the brush as a variant. Select **Brushes palette: Brushes: Variants: Save Variant**. Type in **Row Ducks**, and click **OK**. You now have a variant called *Row Ducks*.

I decided I wanted to paint flocks of ducks. To do so, I had to capture several ducks as a brush tip.

1. Choose **Window**: the RIFF file containing your duck floater.

2. Choose **Effects: Orientation: Free Transform**, turning the floater into a reference floater. Now you can duplicate the duck shape by holding **Option**, Mac; **Alt**, Windows, and clicking and dragging with the left-pointing hand. And you can do the previously mentioned maneuvers to rotate and resize the duplicates. I used **Effects: Orientation: Flip Horizontal** to get the ducks going in the opposite direction (see Figure 12.11).

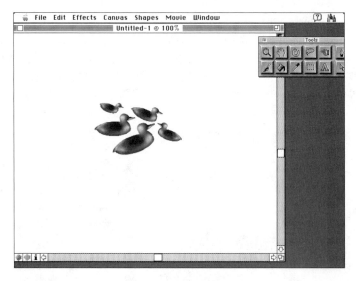

Figure 12.11 Duck shape duplicated and rotated, resized and flipped horizontally.

3. When the ducks are positioned where you want them, click on each with the left-pointing hand and select **Effects: Orientation: Commit Transform**, which turns them back into floaters.

4. Save the file as another RIFF image to keep the floaters and to preserve the image containing the single duck. Choose **File: Clone** to create a cloned image, which drops the floaters into the background.

5. Click on the rectangle in the middle of the Tools palette and click and drag a selection marquee around the ducks.

I went back to the Fat Stroke variant and did Capture Brush again. I chose the **Brushes palette: Controls: Spacing: Spacing/Size 100%** and **Min Spacing: 20.0** and **Controls: Opacity: 100%** and painted, and I had flocks of ducks (see Figure 12.12).

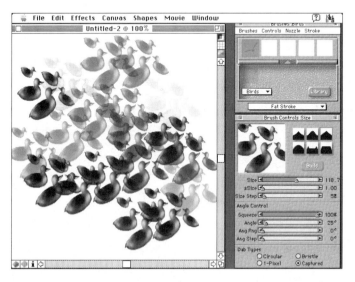

Figure 12.12 Ducks painted with new captured brush.

SUMMARY

Now you know how to create new brush libraries, brush categories and captured brush variants. The next chapter gives you some more brush controls that you can adjust and save to create your own personalized Painter brushes.

13

Advanced Painting Tools

CHAPTER HIGHLIGHTS

- ❖ Adjusting bristle brushes
- ❖ Adjusting watercolors

As you saw in Chapter 7, "Advanced Drawing Tools," you can edit color intensity, grain sensitivity, and other stroke attributes using Painter's myriad palettes and sliders. Some of these settings apply to the paintbrushes, too, so try Chapter 7's recommendations with the Brush category's variants.

Meanwhile, the Brush, Artists, and Water Color categories have their own sets of editing features, and this chapter tells you what they are.

ADJUSTING PAINTBRUSHES

Up through Painter 3, each new version of Painter came with a new set of brushes. In turn, each version introduced new sliders to adjust the new brushes.

While it's nice to have so many choices, not every slider applies to every brush, nor do they dim out if they don't apply. And unfortunately, you can't quickly tell which sliders go with which brushes. I offer this chapter as a reference. You can look up which variants go with which sliders. Listed are all the variants (except Painter 4's Extra Brushes) and below them are what palettes adjust them. I left out the Extra Brushes because they are novelties and set up to work fine the way they are. If you learn what all the settings in this chapter do, then you'll be able to adjust the Extra Brushes, too.

I'd like to point out once again that you don't have to change any of these sliders to use Painter. All the brush variants are perfectly usable as is. But it is nice to know how to adjust them to get the exact effect you seek.

Single-Stroke Brushes

When **Single** is selected in **Brushes palette: Controls: Spacing**, the sliders in the Spacing palette apply.

	Category	Variant
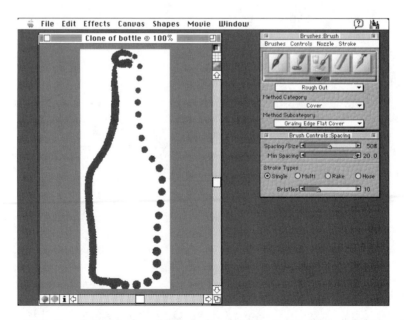	Brush	Graduated Brush, all Rough Outs
	Artists	Seurat, Impressionist, Flemish Rub, Piano Keys
	Brushes palette: Controls: Spacing palette: Spacing/Size and Min Spacing sliders	Spacing/Size and Min Spacing affect space between brush dabs (see Figures 13.1 and 13.2)

Figure 13.1 Rough Out before (l.) and after (r.) Min Spacing moved to the right.

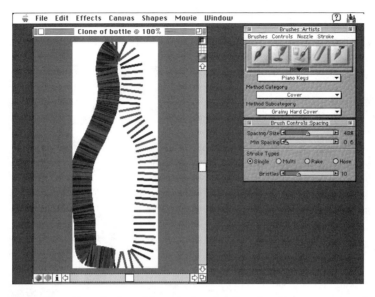

Figure 13.2 Piano Keys before (l.) and after (r.) Spacing/Size moved to the right.

Multibristle Brushes

When **Multi** is selected in **Brushes palette: Controls: Spacing**, the sliders in the Spacing palette apply.

	Category	Variant
	Brush	Hairy Brush
	Artists	Van Gogh
	Brushes palette: Controls: Spacing palette: Spacing/Size, and Min Spacing sliders	Spacing/Size and Min Spacing affect space between bristles. Bristles adjusts a stroke's bristle count (see Figure 13.3)

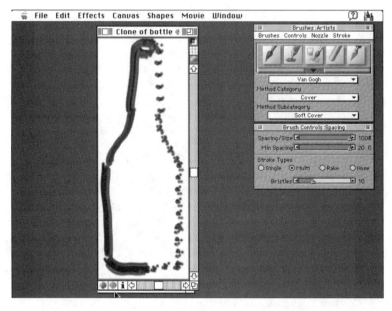

Figure 13.3 Van Gogh before (l.) and after (r.) Spacing/Size and Bristles sliders moved to the right.

Rake Brushes

When **Rake** is selected in **Brushes palette: Controls: Spacing**, the sliders in the Brushes palette: Controls: Rake palette apply. You can also use the **Brushes palette: Controls: Spacing: Bristles** slider.

	Category	Variant
	Brush	Penetration Brush
		Camel Hair Brush

Category	Variant
	Oil Paint
	Cover Brush
	All Loaded Oils
	Big Wet Oils
	Digital Sumi
	Brushes palette: Controls: Rake palette

Contact Angle

The Contact Angle affects stroke density (see Figure 13.4).

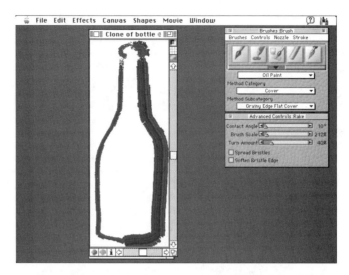

Figure 13.4 Oil Paint before (l.) and after (r.) (default setting)
Contact Angle moved to the right.

Brush Scale

Brush Scale controls stroke size (see Figure 13.5).

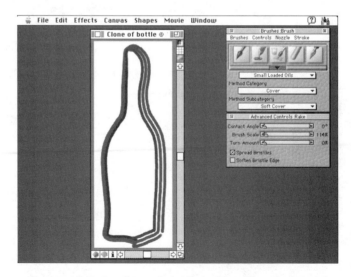

Figure 13.5 Small Loaded Oils before (l.) and after (r.)
Brush Scale moved to the right slightly.

Turn Amount

Turn Amount makes bristles appear to turn (see Figure 13.6).

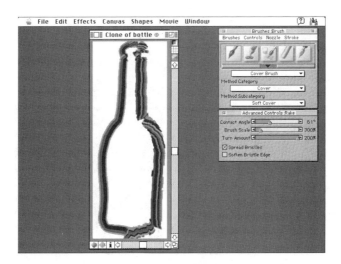

Figure 13.6 Cover Brush before (l.) and after (r.) Turn Amount moved to the right.

Spread Bristles

Spread Bristles joins bristles at the stroke tip (see Figure 13.7).

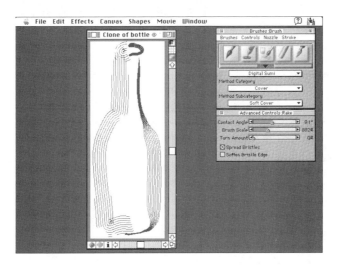

Figure 13.7 Digital Sumi before (l.) and after (r.) (default setting) **Spread Bristles** is checked. You'll see the difference only if you're using a pressure-sensitive stylus.

Soften Bristle Edge

Soften Bristle Edge smoothes out stroke edges (see Figure 13.8).

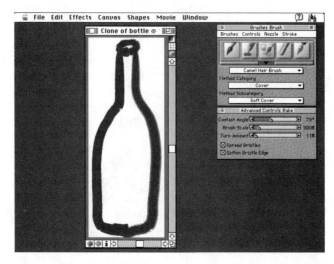

Figure 13.8 Camel Hair Brush before (l.) and after (r.) **Soften Bristle Edge** is checked.

Bristle Brushes

When **Bristle** is selected in the **Brushes palette: Controls: Size** palette, the sliders in the Brushes palette: Controls: Bristle palette apply.

	Category	Variant
	Brush	Ultrafine Wash Brush
		Smaller Wash Brush

Category	Variant
	All Loaded Oils
	Big Wet Oils

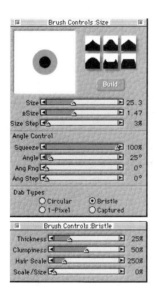 Brushes palette: Controls: Bristle palette

Thickness

The Thickness Slider controls bristle volume (see Figure 13.9).

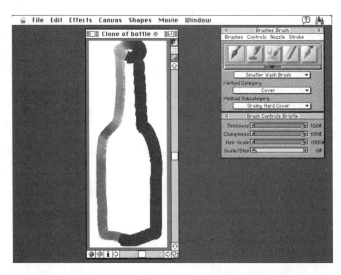

Figure 13.9 Smaller Wash Brush set up to show before (l.) and after (r.) the Thickness slider is moved to the right.

Clumpiness

The Clumpiness slider makes strokes irregular (see Figure 13.10).

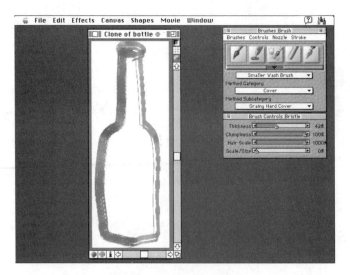

Figure 13.10 Smaller Wash Brush set up to show before (l.) and after (r.) Clumpiness is turned up.

Hair Scale

Moving the Hair Scale slider to the right thickens individual bristles (see Figure 13.11).

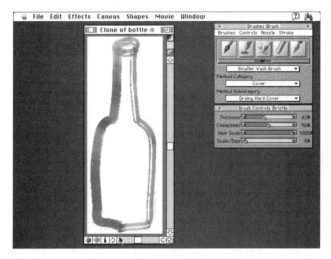

Figure 13.11 Smaller Wash Brush set up to show before (l.)
and after (r.) Hair Scale is turned up.

Scale/Size

Scale/Size controls the size variation of a stroke's bristles. Moving the slider up produces more variation and makes the bristles appear larger. Move the Size palette: ±Size slider up to see the effect (see Figure 13.12).

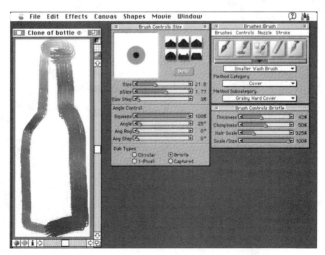

Figure 13.12 Smaller Wash Brush set up to show before (l.) and after (r.)
Scale/Size is turned up. Notice that ±Size in the Size palette is way up.

Watercolors

When you select the **Water Color** variants, the Brushes palette: Controls: Water palette applies.

	Category	Variant
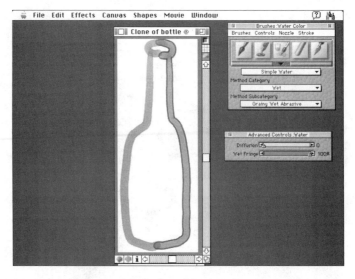	Water Color	All except Diffuse
	Brushes palette: Controls: Water: Wet Fringe	

Wet Fringe

Wet Fringe controls color pools at stroke edges (see Figure 13.13). Pooling can be adjusted after strokes are applied and before choosing **Canvas: Dry**. You can globally edit the pooling as long as you don't choose **Canvas: Dry**. If you want different amounts of pooling, paint several strokes, dry them, adjust Wet Fringe, and paint several more.

Figure 13.13 Water Color strokes before (l.) and after (r.) Wet Fringe is turned up.

Water Color   All

Diffusion

Diffusion controls how much Diffuse Water appears to seep into paper (see Figure 13.14); it works on all brush strokes in the Wet Paint layer. Adjust before applying strokes (opposite of Wet Fringe).

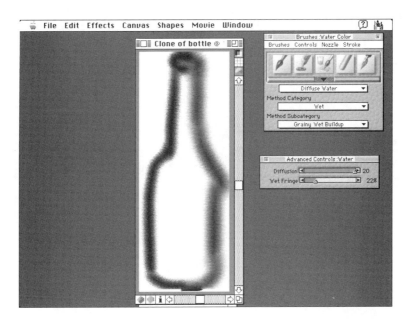

Figure 13.14 Diffuse Water stroke before (l.) and after (r.) Diffusion is turned up.

SUMMARY

Will you ever use any of the sliders discussed in this chapter? Based on conversations I've had with Painter artists, the answer is maybe. Some artists never touch these controls, others fine-tune them to get the exact brush they want. It's nice to know Painter has these brush-editing devices just in case you do need them.

14

Using Painter's Advanced Painting Tools

CHAPTER HIGHLIGHTS

- ❖ Oil painting
- ❖ Watercolor
- ❖ Airbrush

This chapter includes "real-world" examples of paintings created in Painter. They exemplify not only Painter's wealth and breadth of powerful tools, but also the top-flight talent of the artists working with Painter today.

You'll see in this chapter's exercises that artists find their own methods for working with Painter, just like they do when they paint traditionally. As previously mentioned, breaking Painter's tools into drawing and painting sections is a way to explain the program in smaller chunks. However, you'll see in this chapter that artists will use other tools in addition to the paintbrushes to get a desired paint effect.

Also, this chapter contains images that were painted from scratch, not as clones of photographs. Paintings that originated as photos are discussed in the photo-manipulation chapters later in this book.

Be sure to take a look at this chapter's images on the *Fractal Design Painter* 4 *Complete* CD. Zoom way up and you'll see the great detail that went into all of the paintings.

MOSAICS

Painter 4's hot new paintbrush is the mosaic feature. California-based illustrator Chelsea Sammel uses her traditional art background to get the most out of this cutting-edge tool (see Figure 14.1).

Figure 14.1 *New Mosaic* by Chelsea Sammel.

The manual covers thoroughly how to create a mosaic painting. Go through the Mosaics chapter there first to get the basics for creating mosaics. What follows here are some of Chelsea's tips for creating mosaics with a natural feel.

Chelsea says she tries to randomize the tiles as much as possible to individualize the painting.

For example, "tiles vary in color, so I always vary the colors" by adjusting the Color palette: ±HSV sliders, says Chelsea. "I put ±H at **10–15%** and ±S and ±V at **20–25%**."

In the Canvas: Make Mosaic dialog box, Chelsea chooses **Settings: Randomness** and moves up the sliders to randomize tiles. Then she chooses **Settings: Dimensions** and does her painting, adjusting the sliders as she goes along.

She uses the second icon to the right for erasing guidelines. For example, she drew the form for the leaves in *New Mosaic* because she wanted the tips to come to a point, then she erased out the guides by clicking on the second icon and painting in the image.

Another method Chelsea uses for individualizing the tiles is colorizing them by choosing the third icon and painting over the tiles. She chooses **Darken** and **Lighten** and shades and highlights the tiles.

When the tiles are the way she wants them, Chelsea chooses **Render Tiles into Mask**, which puts the tiles' outlines into the mask layer. She then clicks **Done** and adds surface texture. "Tiles would have a little texture," Chelsea notes, so she chooses **Art Materials: Paper palette: Basic Paper** and **Effects: Surface Control: Apply Surface Texture: Using Paper Grain**.

The final touch is to choose **Effects: Surface Control: Apply Surface Texture** again, this time choosing **Using menu: Mask** and adjusting the Softness slider, which gives the tiles three-dimensionality.

AIRBRUSH

Based in Dallas, Chet Phillips is an experienced traditional illustrator who now produces computer artwork for advertising agencies, corporations, newspapers, magazines, book publishers, and occasional gallery shows. Chet creates his artwork in many styles, from the scratchboard technique you saw in Chapter 8 to the next few paintings in this chapter. "*Mimosa Memories* (see Figure 14.2) is pretty much straight Airbrush," says Chet.

Figure 14.2 *Mimosa Memories* by Chet Phillips.

"I used the Pens' Scratchboard Tool variant for some of the detail in the mimosa petals and leaves." With the Airbrush's **Fat Stroke** variant selected, Chet changed the Brushes palette: Method Subcategory to **Grainy Soft Cover** and painted "with a canvas paper texture for the ground area."

The *Night Owls* diner piece pays homage to Edward Hopper's *Nighthawks* painting (see Figure 14.3).

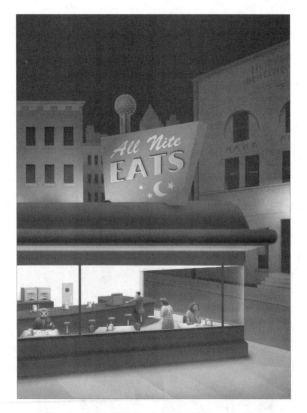

Figure 14.3 *Night Owls* by Chet Phillips.

"I created it for *The Dallas Morning News* for a story about places to eat that are open 24 hours for their weekend guide," says Chet. Chet used **Effects: Surface Control: Apply Lighting** to create the street lighting. The sign letters were embossed using **Effects: Surface Control: Apply Surface Texture using Mask**. Creating type is discussed later in the book. *Summer* (see Figure 14.4) is a self-promotional piece.

Figure 14.4 *Summer* by Chet Phillips.

Chet began the image with a real-time pencil sketch that he scanned. He opened the scan in Painter and turned on **Tracing Paper**. (Select **File: Clone**. Choose **Edit: Select All** [**Command+A**, Mac; **Ctrl+A**, Windows]. Press **delete**, Mac; **Backspace**, Windows. Choose **Canvas: Tracing Paper** [**Command+T**, Mac; **Ctrl+T**, Windows].) He then used the Chalk's **Artist Pastel Chalk** with the Method Subcategory switched to **Soft Cover** "to block in areas of the figure and the water." Then, using the Liquid's **Distorto** tool, he blended the water and created the ripples. He highlighted with the Airbrush's **Fat Stroke**. Then Chet used a combination of the Chalk's **Artist Pastel Chalk** with the Method Subcategory switched to **Grainy Soft Cover** and the Airbrush's **Fat Stroke** to give detail to the figure's face and goggles. Open up the image on the CD and zoom up on these areas to see the detail. It's amazing. Then Chet used the Pens' **Scratchboard** Tool to paint the design on the pool wall.

Chet "created a paper texture with a grid shape to apply to the pool side" as both a color overlay with white and then as a surface texture.

Here's a fairly simple way to do that:

1. Start a new image (**File: New**, click **OK**).
2. Select **Effects: Esoterica: Grid Paper**. The Grid Options dialog box appears. This is a special effect, not the nonprinting grid layer.

3. Click on the **Grid Color** square. In the dialog box, choose **black** and click **OK**. A grid now covers your image.

4. Choose **Edit: Select All** (**Command+A**, Mac; **Ctrl+A**, Windows).

5. Choose **Art Materials: Paper: Capture Texture**. The Save Texture dialog box appears. Click **OK**. The selection is now a paper tile in the Paper palette.

6. Select the pool wall with the **Lasso**, then choose **white** in the Color palette, and choose **Effects: Surface Control: Color Overlay**. The Color Overlay dialog box appears. Click next to **Hiding Power**. You may have to check **Paper palette: Invert Grain** for the grid to be white. Click **OK**. A white grid now covers the pool wall.

7. Select **Effects: Surface Control: Apply Surface Texture**. I played around with different settings and got different results. Choose **Using menu: Paper Grain** or **Image Luminance**. Either works; they give different effects. Also try checking and unchecking **Paper palette: Invert Grain** and adjusting the Amount slider. Click **OK**.

Next, Chet made the reflection. With the pool wall still selected, he made it a floater copy (choose the **Tools palette**: left-pointing hand, press **Option**, Mac; **Alt**, Windows, click on the selection), flipped it vertically (**Effects: Orientation: Flip Vertical**), and brought Controls: Opacity down to **25%**. He clicked and dragged on the floater with the left-pointing hand and "brought it down to area below the wall to create a reflection. Then I used the Liquid's **Distorto** tool to blend with pool water." He chose **Edit:Drop** to drop the floater.

For the sky, Chet made custom gradation with six different blues (**Art Materials: Grad: Edit Gradation**). He airbrushed the cloud with the **Fat Stroke** variant. Chet "frisketed areas for hedges (select with **Lasso**), filled with green (**Effects: Fill**), and airbrushed texture with grainy soft buildup (**Method Category: Buildup; Method Subcategory; Grainy Soft Buildup**).

Chet created the frame area around the outside of the image by first adding white space with **Canvas: Canvas Size**, chose **blue**, and applied **Effects: Fill**. Then Chet applied two different custom-made paper textures of abstract shapes with **Effects: Surface Control: Color Overlay** "to give the blue a refracted light/water texture."

For the *Fallen Angel* piece (see Figure 14.5), Chet selected the top of the image with the middle rectangle in the Tools palette and used **Effects: Fill** to fill it with green for the forest. Then he selected the bottom portion and filled it with blue for water. He then painted the leaves, branches, shoreline, and the figure and filtered light using the Chalk's **Artist Pastel Chalk** variant alternating between **Method Subcategory: Grainy Soft Cover** and **Method Category: Buildup, Method Subcategory: Grainy Soft Buildup**. He painted the horizontal lines in the lake area with the **Artist Pastel Chalk** and Airbrush's **Fat Stroke** and then smudged them with the Water's **Just Add Water**.

Lastly, using the rectangle from the middle of the Tools palette, Chet selected the area from the shoreline to the middle portion of the forest area, chose the **Tools palette**: left-pointing hand, pressed **Option**, Mac; **Alt**, Windows, then clicked on the selection to copy it as a floater. He flipped it vertically (**Effects: Orientation: Flip Vertical**) and clicked and dragged it over the water. He lowered Controls: Opacity to **45%**. He reworked the figure's reflection in red and oranges and smeared with **Just Add Water**.

WATERCOLOR TECHNIQUES

Westchester, NY–based illustrator Denise Devenuti does computer illustration and multimedia interface design for web sites and CD-ROMs. *Muffin Patch* (see Figure 14.6) is a poster she painted for her brother's muffin shop using Painter's Water Color brushes. The following steps show how she did it.

Figure 14.6 *Muffin Patch* by Denise Devenuti.

Denise started out by sketching the image real time (see Figure 14.7).

Figure 14.7 Sketch for *Muffin Patch*.

She scanned it at 300 ppi into Photoshop, where she deleted unwanted lines. Next, Denise brought the image into Painter, where she laid down color with the Water Colors' **Simple Water** variant (see Figure 14.8).

Figure 14.8 Denise started to paint color with Water Color's **Simple Water** variant.

Denise used the Eraser's **Ultrafine**, **Small**, and **Medium** variants to erase unwanted lines as she went along. While the water color is in the *wet layer*, that is, before you choose **Canvas: Dry**, you can erase what's in the underlying image without affecting the watercolor strokes. Similarly, if you erase with the Water Color's **Wet Eraser**, you can erase the watercolor strokes without hurting what's in the underlying image.

As she painted, Denise used various paper textures in the Art Materials: Paper palette to create the look of baked muffins including **Mountains** (Texture Sampler library, Mac; coolsamp.pap,Windows), **Basic Paper**, **Rougher**, (both in the default paper library) and **Mottled** (more Wild Textures library, Mac; Morewild.pap, Windows). She adjusted the Paper palette: Scale slider from **100%** to **300%**, depending on the desired effect.

She blended the colors by lowering the Controls: Opacity and Grain sliders and painting another layer of color. She also blended colors by using the **Pure Water Brush** but "this often removed too much color instead of blending evenly," Denise reports.

Denise then created the fruit in the muffins by coloring with the **Simple Water Brush** and then stroking it with the **Diffuse Water** variant with the Controls: Opacity and Grain both at **50%**. Next, Denise painted the crumbs at the top of some of the muffins with the **Spatter Water** variant. Then Denise created the leaves using the **Charcoal Soft Charcoal** and **Default** variants (see Figure 14.9).

Figure 14.9 Leaves added with Charcoal.

Then she blended the colors in the leaves using the Water's **Just Add Water** variant. She used the Liquid's **Distorto** variant to "give the swirl effect to the leaves," Denise notes. And she used the **Eraser** to clean up edges. Then it was time to create the muffin bases (see Figure 14.10).

Figure 14.10 Muffin base added.

Denise painted the muffin bases with the same **Simple Water**, **Diffuse Water**, and **Pure Water** variants of the Water Color with **Regular Fine** texture chosen in the Art Materials: Paper palette and the Paper palette: Scale slider set at **200%**. Once the painting was done, Denise saved the document in the Photoshop format. In Photoshop she added a gradation in the background and adjusted colors.

CUSTOMIZING PAINTER'S BRUSHES

Northern California–based artist Jeremy Sutton likes to custom-tailor Painter's brushes to paint his portraits like *Picasso* (see Figure 14.11).

Figure 14.11 *Picasso* by Jeremy Sutton.

"When I look at Picasso's face I see a dynamic combination of playfulness, aggression, and passion. It was this fiery mix of qualities, his vibrant zest for life, that I wanted to capture in this portrait," Jeremy says. "I chose to use *The Dream*, a painting that depicts a dreaming lady, to represent the sensual side of Picasso" (see Figure 14.12).

213

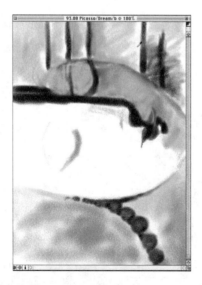

Figure 14.12 *The Dream.*

"His aggression and anger seemed well expressed in the screaming horse of his *Bullfight*, and this I chose for a second image," says Jeremy (see Figure 14.13).

Figure 14.13 *Bullfight.*

Chariot

Dorothy Simpson Krause

*Catherine and
Jacqueline*

Nomi Wagner

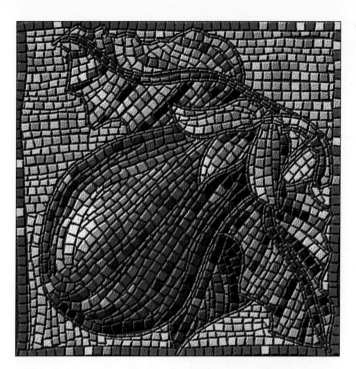

New Mosaic

Chelsea Sammel

Controller

Steve Campbell

Picasso   Jeremy Sutton

Winter Solstace   Bonny Lhotka

Mimosa Memories

Chet Phillips

Summer

Chet Phillips

One Yellow Tulip

Chelsea Sammel

Electric Apples

Chelsea Sammel

Muffin Patch

Denise Devenuti

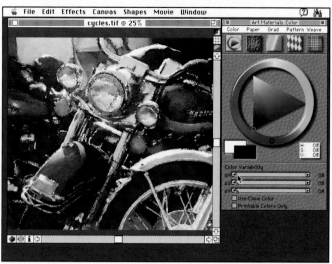

Cycles

Michael Savas

Boy

Michael Savas

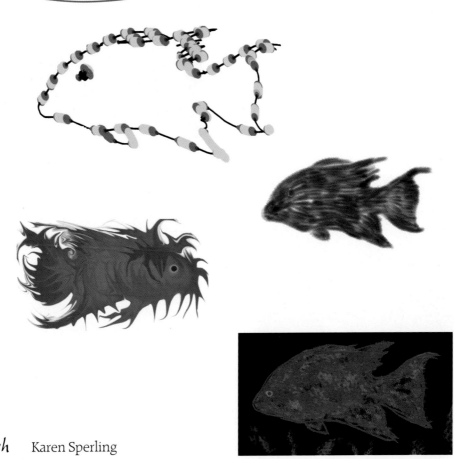

Fish   Karen Sperling

Poker Cat

Jason Fruchter

Night Owls

Chet Phillips

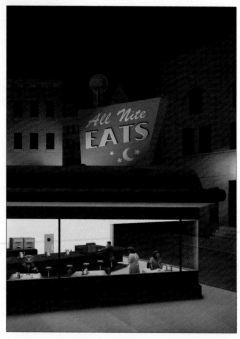

Superman™ ©1996 *DC Comics*

Jose Marzan

"Both images are real Picasso paintings that I painted my own copies of while looking at prints of them. Everything in the paintings is original painting, but they were based on two original paintings by Picasso."

Jeremy usually paints with any chosen brush set either to **Grainy Soft Cover** or **Grainy Soft Buildup** chosen in the Brushes palette: Method Subcategory pop-up menu, so that he can "introduce different paper textures" as he paints. He sets up the Brushes palette: Controls: Sliders palette so that Size, Grain, and Opacity are all set to **Pressure**. "This allows convenient control of subtle effects and detail" by controlling the stroke aspects by varying stylus pressure.

Once he had painted *Dream* and *Bullfight*, with *Bullfight* as the current image Jeremy selected **File: Clone Source: Dream**. He used the Cloners' **Soft Cloner** brush with the Method Subcategory set to **Grainy Soft Cover Cloning** "to subtly introduce portions of the *Dream* image into the *Bullfight* image."

Then Jeremy painted Picasso's face using the Chalk to "build up the portrait over the top of the background I created." He switched to the Crayons for the "dark areas like eyelashes and pupils." He set up both tools so that brush width would vary based on how hard he pressed the stylus in the Brushes palette: Controls: Sliders palette. He used the Liquid's **Distorto** variant to blend elements (see Figure 14.14).

Figure 14.14 Picasso beginning to emerge.

Lastly, Jeremy created a cubist design using Xaos Tools Paint Alchemy, a Mac program (see Figure 14.15).

Figure 14.15 Cubist design.

He then set that image as the clone source and "cloned in certain edges and blocks to provide an underlying hint of cubist forms."

PAINTING WITH OIL PASTELS

Kerry Gavin has been an illustrator for nearly 20 years, and until a couple of years ago, he worked in traditional media, primarily watercolor, technical pen, and airbrush. Now his tool of choice is Painter. He uses Painter's floaters to move image elements around and he paints with the Chalk and Water to get the look of Craypas, a brand of oil pastels. The following section shows some of Kerry's paintings (Figure 14.16) and the steps he did to create them.

Figure 14.16 *The Toast.*

1. Draw the bottle shape with the Pen tool.

2. If the shape isn't filled with a color, press **Return** Mac; **Enter,** Windows, click next to **Fill**, and click **OK**. The shape is now filled with the current color in the Color palette.

3. Paint with the chalk. The shape becomes a floater. Smear with the Water's **Just Add Water**.

4. Create the pouring shape the same way; paint the swirls with the Liquid's **Distorto** variant.

Kerry created the label in a separate document with the same tools and copied and pasted it into the main image as a floater. Use **Effects: Orientation: Free Transform** to turn the floater into a reference floater. Then, with the left-pointing hand selected, press **Command**, Mac; **Ctrl**, Windows, and click and drag on a corner point, letting you rotate the label floater into the correct angle with the bottle. When done, select **Effects: Orientation: Commit Transform**. The floater is set. Says Kerry, "I used a really fat Chalk (adjust the width in Brushes palette: Controls: Size) and created the yellow background highlight." Kerry used a similar technique to paint *Dinner at Kintaro* (see Figure 14.17).

Figure 14.17 *Dinner at Kintaro.*

1. Kerry used the oval in the upper-right corner of the Tools palette (click and hold on the rectangle and it becomes an oval) and drew several circular shapes to create the dish.

2. Next, combine the shapes and make them into a floater. To do so, choose the **Tools palette:** left-pointing hand and **Edit: Select All** (**Command+A**, Mac; **Ctrl+A**, Windows). The shapes are all selected. Choose **Objects: F. List: Group** and then **Collapse**. The shapes become one floater.

3. Kerry created the various pieces of sushi as shapes, then turned them into floaters and painted in them with the Chalk and Water, as previously described. He also created the chopsticks in this document.

4. Back in the dish image, Kerry clicked outside the bowl with the left-pointing hand to deselect, chose a "warm gray tone" and chose **Effects: Fill**. Then he chose **Effects: Surface Control: Apply Lighting** "for a kind of photographic effect."

5. Kerry next copied and pasted the sushi and chopsticks floaters from the other image into the main one.

6. Last, Kerry created shadows for the chopsticks and the dish floaters using **Effects: Objects: Create Drop Shadow**.

OIL PAINTING

Indiana-based artist Richard H. Biever has devised a method to get his rich oil painting look (see Figure 14.18) by smearing Chalk strokes with the Water's **Water Rake** variant.

Figure 14.18 *African Princess* by Richard H. Biever.

This is how Richard created *African Princess*. He started sketching the general outline and position of the figure with the Chalk's **Artist Pastel Chalk** (see Figure 14.19).

219

Figure 14.19 Original sketch.

"I did this right on the computer," Richard notes. "I wasn't working from a photo, and nothing was scanned. I simply started drawing." Then Richard applied large flat strokes of color with the Chalk and the Brushes palette: Controls: Size slider moved up. "I detailed the face a bit to get a feel of the mood and character of the woman," Richard adds (see Figure 14.20).

Figure 14.20 Colors painted in.

"In order to reduce the file size, I cropped just the area of the head to work on the face," says Richard. To crop an image, select the desired area with the middle rectangle in the Tools palette, then select **Edit: Copy** then **Edit: Paste: Into New Image**. "I liked the look of the picture cropped so much that I decided to leave it that way," he adds. "With it cropped though, I didn't like the purple gown so I made it white and developed the face a little further," says Richard (see Figure 14.21).

Figure 14.21 Gown recolored and face developed.

Richard notes, "the areas around the face are purposefully a bit blurry to accentuate the face. I also made her neck a bit thinner than real to give her a little more elegance. That's really all there was to it, which sounds simple and easy but I really have to work to get the final result. Most of my paintings must evolve into what they are; they were not created in the first session. The forms must be coaxed from the canvas."

ANOTHER KIND OF OIL PAINTING

Chelsea Sammel created her painting *One Yellow Tulip* (see Figure 14.22) using the Brush's **Coarse Hairs** and **Loaded Oils** variants.

Figure 14.22 *One Yellow Tulip* by Chelsea Sammel.

First she painted the underpainting with the **Loaded Oils**, then, to "make it (the image) more delicate," she went over the strokes with the **Coarse Hairs** brush.

SUMMARY

You have now seen a vast range of paint styles by working artists who use Painter as their medium of choice. I hope this chapter inspires you to create your own Painter masterpieces.

Part IV

Drawing and Painting Accessories

15

Using Paths, Floaters, and Shapes

CHAPTER HIGHLIGHTS

❖ Using paths
❖ Using floaters
❖ Using shapes

Painter 4 includes technology that Mark Zimmer and Tom Hedges invented in 1990, namely *Shapes*. Shapes are vector selections that float above the bitmapped image area. Mark and Tom first introduced them in ColorStudio, their image manipulation program that predated Photoshop.

I wrote the Shapes manual and it's interesting how far computer art has come since then and the good use that artists now make of the shapes features, in addition to Painter's other selection tools, as you'll see in this chapter. Once you master Painter 4's selection tools, you're going to enjoy their power. And if you use Adobe Illustrator, then you'll really like the way Painter's selection tools now work.

Selections come in many forms in Painter, namely *paths*, *floaters*, and *shapes*. What each does is the same, that is, it isolates an area of your image. Once an area is isolated, you can do things to it. These things include painting in it, moving it, or adding an effect to it. It's that simple.

What's complex is deciding whether a particular design problem calls for a path, a floater, or a shape. Experience is really the best guide, and after you work with the paths, floaters, and shapes a lot, you begin to get a sense about which is best in a particular situation. Meanwhile, working with paths, floaters, and shapes—especially activating and editing them—can be complex, and again, experience is the best teacher.

And, unfortunately, the various kinds of selections are used synonymously sometimes, causing some confusion. For example, in the Objects: F. List palette, you can select **Drop with Mask** to drop a floater with its marching ants, which are really called a path.

In learning version 4 I found that if I ignored all the terms and just sort of used the tools to do a specific task, then things became clear. Along the same lines, this chapter's tutorial showing how Ben Barbante used shapes, paths, and floaters to paint an airbrushed painting should help make Painter's selection tools seem less mysterious to you.

PAINTING WITH SHAPES

"I approached *Synchronous Harmony* (see Figure 15.1) in much the same manner as an airbrush painting using friskets," says San Francisco–based illustrator Ben Barbante, who is also art director at InfoWorld.

Figure 15.1 *Synchronous Harmony* by Ben Barbante.

"I created shapes to define areas to be masked. The background elements, the dolphin, and the swimmer were created in separate documents and pasted together at a later stage."

The following steps show how Ben created *Synchronous Harmony*.

First Ben drew the dolphin and swimmer, scanned them in, and traced them with shapes.

1. Draw the dolphin and swimmer "real time" and scan them in as a 144 ppi PICT file.

2. Turn on Tracing Paper (select **File: Clone**. Choose **Edit: Select All** [**Command+A**, Mac; **Ctrl+A**, Windows]. Press **delete**, Mac; **Backspace**, Windows. Choose **Canvas: Tracing Paper** [**Command+T**, Mac; **Ctrl+T**, Windows]).

3. Trace the scanned PICT template using the Pen tool. To color a shape, select it by clicking on it with the left-pointing hand (if the shape isn't already selected) and press **Return**, Mac; **Enter,** Windows. The Set Shape Attributes dialog box appears. Click on the **Fill square** on the dialog box's right-hand side, and choose a color in the Color palette. The Fill square and the shape turn the selected color. Click **OK**. You can also double-click on the **Fill Color square**, which brings up a color picker where you can choose a color (see Figure 15.2).

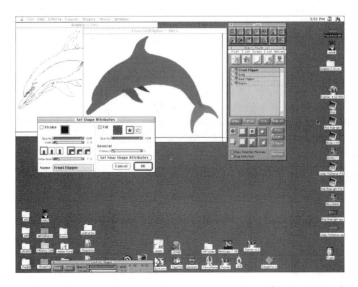

Figure 15.2 Shapes are traced in the clone and then filled with color using **Set Shape Attributes**.

Next, to keep things organized, Ben named each shape in the Objects: F. List palette (see Figure 15.3).

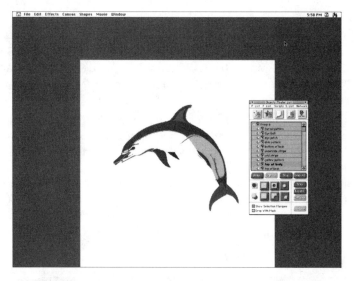

Figure 15.3 Shapes named in the Objects: F. List palette.

Here's how you name a shape:

1. Select the shape (either click on it with the Tools palette: left-pointing hand or click on its name in the F. List palette). Press **Return** Mac; **Enter,** Windows. The Set Shape Attributes dialog box appears as before.

2. Type in the new name in the dialog box's lower-left corner.

3. Click **OK**. The name you typed now appears in the Objects: F. List palette.

Next Ben gave his shapes an airbrushed look by painting in each shape with the Brushes palette: Airbrush's **Fat Stroke** variant (see Figure 15.4). When you paint or apply an effect in a shape it becomes a floater.

"When areas within floaters need to be blended together, I convert them into selections," Ben notes. For example, if you look at Figure 15.5, the rib and torso were separate areas and had to be blended.

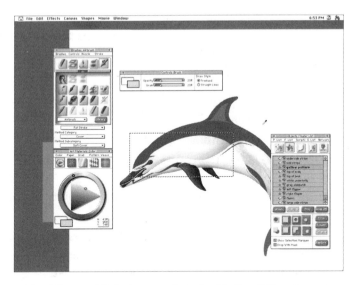

Figure 15.4 Areas painted with the Airbrush.

Figure 15.5 Floaters turned into selections.

Turning floaters into selections requires dropping the floater into the background image. So the first thing you want to be sure of is that you have one part of the image, say the swimmer, in its own document.

The following shows how to convert a floater into a selection.

1. Select a floater by clicking on it with the Floaters tool (the left-pointing hand in the Tools palette).

2. Click **Objects: F. List: Drop with Mask**.

3. Click **Objects: F. List: Drop**. The floater becomes part of the background image.

4. To see the path, click **Objects: P. List**: third **Visibility** button (next to the eye).

To paint within the path, choose a brush, click the **Objects: P. List**: third **Drawing** button (next to the pencil) and paint. The paint goes inside the path but not beyond it. To paint outside of the path, click the **Objects: P. List**: second **Drawing** button (next to the pencil). Now you can paint in the area beyond the path but not in the space inside it.

The way to blend two image areas like the rib and torso would be to drop each area's floater with its mask. Once the floaters are incorporated into the image, you can then activate their paths and paint inside the two areas as long as both paths' marching ants are active. To activate an inactive path, click on it with the Selection Adjuster tool (hold on the left-pointing hand in the Tools palette and you'll see a left pointing hand on top of a selection. That's the tool you want). Press **Return**, Mac; **Enter**, Windows. Repeat to deactivate. Be careful—if you click on the path with the Floater tool (the left-pointing hand) by mistake, then it will become a floater, which you don't want to happen yet.

After you are done dropping floaters, activating and deactivating paths, and painting, you'll want to float the image again so that you can bring it into the main image.

First, activate all the paths, showing their marching ants. Do so by selecting the **Tools palette: Selection Adjuster** tool and clicking and dragging a marquee around all the paths. You can instead press the **Shift** key, click on each path's name in the Objects: P. List palette, and press **Return**, Mac; **Enter,** Windows. With the Floater Adjuster tool (the left-pointing hand without the selection), click on the group of paths. They combine into one floater. You can click **Objects: F. List: Trim** to reduce the floater's bounding box.

Next Ben created the background within the circle. First he drew a circle shape.

1. Select **File: New**. A new images appears.

2. Click and hold on the **rectangle** in the Tools palette's upper-right-hand corner to access the oval shapes tool. Press **Shift** to constrain the tool to a circle and click and drag in the image. You now have a circle shape.

3. Press **Return**, Mac; **Enter,** Windows. The Set Shape Attributes dialog box appears. Deselect **Fill**. Click **OK**. The shape seems to disappear.

4. Click on the **Tools palette: hollow arrow**. The shape reappears as a blue line.

5. With the hollow arrow, click and drag a selection marquee around the circle. Its selection points appear.

6. Choose the **Tools palette: scissors**. Click anywhere on the circle that isn't a selection point. You create a new point, splitting up the circle. Click elsewhere on the circle, which creates another new point and segment. The section between the two points is now separate from the rest of the circle.

7. Click and hold on the hollow arrow to access the solid arrow. Click and drag on the segment you just created. It comes away from the circle.

8. Choose the **Pen** tool. Click on one end of the segment and then the other. The segment closes and is now a new shape.

You can click on the two ends to close up the top semi-circle and the bottom semi-circle. But you're left with two disconnected segments in the middle (see Figure 15.6).

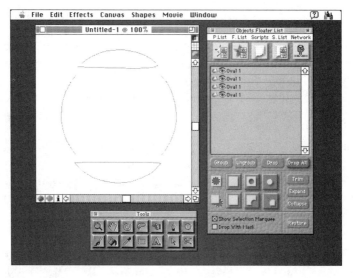

Figure 15.6 The circle after the top and bottom portions are connected.

To join the middle segments, with the hollow arrow, click and drag a marquee around the bottom point of one, then press **Shift** and do the same to the other. Then choose **Shapes: Join Endpoints** (**Command+J**, Mac; **Ctrl+J**, Windows). A line then connects the two points.

Ben created three separate shapes, one each for the sky, the water surface, and the underwater. He then created three new images, one containing the sky, one containing the water surface, and one containing the underwater.

First create an image for the sky, which you'll fill with a top-to-bottom gradation.

1. Select **File: New** and click **OK**. A new image appears.

2. Choose a **dark blue** in the Color palette. Click on the rear **rectangle** in the Color palette, choose a **light blue**, and click back on the front **rectangle** in the Color palette.

3. Click and drag the **Grad** icon to tear off the palette. Click on the **overlapping rectangles** icon in the Grad palette (it may be inside the drawer). Close the drawer and drag on the red dot on the front panel until the dark blue is at the top of the Grad Preview.

4. Select **Effects: Fill**, click next to **Gradation**, and click **OK**. You now have a sky.

Ben painted the clouds with the **Brushes palette: Brushes: Brush Looks: Erase Clouds** brush look.

234

Then Ben created a new image for the water surface and did a graduated fill as described above. He painted the waves using the **Brushes palette: Dodge** and **Burn** tools and the Brush's **Brushy** variant.

Then he created a third image for the underwater, filled it with a gradient, and used **Effects: Surface Control: Apply Lighting**.

The next step was to bring these various images into the main image. Ben composited the floaters to map each area to each shape (see Figure 15.7).

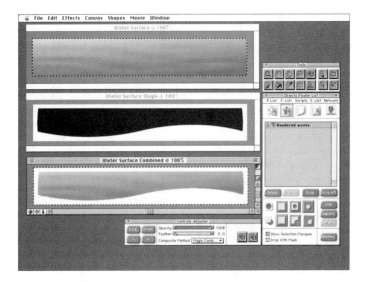

Figure 15.7 The water created with a composited floater.

The following steps show how to composite floaters.

1. Select the middle section of what was once the circle by clicking and dragging around it with the hollow arrow.

2. Press **Return**, Mac; **Enter,** Windows. The Set Shape Attributes dialog appears. Click next to **Fill**. The shape in the image fills with color. Choose **black** in the Color palette to fill the shape with black. Click **OK**.

3. Click **Objects: F. List: Drop**. The black shape is rendered into the image.

Next you'll bring in the water surface.

1. Open the image you created for the water surface (or create one now).

2. Choose **Edit: Select All (Command+A**, Mac; **Ctrl+A**, Windows).

3. Choose **Edit: Copy**.

4. Choose **Window: image containing the black shape**.

5. Choose **Edit: Paste: Normal**. The water surface comes in as a floater.

6. With the left-pointing hand selected in the Tools palette, select **Controls palette: Composite Method: Magic Combine**. The water surface is mapped to the black image shape and the area outside the black shape is masked.

Once the other image elements were brought in, the final touch was to paint the splashes and foam using the **Brushes palette: Brushes: Brush Looks: Erase Clouds** brush look. For the splashes, Ben customized the Erase Clouds. He moved up the Brushes palette: Controls: Size: ± Size slider; the Controls: Opacity slider; and the Brushes palette: Controls: Random: Dab Location Placement slider. He also set the Brushes palette: Controls: Sliders: Jitter and Opacity sliders to **Pressure**, so that the "harder you push the stylus, the further apart the splashes appear."

SUMMARY

That's how versatile Painter's selection tools can be. I hope seeing how Ben Barbante was able to maximize the tools' potential will give you some incentive to learn these tricky but useful Painter options yourself. Next is the paper chapter, where you'll see how Steve Campbell uses selections, in his case, to add paper textures to his art.

16
Working with Paper

CHAPTER HIGHLIGHTS

- ❖ Creating paper textures
- ❖ Editing paper textures
- ❖ Applying paper textures

Paper textures are one of the things Painter does best.

As you saw in previous chapters, your brush or drawing tool can react to the paper texture chosen in the Paper palette, which means you can have a variety of textures going on within the same image (see Figure 16.1). I did the quick sketch in Figure 16.1 with the Chalk's Large Chalk variant and various textures from Fractal's Nature Paper Texture collection.

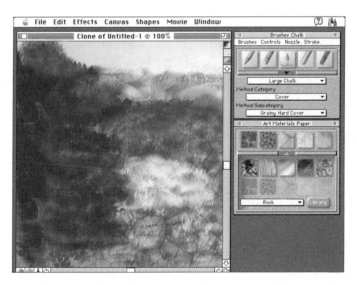

Figure 16.1 Draw or paint with a variety of textures by choosing them in the Paper palette. Textures in Nature collection by Fractal Design.

You can also add paper texture as a special effect in Painter as you'll see later in this chapter. Select **Window: Art Materials: Paper palette**. You'll use this palette throughout this chapter.

GRAINY METHOD BRUSHES

As previously mentioned, a variant must have the word *Grainy* in its Brushes palette: Method Subcategory to interact with paper grain. You can give any variant paper grain interactivity by choosing a Grainy method in its Method Subcategory; you can shut off a variant's grain sensitivity by switching to a non-Grainy method.

SLIDERS PALETTE

Chapter 7, "Advanced Drawing Tools," discusses the Brushes palette: Controls: Sliders palette: Grain slider. It's worth mentioning again. You can get all kinds of interesting paper texture effects by setting the Sliders palette: Grain slider on all the different choices. See Chapter 7 for details.

EDITING GRAINS

Painter's paper textures are usable as is, but pretty soon you'll find yourself wanting to adjust grain to suit a particular image or effect.

Grain Slider

As you've seen in previous chapters, the simplest way to edit paper grain is to adjust the Controls palette: Grain slider. Moving the slider to the left gives you more paper texture in a brush stroke, moving the slider to the right puts more color into the stroke, hiding more paper grain (see Figure 16.2).

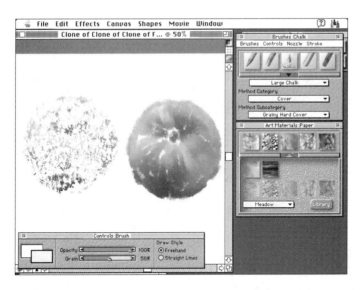

Figure 16.2 Strokes with the Controls: Grain slider moved to the left (left) and to the right (right). Texture from the *Artistry* Paper Collection vol. 1 created by Pete McCabe.

The Grain Slider works with all Grainy method brushes except those with Grainy Soft Buildup. For example, if you draw with the Pens' Smooth Ink Pen, adjusting the Grain slider will have no effect.

Adjusting Grain Scale

You can use the paper textures to conjure up all kinds of effects by doing something as simple as adjusting paper scale using the Paper palette: Scale slider. The slider's default setting is **100%**; moving the slider to the left makes the paper grain smaller, moving it to the right makes it bigger (see Figure 16.3). When you resize the texture, the Preview window on the Paper palette front panel shows the change.

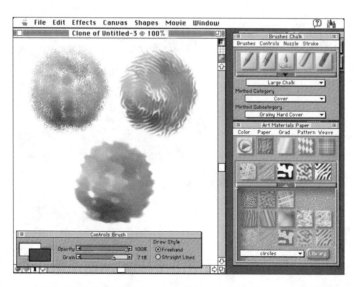

Figure 16.3 Circles in the More Wild Textures library on the Mac or MOREWILD.PAP in Windows, with the Scale slider at **34%** (top, left), **100%** (top, right), and **300%** (bottom).

Inverting Paper Texture

Another quick edit that produces interesting results is checking the Paper palette's **Invert Grain** box. When you draw or paint on textured paper, color coats the peaks and ignores the valleys. Checking the **Invert Grain** box reverses the relationship, so that color will cover what was ignored before. The result is a duotone effect. Invert Grain works with both brushes and Effects menu items. So you can create duotone paper by either painting or applying an effect, checking **Invert Grain**, choosing a new color, and painting again or reapplying the effect.

Randomizing Paper Grain

Sometimes you want to texturize part of your image with an unrecognizable paper grain. For example, you may want texture in a carpet but not an even, recognizable texture. You can "mess up" textures to look uneven by checking **Brushes palette: Controls: Random: Random Brush Stroke Grain**.

The Airbrush's Spatter Airbrush variant was created with **Random Brush Stroke Grain** checked. Select the **Spatter Airbrush** variant, select a big-grain paper, and paint. Uncheck **Random Brush Stroke Grain** and you have an evenly tiled pattern (see Figure 16.4).

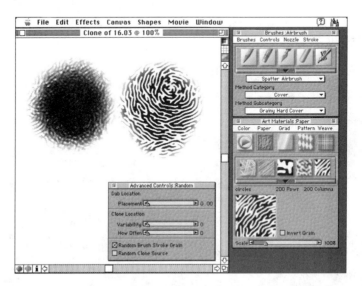

Figure 16.4 Spatter Airbrush stroke with **Random Brush Stroke Grain** checked (left) and unchecked (right).

CREATING PAPER TEXTURES

Painter comes with many paper libraries from which to choose. As many as there are, however, you may not find the exact paper texture that you want. If that happens, you can create your own using **Paper palette: Paper: Capture Texture** and **Make Paper Texture**.

Capture Paper Texture

Capture Paper Texture lets you select anything in your image and save it as a tile in the Paper palette.

This means that you can transform anything into a paper grain, including original art or photos, recognizable shapes or abstract designs, gradations or weaves—anything.

The next exercise shows how I created a paper texture called Scrambled Eggs from an abstract design (see Figure 16.5). I created Figure 16.5 by applying **Scrambled Eggs** with **Effects: Surface Control: Color Overlay** and **Apply Surface Texture**, covered later in this chapter.

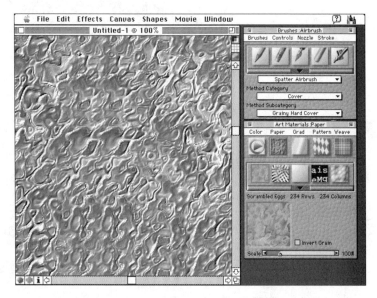

Figure 16.5 Scrambled Eggs paper texture.

Creating Abstract Paper Texture

I created my Scrambled Eggs paper texture using **Express Texture** and **Glass Distortion**. First you'll draw some lines.

1. Select **File: New**. Select **inches** in the pop-up menus next to Width and Height and type in **1** for each. Type **250** next to Resolution. Click **OK**. A new image appears.
2. Choose the Pencils' **2B Pencil** variant.
3. Choose **black** in the Color palette.
4. Draw some strokes (see Figure 16.6).

5. Choose **eggscape** in the Paper palette and choose **Effects: Surface Control: Express Texture**. The Express Texture dialog box appears.

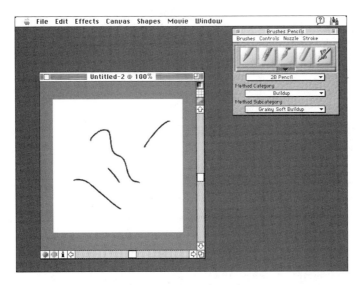

Figure 16.6 Pencil strokes.

6. Move the sliders around until you like what you see in the Preview window (see Figure 16.7).

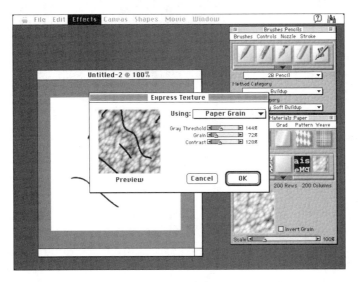

Figure 16.7 The Express Texture dialog box.

243

7. Choose **Effects: Focus: Glass Distortion**. The Glass Distortion dialog box appears. Choose **Paper Grain** in the Using menu and set the sliders to the following settings:

Softness	**3.5**
Map	**Angle Displacement**
Amount	**.23**
Variance	**14.00**
Direction	**0°**

8. Click **OK**.

Now it's time to make this pattern a paper texture.

1. Choose **Edit: Select All** (**Command+A** on the Mac; **Ctrl+A** in Windows).
2. Choose **Paper palette: Paper: Capture Texture**. The Save Texture dialog box appears. Type in the name of your new texture and click **OK**. Your texture now appears as an icon in the Paper palette drawer.

Now you'll draw with the new texture.

1. Select **File: New**, type **4** next to Width and Height, and click **OK**. A new image appears.
2. Choose the Chalk's **Large Chalk** variant.
3. Click on the new texture in the Paper palette if it isn't already selected.
4. Draw in the image. The grain appears in the stroke (see Figure 16.8). I drew Figure 16.8 freehand (no underlying image) with the Scale slider at various positions, lower for the cup, higher for the table.

Make Repeating Texture

Choose **Paper palette: Paper: Make Paper Texture**. Make Paper Texture creates geometric patterns that you can save as grains in the Paper palette. Check the manual for information about using Make Paper Texture.

Using Soft Grain Colorize

Soft Grain Colorize is a Method Subcategory in the Eraser Method Category that lets you add two colors to an image based on the grain chosen in the Paper palette. This effect is good for painting in broad areas. Choose a brush, then change the Method Category pop-up menu to **Eraser**. Change the Method Subcategory pop-up menu to **Soft Grain Colorize**. Choose a light color in the Color palette. Click on the **rear rectangle** in the Color palette and select a darker color. Click back on the **front rectangle**. Select a paper texture in the Paper palette and paint in the image. The selected paper texture appears in the image, and the peaks and valleys are filled in with the rectangles' colors.

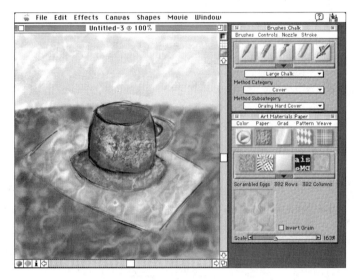

Figure 16.8 Chalk sketch with **Scrambled Eggs** texture selected in Paper palette.

TEXTURE AS A SPECIAL EFFECT

Now that you've seen how to create and edit paper textures, take a look at some of the different ways you can add paper grain to part or all of your image.

Before you choose an effect, it's always good to pick a paper texture first. However, one of the nice things about these dialog boxes is that you can click outside of them. You can pick a different grain while you're inside a dialog box, and you can open the Paper palette drawer, click on **Library**, locate another set of textures in your system, come back into the Library, and pick one of the new grains—all without closing the dialog box. You can also do any paper texture adjustments while the dialog box is still open, including inverting the grain and changing paper scale.

Effects: Surface Control: Dye Concentration

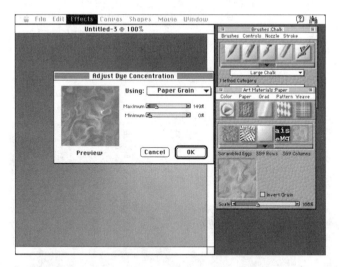

If you think of texture as a group of peaks and valleys, the Maximum slider controls the dye on the peaks, and the Minimum slider controls the dye in the valleys. You can set Maximum as high as **800%**. The lower you set the Minimum slider, which can be as low as **0%**, the higher the contrast will be between peaks and valleys. The higher the Minimum slider, the flatter the paper will appear.

Effects: Surface Control: Apply Surface Texture

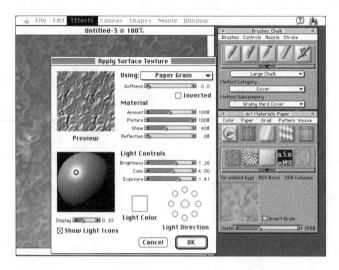

The most straightforward way to apply paper grain to your image is with **Apply Surface Texture**. Choose **Paper Grain** in the Using menu and the currently selected grain in the Paper palette appears in the image.

Do **Apply Surface Texture** to the same image whose dye concentration you just adjusted, and the paper pops out. Move the Shine slider to **0%** for a matte surface.

Effects: Surface Control: Color Overlay

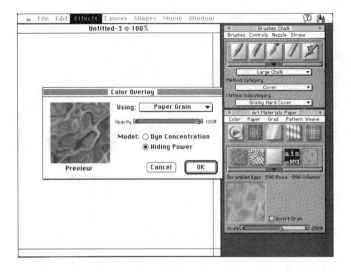

Color Overlay adds the currently selected paper and color to the image. Do **Color Overlay**, check **Invert Grain** in the Paper palette, choose another color, repeat **Color Overlay**, and you get a duotone effect.

Effects: Tonal Control: Adjust Colors

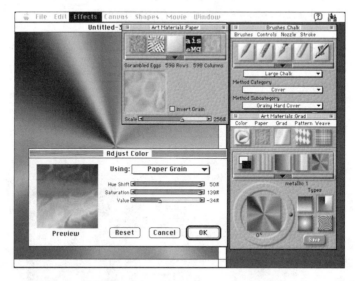

Use **Adjust Colors** to add the chosen texture in the Paper palette while shifting hue, value, and saturation.

APPLYING TEXTURES IN AN IMAGE

One artist who works extensively with Painter's paper texture features is Steve Campbell. He used most of the tools discussed in this chapter to create his image, Controller (see Figure 16.9).

Originally from Kansas City, MO, the San Francisco–based artist spent much of his time drawing traditionally until 1988, when the Mac became his primary illustration tool. Steve's award-winning art has been featured in gallery shows and publications.

Asked what inspired him to create *Controller*, Steve says "a synergistic rush from working on a multimedia project (the organized chaos of the intersecting realities) and the feeling of using a web browser." His artistic influences in general include Max Ernst, Pamela Coleman Smith, Jackson Pollock, Fritz Lang, Tantric Art, and The Brothers Quay, along with Latin American contemporary art.

Figure 16.9 *Controller* by Steve Campbell.

Steve used selections and floaters to mask image areas. Since this is a paper chapter, the following discussion focuses on the use of paper. See Chapter 15 for information about creating and using selections and floaters.

Steve began *Controller* by sketching with the Pencils' 2B Pencil variant. "Nearly all basic elements are laid into the initial sketch, some color laid in with Water Colors including Spatter Water, among others," says Steve (see Figure 16.10).

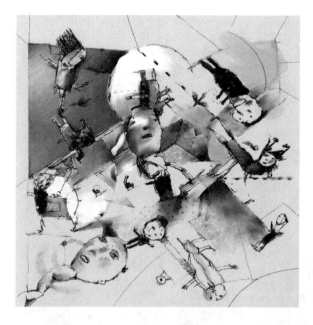

Figure 16.10 Initial pencil sketch with some color applied with Water Color.

Next Steve made selections and applied color (**Effects: Fill, Effects: Surface Control: Color Overlay**) (see Figure 16.11).

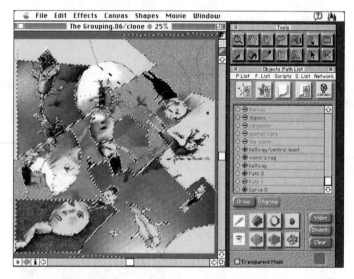

Figure 16.11 The selections that Steve filled with color.

He added areas and divided up his initial color breaks. He added some more color, began breaking up the image and adding more structure. "The idea was to create the feeling of intersecting dimensions," Steve notes. "I further elaborated on this idea using lighting (**Effects: Surface Control: Apply Lighting**) within selections." Steve continued tweaking color and laying in sections, focusing on depth and dimensionality, adding more brushwork. "I probably used every tool in the Painter palette while working on this, but I most often used Chalk, Brush and Water Color" (see Figure 16.12).

Figure 16.12 The image so far.

Then Steve did "a lot of experimentation with just piling up textures." He applied one color with a texture-aware brush (having the word **Grainy** in the Brushes palette: Method Subcategory), reversing the grain (**Paper palette: Invert Grain**) and laying in another color. He also created textures (**Paper palette: Paper: Capture Texture**). He used **Effects: Focus: Glass Distortion** in the yellow "wall" area, top center, and left. Steve made a paper texture out of a "photograph of a mass of tattered handbills on a telephone pole." He applied them in the upper-right corner using **Effects: Surface Control: Dye Concentration** and **Apply Surface Texture**. "Throughout this I was constantly rotating the page and working on the image at different orientations. I wanted it to work upside down as well as right side up, plus it was a real joy to be able to do this with software! I rotate the page all the time making real world pencil sketches," Steve adds. At this point, he used the **Eraser** and **Bleach** variants to "cut stuff back out of the image." He then added floaters. "The figure at lower right was glued together from a small toy with wheels and a doll's face, and then video grabbed, traced with Adobe Streamline and edited and distorted as a postscript document in Illustrator, then rasterized in Photoshop. Suggestions of conflicting 3D planar constructions brought up more." He then did "more and more brushwork" using the Brush's **Hairy Brush**, **Brushy**, and **Loaded Oils** variants (see Figure 16.13).

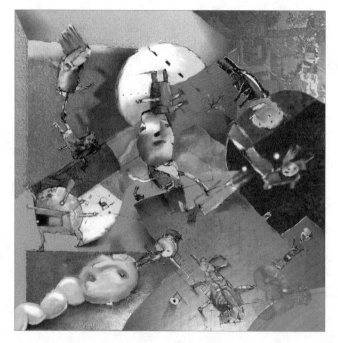

Figure 16.13 Texture added in upper-right corner, Glass Distortion applied to rear wall, other textures added with brushes, figure in lower right added.

"I fattened up the slug-like character at lower left and gave him a mask using a floater created from a video grab of an iron antique piggy bank shaped like a clown. I added lighting and more and more brush strokes, rotating the page. I moved the floaters around to see where they looked best. I added an L shaped floater to upper right to force the image back into two dimensions when you look at that area" (see Figure 16.14).

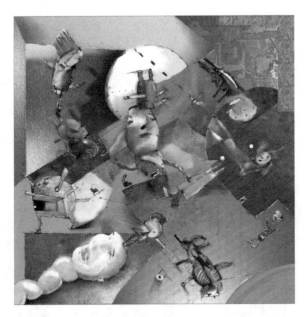

Figure 16.14 Lower-left slug fattened up, floaters moved around.

Steve then added more floaters (see Figure 16.15).

Figure 16.15 More floaters added.

The last step was to finalize the floaters' positions and add more lighting and texture (see Figure 16.16).

Figure 16.16 Floaters are placed in final positions.

The final piece (Figure 16.9) had some color changes done in Photoshop.

SUMMARY

You've now seen how to work with paper in Painter and how one artist uses it to create his images. The next chapter is for nonartists who need some information about using color in their artwork.

17

Working with Color

CHAPTER HIGHLIGHTS

❖ Color theory tips
❖ Some color observations

If you've been reading this book cover to cover, then you already have a good idea of how to work with color in Painter. You've already seen the elements of the Color palette in action, including the ±HSV sliders, the overlapping rectangles, and the white HSV box. In Chapter 7, "Advanced Drawing Tools," you saw how to control color intensity.

This chapter covers color theory and is aimed at non-artists to help with your painting and drawing. At the end are some comments about screen color vs. output color.

USING COLOR IN ART

Artists have an advantage over nonartists when using Painter, because they have studied color theory and know how to use color when drawing and painting.

The good news is that there are many books available that explain color theory, and the nonartist can gain knowledge fairly quickly for effective color use. As is the case with most art-related skills—and most computer interactions—trial and error are the best teachers; the more you use color, the better you get at working with it.

It's not within the scope of this book to explain color theory, but I offer a few tips to get you started. The following information comes from *The Artist's Handbook* by Ray Smith (Alfred A. Knopf, publisher, 1993), an invaluable guide to basic art theory and materials.

Using color is all about how colors are related to each other on the color wheel (see Figure 17.1) and how they are mixed together and positioned next to each other within an image.

Figure 17.1 The color wheel.

Artists use color theories espoused by Michel-Eugène Chevreul, who in 1839 published a work on the principles of harmony and contrast of colors. The following are some of his principles.

The *primary* painting and drawing colors are red, blue, and yellow, each displayed in Figure 17.1 at the tip of an equilateral triangle. Draw a circle around the triangle, and you have a *color wheel*. When you mix two primary colors together, you get a new color called a *secondary color*. The secondary colors are orange, green, and purple. Each secondary color appears on the color wheel between two primary colors, indicating that you get orange when you mix red with yellow; green when you combine yellow and blue; and purple by blending blue and red.

Notice that in Figure 17.1 you see dotted lines going across the circle connecting opposite colors. Colors opposite one another on the color wheel are *complementary* colors, so red's complement is green, yellow's complement is purple, and orange's complement is blue. When you mix complementary colors, you get gray, brown, or black, depending on the colors. Art students learn from the start that the way to darken a color is not to add black but to add the color's complement.

Painter's colors follow the same set of rules as their real-life counterparts. As you saw in earlier chapters, you can mix primary colors to get secondary colors. Also, placing primary colors next to each other makes them appear to mix, a painting effect used by the pointillists with the placement of multicolored dots.

To see this in action, choose the Artists' **Seurat** variant (Georges Seurat was the best-known pointillist). Move the ±HSV sliders in the Color palette all the way to the left. Choose **yellow** with the following settings in the white box in the Color palette: H: **51%**, S: **100%**, V: **50%**. Paint two spheres; select **blue** with the following settings in the white box in the Color palette: H: **85%**, S: **100%**, V: **50%**. Paint a separate blue sphere. Now paint within one of the yellow spheres, leaving space between the yellow and blue dots. You should now have a yellow sphere, a blue sphere, and a yellow-and-blue sphere. Notice that in the yellow-and-blue sphere, green seems to appear. The Seurat brush is a Cover Method brush; the dots are not mixing together, but you start to see green because the adjacent dots appear to mix together. This mixing effect works best with colors that are similar to each other, that is, a yellow that is more green and a blue that is more green. Using a yellow that is more orange and a blue that is more purple will result in a dulling effect.

Paint complementary colors next to one another and they appear to vibrate. Paint a red Seurat sphere and then paint green dots on it and watch the colors vibrate. When you put a primary next to a secondary color, the colors also vibrate because they cast their complements onto their surroundings, that is, red tends to color the surrounding space green, yellow makes it violet, and blue turns it orange. For example, paint a red sphere and then paint an orange one next to it. The red appears to be more of a violet red because of the blue cast that the orange induces.

Because colors "give off" their complement, another thing to keep in mind is what color you make your background. Painting on a white background makes colors look more brilliant because their complements are added to the white. Paint red dots on white and they beam out from the screen.

Colors appear lighter on a black background because of the way the complements combine with the black. Select **black** in the Color palette, select **Effects: Fill**, click **Current Color**, and click **OK**. Select **red** in the Color palette and paint, and the red looks even more brilliant.

Using a gray background will also intensify colors because the gray takes on the cast of the complements. Fill the image with gray this time, then paint with orange, and then with blue and watch the colors shimmer.

Meanwhile, isolating colors with black or white boundaries will reduce their mixing effect and give you purer colors. Stained glass is a perfect example of color purity enhanced by black borders.

Hue is just one characteristic of color. The other two characteristics are *saturation*, or intensity, and *value*, or relative lightness or tone. You adjust saturation in Painter by clicking in various locations from left to right in the triangle in the Color palette.

Colors have intrinsic values. Yellow is the lightest color; purple is the darkest. You change all colors' values by adding white, which gives you a tint of the color; gray, which produces a tone of the color; and black, which gives you a shade of the color. In Painter, you get the effect of adding white, gray, and black by choosing values from top to bottom in the triangle in the Color palette.

Understanding saturation and value can also help when mixing colors and choosing adjacent colors. Chevreul recommended, for example, that when you place similar colors side by side, lowering the tone of one would make the other appear more brilliant. Paint two spheres with the same highly saturated blue (one from the right-hand corner of the triangle). Choose a different blue in the color ring but still select the right-hand corner of the triangle, and paint some color in the first sphere. Now select a lower value for the same blue by choosing a tone over to the left in the triangle, then paint in the second sphere. Notice that the original blue dots look brighter in the second sphere next to the lower-toned blue than they do in the first sphere next to the highly saturated blue.

Artists are mindful of their colors' overall intensity within an image. You can use *high-key* or *low-key* color schemes. High-key refers to bright, highly saturated colors; low-key colors are unsaturated tints and shades. Now that you have a basic understanding of color, perhaps you can find more possibilities for all of Painter's color tools.

SOME COLOR OBSERVATIONS

When talking about color in Painter or in any software program, the question is always, "How do I get what I see on screen to look like what I print out?"

I addressed this question a bit in Chapter 3 when talking about printing. I want to add some more personal experience specifically about color here.

I have written that you should check Printable Colors Only in Painter's Color palette to ensure that printed colors match the ones on screen. However, my actual experience has been the opposite. Generally, what I see on screen has nothing to do with what the output looks like. And for some reason, choosing **Effects: Tonal Control: Enforce Printable Colors** while changing the on-screen colors produces final output that resembles the file's original colors. I've been getting vibrant reds to print out properly, which is sometimes a feat in itself. These reds appear to be red in the original file. When I choose **Enforce Printable Colors** they turn purple on-screen, and then they print out red in the final output.

As I mentioned in Chapter 3, experience is the best tutor when it comes to output and you'll only know how to do it after you've done it. Also, until there's an industry color standard that all software and hardware manufacturers abide by, outputting files will continue to require a bit of guesswork.

SUMMARY

Now you have the basics of color theory to help you when deciding what colors to use in your Painter compositions. I would heartily recommend learning all you can about color theory. Knowing how colors work together can really add to your images' impact.

18

Working with the Image Hose

CHAPTER HIGHLIGHTS

- ❖ Creating an image hose nozzle from floaters
- ❖ Creating an image hose nozzle using the grid
- ❖ Creating a two-rank image hose nozzle
- ❖ Creating a three-rank image hose nozzle

The Image Hose sprays images called *nozzles* and is ideal for creating repeating patterns, textures, and crowds of things like snow, gardens, and forests. You can either use Fractal's nozzles or create your own. Nozzles can comprise either floaters or elements painted along a grid. You activate the grid, create a background, and then paint the elements into the mask with a Masking variant, using it like a cookie cutter.

Fractal Design has released its first collection of Image Hose nozzles on a CD called *The Garden Hose*. Created by California-based artist Dennis Berkla, the Garden Hose CD images feature 25 plants (more than 100 different nozzles) including grasses, clover, violets, eucalyptus, jasmine, bamboo, berries, plum, acacia, and oak. There's a sample on the CD with this book.

This chapter includes examples from the Garden Hose collection to show how to construct nozzles with hand-painted floaters. Chapter 24, "Using the Image Hose," shows how to make nozzles from photograph floaters. Chapter 11, "Special Effects Brushes," described how to use the Image Hose and its variants. You can review that chapter and then come back here to find out how to whip up an Image Hose nozzle.

IMAGE HOSE RANKS

Image Hose nozzles come in three varieties: one rank, two-rank, and three-rank. Each level determines how many characteristics the nozzle elements will have.

Take an apple. If you create a one-rank nozzle containing apples, the apples can have one characteristic that varies. Let's say size. So as you paint with this one-rank image hose, you would get varying sizes of apples.

Note that you can paint a one-rank nozzle without any governing characteristic. Paint a bunch of apples and paint with the nozzle, and you get a spray of random apples, ideal, say, to coat the ground of a painting showing a rustic fall scene.

In a two-rank nozzle, the apples can have two characteristics that vary, for example, size and color. So with a two-rank nozzle, you can paint various sizes of apples in various colors. A three-rank nozzle gives you three choices, so your apples can be various sizes, colors, and point in various directions.

It's that easy. The rest of this chapter discusses how to create these nozzles to paint the desired way.

ONE-RANK IMAGE HOSE NOZZLES

You can hand-paint Image Hose nozzle elements, float them, and then group them into a nozzle and paint with them (see Figures 18.1 and 18.2).

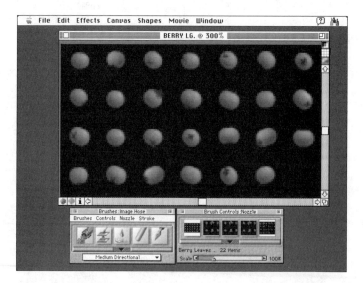

Figure 18.1 Berry lg., Mac; Berry_l.rif, Windows, Garden Hose nozzle by Dennis Berkla for Fractal Design.

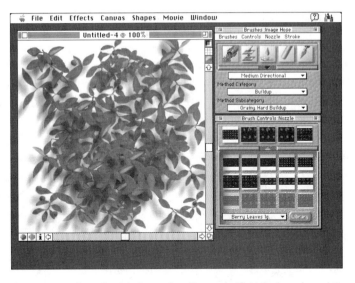

Figure 18.2 Image painted with Berry lg. (Berry_l.rif, Windows) and Berry Leaves lg. (Berlvs_l.rif, Windows) from Garden Hose.

Berry lg. (Figure 18.1) is an example of a simple random nozzle. Notice that in this nozzle Dennis painted the berries in no particular order. To make this nozzle, Dennis painted a number of berries and converted each one into a floater. The following steps show how.

Creating Image Hose Nozzles from Hand-Painted Floaters

First you'll paint a berry.

1. Select **File: New**. The New Picture dialog box appears. Dennis typed in **168** pixels for Width, **96** pixels for Height, and **72** next to Resolution. Click **OK**. A new image appears.

2. Paint a berry.

Next you'll create a path for the berry and float it.

261

1. Select the Tools palette's **Lasso** tool. Click and drag around the berry to select it. This tool is new in Painter 4 and takes a bit of getting used to. Once it becomes familiar, you'll see it is very useful. If you draw a continuous path connecting the beginning and end points, then the path turns into marching ants. If you don't connect the points, then it remains an open path. This is a good thing, actually, though it may not appear to be at first. That is, you can let go, and then, if you click on your end point and continue creating the path all the way to the starting point, then let go, the path turns into marching ants. In previous versions of Painter, you couldn't let go in the middle of a freehand selection. Pressing **Return**, Mac; **Enter**, Windows also closes the open path.

2. Click on the **Floaters** tool (the left-pointing hand) in the Tools palette. Click on the berry. It's now a floater.

3. Click **Objects: F. List: Trim**. The rectangle around the floater is trimmed.

4. Click outside the berry with the Floaters tool to deselect the berry.

Continue to paint, select, and float berries.

Once all the berries are floated, group them, give them drop shadows, and then make them into a nozzle.

1. With the **Floaters** tool (the left-pointing hand) in the Tools palette selected, press **Command+A**, Mac; **Ctrl+A**, Windows. All the floaters are selected (being able to select the floaters this way is new in Painter 4).

2. Click **Objects: F. List: Group** (**Command+G**, Mac; **Ctrl+G**, Windows) to place the floaters into a group.

3. Choose **Effects: Objects: Create Drop Shadow**. The Drop Shadow dialog box appears. Use the default settings and click **OK**. Each element now has a drop shadow.

4. Next, click on the **triangle** next to Group in the Objects: F. List to open the group. You'll see several groups of items with their drop shadows. Click on each group then click **Collapse**. This makes the item and its shadow into one floater. Then click the **Trim** button, trimming the area around the new, combined floater.

5. Click on the **triangle** again next to Group in the Objects: F. List to close the group.

6. Select **Brushes palette: Nozzle: Make Nozzle From Group**. A new document appears with the floaters.

7. Save this new image as a **RIFF**, Mac; **.RIF**, Windows, called **berries**.

8. Close this image and the one you used to create the berries.

Now you'll paint with the new nozzle.

1. Select **File: New**. Type **500** pixels next to Width and Height. Click **OK**. A new image appears.
2. Select the **Image Hose** in the Brushes palette.
3. Choose **Brushes palette: Nozzle: Load Nozzle**. A dialog box appears. Locate and select the berries nozzle you just created and click **Open**.
4. Paint in the image. Berry nice!

That's how to create an Image Hose nozzle with random elements. If, however, you wanted your nozzle to have elements that appear based on a specific characteristic, you have to do things a bit differently.

Say you want the items to vary based on size. You would create the elements from the smallest to the biggest, from left to right, row to row. In this case, you would have the smallest berry in the upper-left-hand corner, the biggest one in the lower-right-hand corner, and all the other berries in size order in between. Not only do they have to appear in the image in the correct order, but also in the Objects: Floater List palette. The left-hand floater should be at the top of the list, followed by the next floater, down to the right-hand floater, which should be at the bottom of the Floater List palette. If a floater is out of order, click on its name in the Floater List palette and drag it to the correct position in the Floater List palette.

ADJUSTING THE IMAGE HOSE

Chapter 11 went over each of the Image Hose variants and what they do. Now you're going to find out how the variants were created so you can adjust them and make your own.

Like everything else in Painter, the Image Hose variants are preprogrammed choices made for you. You can set up variants yourself as well. The Image Hose variants are variations of the sliders in the Brushes palette: Nozzle and Brushes palette: Controls: Size, Spacing, and Random palettes.

In the Image Hose variants' names, the words *small*, *medium*, and *large* refer to the amount of space between nozzle elements as they're sprayed in the image; they were set up with the Brushes palette: Controls: Size and Spacing palettes. Move the Brushes palette: Controls: Size palette: Size slider and Spacing palette: Spacing/Size and Min Spacing sliders to the left to reduce the space between sprayed nozzle elements. Move them to the right to increase the space. Experiment by moving the Size and Spacing sliders and painting in the image and you'll see how they operate.

Then there are the words *Linear* and *Spray*, which are controlled by Brushes palette: Controls: Random palette: Dab Location Placement. Move the Dab Location Placement slider to the right to spray the nozzle elements more randomly, move the slider to the left to place the elements in a row. The variants with the word Spray in them were made with the Dab Location slider moved to the right and the Linear variants were created with the slider to the left.

Meanwhile, in the variants, *Sequential*, *Random*, and *Directional* all refer to slider choices in the Brushes palette: Nozzle palette. The Nozzle palette sliders work like the sliders in the Brushes palette: Controls: Sliders palette. The Nozzle palette sliders tell Painter what to base item selection on. For example, you can base the selection on *Direction*, or which way you drag, *Pressure*, or how hard you press a pressure-sensitive stylus, and so on. *Sequential* means that the nozzle elements are sprayed sequentially from left to right in the first row, and when that row is completed, they're selected left to right in subsequent rows.

If you have a pressure-sensitive stylus, set the Rank 1 slider on **Pressure** and paint. You'll see that the amount of pressure you apply is what determines which element is chosen. If you press lightly you get the first floater in the nozzle, and if you press heavily you get the last one; pressing in between gets the middle floaters.

Setting the slider on **Direction** chooses different floaters based on which way you drag. **Random** selects elements randomly; **Source** chooses floaters based on light and dark areas of a source document in a cloned document.

As in the Sliders palette, *Bearing* and *Tilt* are settings for CalComp, Wacom and Hitachi tablet users and should give you different elements based on how you tilt the stylus. Setting Rank on **Velocity** means that floater selection will depend on how fast you drag in the image. Selecting **None** means you will only get the lower-right-hand floater as you paint in the image.

You can save changes to Image Hose variants just as you can save changes to variants of other brushes.

For example, say that you like the Rank 1 slider set at **Pressure** and you want to save that slider setting as a variant. Just save the setting as a variant in the usual way. Select **Brushes palette: Brushes: Variants: Save Variant**. The Save Variant dialog box appears. Type in a name for the variant, like **Pressure**, and click **OK**. Pressure now appears in the Image Hose Variants pop-up menu in the Brushes palette.

NOZZLES CREATED IN THE MASK USING THE GRID

Nozzle elements can be painted in the mask layer using the grid as a guide instead of by grouping floaters.

The mask is another selection tool like the paths, shapes, and floaters. Using the mask, you isolate areas of your image. In the case of nozzles, you use the mask to isolate nozzle element areas. The grid is a series of guidelines to help you line things up.

Use the mask/grid combination instead of floaters if you want to create a background texture and then paint the elements into the background mask. You'll also use the mask/grid for complex nozzles where it would just get too cumbersome to try to order numerous floaters in the Floater List palette.

The next exercise shows how I painted a snowflake nozzle using the mask/grid (see Figure 18.3).

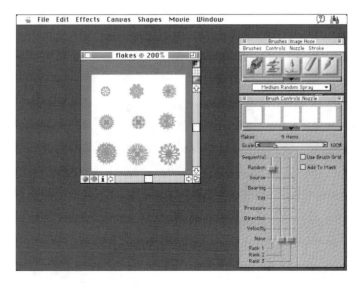

Figure 18.3 Snowflake nozzle with **mask** turned on.

Creating a Nozzle Using the Mask/Grid

First turn on the grid to use it as a guide.

1. Start a new image that is 90 X 90 pixels at 75 ppi.

2. Select **Canvas: Grid: Grid Options**. The Grid Options dialog box appears.

3. Type in **30** next to Horizontal Spacing and Vertical Spacing, click next to **Transparent Background**, and click **OK**.

4. Click on the grid icon in the image window's upper-right-hand corner. A grid appears with three spaces across and three spaces down.

Because snow is white, you already have the snow—it's the image. You just have to create the flakes. In this instance, it's a lot easier to paint in the mask than to start making floaters. So the thing to do is to cut the snowflakes into the mask. I know this is supposed to be painting from scratch, but I thought of a great short-cut using the Growth effect, as you'll see. If you prefer, you can paint in the mask with the Masking brushes instead.

1. Choose **black** in the Art Materials: Color palette.

2. Choose **Effects: Esoterica: Growth**. The Growth dialog box appears.

3. Check **Hard Edges** and **Fractal**, and, using the Preview as your guide, move the sliders until you see a snowflake pattern you like (see Figure 18.4).

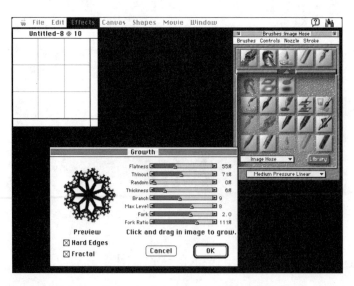

Figure 18.4 The Growth dialog box with a snowflake pattern.

4. With the Growth dialog box open, click and drag a snowflake in each grid square. Vary the sizes, putting the smallest snowflake in the upper-left-hand corner, making them gradually bigger and painting the largest snowflake in the lower-right-hand corner, as you see in Figure 18.3. Stay inside the grid. When you have nine flakes, click **OK**.

5. Click on the grid icon to shut off the grid.

6. To put these flakes into the mask, choose **Edit: Mask: Auto Mask**. The Auto Mask dialog box appears. Choose **Image Luminance** in the Using menu and click **OK**. The flakes are now in the mask. Choose **Edit: Select All** (**Command+A**, Mac; **Ctrl+A**, Windows). Press **delete**, Mac; **Backspace**, Windows. The black lines disappear but the flakes remain in the mask. To see them, click **Objects: P. List**: middle **Visibility** button. You see the flakes.

7. Save this file as a **RIFF** on the Mac or a **.RIF** in Windows.

Leave this image open so that as you paint you can see how the nozzle elements appear based on their position in the nozzle file. However, you don't have to leave it open to paint with the nozzle.

I then painted a simple background to show off the snowflakes better (see Figure 18.5).

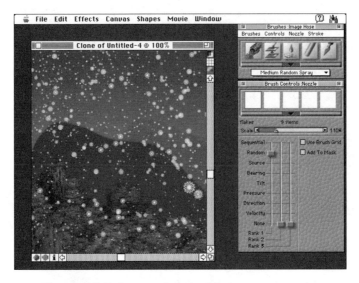

Figure 18.5 Snow painted with the snow nozzle.

First you'll create a sky.

1. Select **File: New**. Type **500** next to Width and Height and **150** next to Resolution and click **OK**. A new image appears.

2. Choose a **dark blue** in the Color palette. Click on the rear **rectangle** in the Color palette, choose a **light blue**, and click back on the front **rectangle** in the Color palette.

3. Click and drag the **Grad** icon to tear off the palette. Click on the **overlapping rectangles** icon in the Grad palette (it may be inside the drawer). Close the drawer and drag on the red dot on the front panel until the dark blue is at the top of the Grad Preview.

4. Select **Effects: Fill**, click next to **Gradation**, and click **OK**. You now have a sky.

I then created the mountains.

1. With the Pen tool, draw a mountain shape (see Figure 18.6). Press **Return**, Mac, **Enter**, Windows and the Set Shape Attributes dialog box appears. Click next to **Fill** to fill the shape, choose a color in the Color palette, and click **OK**. The mountain turns the selected shade.

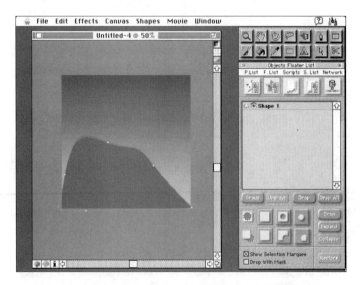

Figure 18.6 Mountain shape drawn with Pen tool.

2. Choose the **Floaters** tool, press **Option**, Mac; **Alt**, Windows, and click and drag a copy of the mountain.

268

3. Choose a color for the rear mountain as above.

4. Click **Controls palette: Back** to send the second mountain to the back (see Figure 18.7).

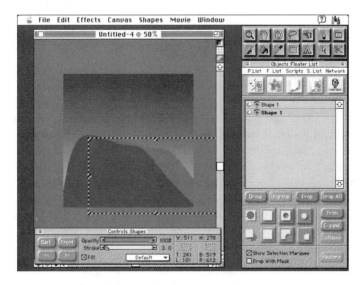

Figure 18.7 Second mountain added.

5. Click **Objects: F. List: Drop All**. The shapes drop into the background.

I painted the trees with the Trees nozzle from the Garden Hose CD.

Next you'll paint with flakes.

1. Select **Brushes palette: Image Hose**.

2. Select **Brushes palette: Nozzle: Load Nozzle**. In the dialog box, find your snowflakes nozzle and open it. The Nozzle Definition dialog box appears. Type **30** next to Item width and Item height because 30 X 30 pixels is the size of each flake. Next to Rank 1 type **9**, which means there are 9 items in the file. Click **OK**.

Paint with your Image Hose. Looks like New York this past winter (or so I heard).

With a pressure-sensitive stylus, set the Nozzle palette: Rank 1 slider to **pressure** then paint. Pressing lightly produces smaller flakes, pressing heavily sprays bigger ones.

The flakes overall might be a bit big. A scale slider has been added to Painter 4, simplifying element resizing.

The nozzle has to be in a library to use the scale slider. The next few steps show you how to create a library and add your nozzle.

1. Select **Brushes palette: Nozzle: Nozzle Mover**. The Nozzle Mover dialog box appears. This is where you'll create your new Nozzle library.

2. Click **New** on the dialog box's right-hand side. A dialog box appears. Type in a name for your new library. I called it **flakes**. Click **Save**. Then click **Quit**.

3. Click the **Library** button in the Nozzle palette drawer. Locate your new flakes library and click **OK**.

4. Load your nozzle with **Brushes palette: Nozzle: Load Nozzle**. Choose **Brushes palette: Nozzle: Add Nozzle to Library**. The Save Nozzle dialog box appears. Type in the name of your nozzle and click **OK**. It now resides in the flakes library. I found that if the nozzle was already loaded, I still had to reload it for the Save Nozzle dialog box to appear.

5. Close the Nozzle palette drawer. Adjust the Scale slider and paint. You'll see varying sizes of snowflakes, depending on the Scale slider position.

Creating Two- Rank Image Hose Nozzles

So far you've seen how one-rank image hose nozzles work. Take a look, now, at how Dennis created a two-rank nozzle.

Plum 2 Rank-R/P is a simple two-rank pressure nozzle taken from the Garden Hose sampler found on the Painter 4 CD (see Figure 18.8).

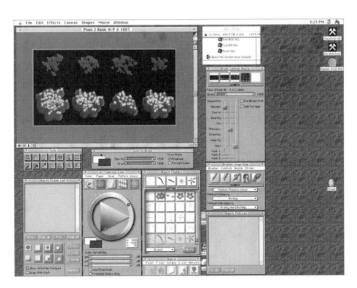

Figure 18.8 Plum 2 Rank-R/P by Dennis Berkla.

To paint with it, click the **Library** button inside the Nozzles palette and choose the **plum.nzl** from the Painter 4 CD **Goodies: Nozzles** folder. Choose **Plum 2 Rank-R/P** from the pop-up menu within the Nozzle palette drawer. Then choose the Image Hose's **2 Rank R-P** variant in the Brushes palette and paint in the image. With a pressure-sensitive stylus, vary how much pressure you apply to the stylus as you paint. Press lightly to paint with the dark leaves, and paint heavily to paint with flowers (see Figure 18.9).

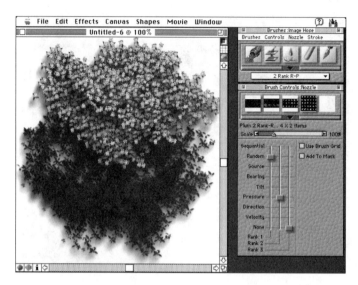

Figure 18.9 Varying stylus pressure selects different nozzle elements.

You saw that a one-rank image hose chooses nozzle elements from left to right, row by row. A two-rank image hose selects nozzle elements vertically from top to bottom.

In the case of the Plum 2 Rank-R/P, there are two rows vertically from which to choose. Using the 2 Rank R-P variant, **P** stands for *pressure* in the second rank, so elements are chosen vertically based on the amount of pressure applied to the stylus. Since there are only two rows, you get leaves by pressing lightly and flowers by pressing heavily. **R** is in the first Rank and stands for *random*, which means that instead of being chosen from left to right, the Rank-1 elements are chosen randomly.

"The benefit of this type of nozzle is that you can paint two kinds of elements, in this case, leaves or flowers, without having to change nozzles," Dennis notes. Dennis created this nozzle using eight floaters and the **Make Nozzle from Group** command, described earlier in this chapter. The floaters were listed in the Objects: F. List palette in the same order as they appear in the nozzle.

After he applied **Make Nozzle from Group**, he designated the image as a two-rank image hose, as follows.

1. Choose **File: Get Info** (**Command+I**, Mac ; **Ctrl+I**, Windows). The File Information dialog box appears.

2. Type **4** by **2** items. This means that each rank has 4 items and that there are two ranks (see Figure 18.10).

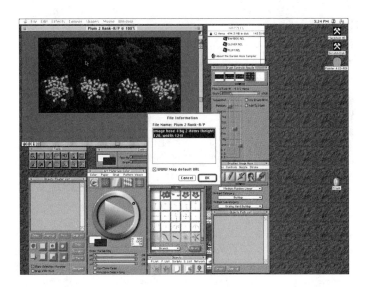

Figure 18.10 File Information dialog box for a two-rank Image Hose nozzle.

3. Click **OK**.

Creating a Three-Rank Nozzle

Mixed Oak 3-RPP sm. on the *Painter 4 Complete* CD is an example of a three-rank Image Hose nozzle in the Garden Hose collection. Says Dennis of the oak nozzle, "It demonstrates how pen pressure can make subtle adjustments in the color of a Scarlet Oak's leaves" (see Figure 18.11).

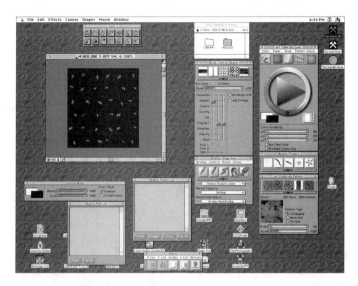

Figure 18.11 Scarlet Oak three-rank nozzle.

Dennis created this three-rank Oak nozzle "to let users control the variability of leaf color during autumn. I observed that leaves at the ends of branches are generally more red than those closer to the trunk. The Oak nozzle lets you recreate the tree's color transition without having to change nozzles," Dennis says.

As you recall:

A 1-Rank image hose chooses elements from left to right.

A 2-Rank image hose chooses elements from top to bottom.

What a 3-Rank image hose does is choose elements from among sets of items.

In the case of the oak leaves, Dennis used three sets of 12 floaters, each set representing a different color: red, green, and yellow-green. You can't tell that the leaves are these colors from the illustration, but you can if you open up the image on the book's CD. The third rank, then, determines which color set a leaf will be chosen from as you paint.

Dennis found that to work as a multiranked nozzle, each row has to have the same number of leaves and an even distribution of leaves throughout the file. So he created rows of leaf floaters.

Then, using the File Information dialog box described earlier, (**File: Get Info** [**Command+I**, Mac ; **Ctrl+I**, Windows], Dennis specified that the file was a 3-Rank nozzle containing 6 leaves in each of 2 rows and that there were 3 groups of rows. Written correctly, it appears as: image hose 6 by 2 by 3 items (height 45, width 42) (see Figure 18.12).

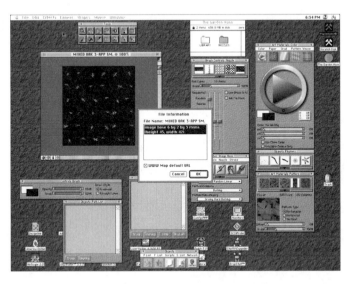

Figure 18.12 Setting up the File Information dialog box for a 3-Rank image hose.

To paint with this nozzle, set the Nozzle palette: Rank 1 slider on **Random** and the Rank 3 slider on **Pressure**. Then the leaves are chosen randomly and the amount of pressure determines from which set a leaf is selected, giving you a red, yellow, or yellow-green leaf, depending on stylus pressure. In the case of the Oak file, the Rank 2 slider has no significance as there is no variation in elements vertically within each set. Had there been a variation in size, for example, then the Rank 2 slider would be set to **pressure** to vary the leaf size.

SUMMARY

After you've done a few image hose nozzles you begin to see the world in textures and repeating patterns. Take a look around; you will probably find some ideas for image hose nozzles just waiting to be created.

Part V

Photo Retouching and Compositing

19

Realistic Photo Retouching

CHAPTER HIGHLIGHTS

❖ Edit a photograph with Distorto
❖ Create transparency with Cloning
❖ Edit with the Image Hose

Realistic photo retouching is a term I made up to describe images retouched in Painter that still look like photographs after the artist is done with them. Not too many people use Painter for realistic photo retouching, turning instead to Photoshop and Photostyler, whose tools lend themselves more logically to photo manipulation.

Still, some artists have found Painter useful for realistic photo retouching. One example is Michael Savas, a self-taught traditional commercial illustrator based in Orange County, California, who creates his art primarily for the advertising industry. Michael used Painter to spice up an image in a print ad for a data backup company (see Figure 19.1).

Figure 19.1 Retouched image by Michael Savas.

279

The headline for the ad was "Large Data Warehouse, Small Backup Window," showing that the company can take all the information in the warehouse, bring it through a small window, and put it in the small storage units. Michael started out with a stock photograph of a warehouse.

Using the Liquid's Distorto variant with the Brushes palette: Controls: Size slider turned up, Michael pulled out a portion of the warehouse to a point (see Figure 19.2).

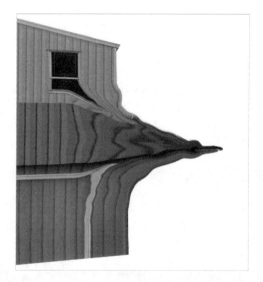

Figure 19.2 A portion of a warehouse pulled to a point with Distorto.

"Be careful not to break the image data, that is, be sure not to create small tears in the image that painting with Distorto can cause," Michael notes. Then he pulled the image in from the sides to give the appearance of a swirl. "This is when the multiple undo feature is very handy," Michael says.

Next, Michael copied and pasted this warehouse image on a stock image of sky (see Figure 19.3).

Figure 19.3 Warehouse pasted into sky image.

He saved this image and cloned it (**File: Clone**). Next, Michael created the Is and Os in a 3D program (although he could have created them in Painter as well), brought them into Painter, turned them into floaters, and made them into an Image Hose nozzle (see Chapter 18 for information about setting up Image Hose nozzles). He sprayed them onto the swirled area using the **Small Random Spray** variant of the Image Hose (see Figure 19.4).

Figure 19.4 *Is* and *Os* sprayed with the Image Hose.

He then painted transparency into the swirled area with the Cloners' **Soft Cloner** variant, which brings back part of the original warehouse/sky image. "I find this is the best way to get complete control of transparency effects," Michael says (see Figure 19.5).

Figure 19.5 Transparency painted into the *Is* and *Os* with the Soft Cloner.

Next, Michael painted the window with the Airbrush and copied and pasted the product shots (see Figure 19.6).

Figure 19.6 Window painted and products brought in.

Next, Michael sprayed the Is and Os on the products with the Image Hose. Michael figured out something that isn't in the Painter manual, that is, setting the Brushes palette: Controls: Sliders palette: Opacity slider to **Pressure**. Then, when he painted with the Image Hose, the nozzle elements' transparency levels were controlled by stylus pressure. Most of the other sliders in this palette are irrelevant with the Image Hose. But when you set the Grain slider to **Pressure** and choose a color for the rear rectangle in the Color palette, then stylus pressure determines whether the nozzle elements will be their own color or the Color palette color. This is a similar effect to the one described in Chapter 11, where you move the Controls palette: Grain slider to the left to add the rear rectangle color to the nozzle elements. Setting the Sliders palette: Grain slider to **Pressure** gives you more flexibility, since you can adjust opacity just by varying stylus pressure. Also, setting the Sliders palette: Jitter slider to **Pressure** means that stylus pressure will vary the amount of space between nozzle elements. Move up the Brushes palette: Controls: Random: Dab Location Placement slider to amplify the effect.

Michael painted the shadows with the Airbrush. "If vignette effects or graded backgrounds are going to be created for print, it is a good idea to add about 2 or 3 percent noise in Photoshop to prevent banding effects," Michael notes.

SUMMARY

You can see from this warehouse image that realistic photo-retouching in Painter isn't so far-fetched after all. The next chapter covers colorizing photographs in Painter, a much more popular concept among those who manipulate photographs.

20

Colorizing Photographs

CHAPTER HIGHLIGHTS

- ❖ Colorizing with Painter's Effects menu
- ❖ Adding color with the cloning brushes
- ❖ Using floaters to colorize
- ❖ Colorizing with the brushes and Effects menu

Painter has some great tools for colorizing black-and-white photographs. Naturally, anything that you've seen in this book so far can be used to colorize photographs, including any of the drawing and painting tools and the Effects menu items, including **Fill** and **Surface Control: Color Overlay**. This chapter shows you some of Painter's other special colorizing effects in addition to the ways working artists colorize photographs using Painter.

Obviously you won't be able to see the results of colorizing photographs on black-and-white pages. Look at the images on the *Fractal Design Painter 4 Complete* CD and the 8-page color insert to see what the different effects look like.

COLORIZING WITH EXPRESS IN IMAGE

One way to color photographs is to use **Art Materials: Grad: Express in Image**, which colorizes using a gradation based on the image's light and dark areas, or *luminance*. This versatile feature has many applications, as you'll see in the following sections.

Applying Multicolored Grads

One use for Express in Image is to add a 1960's-esque psychedelic-type effect to a photograph (see Figures 20.1 and 20.2). The following exercise shows how to use Express in Image with a multicolored grad.

Figure 20.1 *Hampstead Heath* photograph by Karen Sperling.

Figure 20.2 The *Hampstead Heath* photograph colorized using Express in Image with **colorburst** chosen in the Grad palette.

Colorizing Using Express in Image

1. Select **File: Open** and select **FIG2001.TIF** in the Chapter 20 folder on the *Fractal Design Painter 4 Complete* CD.

2. Select **File: Clone**. It's always a good idea to make a clone and leave the original intact.

3. Click **Art Materials: Grad**. The Grad palette appears.

4. Select **colorburst** from the pop-up menu within the Grad palette's drawer, then close the drawer.

5. Choose **Art Materials: Grad: Express in Image**. The Express in Image dialog box appears. Adjust the Bias slider, which gives some wild variations, as you can see in the Preview window. With the Grad palette drawer closed, you can also click on different Orders icons in the lower portion of the Grad palette while you're inside the Express in Image dialog box for other possible color combinations. Click **OK**. The image now has the colorburst colors based on luminance. By the way, I had the top-right **Grad palette: Orders** icon chosen and the Bias slider at **0%** to get that black sky.

Tinting a Photograph with Sepia Tones

Using Express in Image is also useful for specific results, like making a black-and-white photograph sepia-toned, as the next few steps show.

Adding Sepia Tones

1. Select **Edit: Undo**. The photograph is once again black-and-white.

2. Choose **sepia tones** in the pop-up menu within the Grad palette and close the drawer.

3. Click on the top-right **Grad palette: Orders** icon if it isn't already selected.

4. Choose **Art Materials: Grad: Express in Image**. The Express in Image dialog box appears. Set the Bias slider at **0%**. Click **OK**. The image becomes sepia-toned. Click on the top-left **Orders** icon and apply **Express in Image**, and you get a negative of the image. Click on any of the other icons and apply **Express in Image**, and you get various examples of a metallic-looking effect.

COLORIZING USING COLOR RAMPS

Another way to colorize using **Express in Image** is to add a blend of two colors selected in the Color palette, as explained in the next few steps.

Colorizing with Two Colors

1. Select **Edit: Undo**. The photograph is once again black-and-white.
2. With **Art Materials: Grad** selected, click and drag on the **Art Materials: Color** icon, separating out the Color palette from the Art Materials palette.
3. Click on the **overlapping rectangles** icon in the Grad palette. The icon may be within the Grad palette's drawer. Close the drawer.
4. Choose a color in the Color palette. Click on the **rear rectangle** in the Color palette and choose another color. Click back on the **front rectangle** in the Color palette. The Grad Preview window shows the blend between the two colors.
5. Choose **Art Materials: Grad: Express in Image**. The Express in Image dialog box appears. Adjust the Bias slider to taste. Click **OK**. The light and dark image areas fill with the selected colors.

COLORIZING WITH COLOR SETS

You can add colors to images from Painter's color sets or color sets that you create. The following exercise shows how.

Using Color Sets to Colorize

1. You can continue to use the *Hampstead Heath* image. Select **Edit: Undo**. The photograph is once again black-and-white.
2. Choose **Window: Color Set**. The default Color Set appears.

3. You're going to switch to a different Color Set. Choose **Art Materials: Color: Adjust Color Set**. The Color Set palette appears.

4. Click **Library**. A dialog box appears. In your Painter 4: Colors, Weaves and Grads (Colors directory, Windows) folder, select **Earth Tones** on the Mac or **EARTH.PCS** in Windows. Click **Open.** The set you just selected appears on-screen, and the name is listed under Current Color Set in the Color Set palette.

5. Select **Effects: Tonal Control: Posterize Using Color Set**. After a while, the image is posterized with earth tones.

COLORIZING WITH WATER COLOR

One of the nicest ways in Painter to colorize photographs is to paint with the Water Color brushes. Because these variants paint in the Wet Layer, above and separate from the underlying image area, you can hand-tint a photo without the paint actually touching the image. Then, if you make a mistake or decide on a different color, choose the **Wet Eraser** and erase out the color you just painted. As long as you haven't dried the paint using **Canvas: Dry**, the color gets deleted but the image remains in tact. I love the look of black-and-white photographs that are hand-tinted in real time. Using Painter's Water Color brushes on a photograph is the way to get similar results on the computer.

COMBINING BRUSHES AND SPECIAL EFFECTS TO COLORIZE

Judith Moncrieff uses a combination of Painter's brushes and special effects to colorize and composite her images. Take a look at these images on the *Fractal Design Painter 4 Complete* CD to see the differences among them.

Judith is an Assistant Professor of Art and Design in charge of digital imaging, design, and typography at the Pacific Northwest College of Art in Portland, Oregon. Her images have been shown nationally and internationally, with recent exhibits in Massachusetts, Oregon, New York, and Rome. Judith's *Eye of the Soul* (see Figure 20.3) is a composite of a photograph and a scanned rubbing of a fish.

Figure 20.3 *Eye of the Soul* by Judith Moncrieff.

"The background is made up of several layers of manipulation of floaters of a photo I took of pipes on the side of a building in Portland that run storm water into the city system," Judith explains (see Figure 20.4).

By the time she was finished, Judith had 10 separate pipe image floaters. She floated the image the first time by choosing **Edit: Select All** (**Command+A**, Mac; **Ctrl+A**, Windows) and clicking on the selected image with the Floaters tool (the left-pointing hand in the Tools palette). Then she copied the floater by holding **Option**, Mac; **Alt**, Windows and clicking on the floater with the Floaters tool.

She did different things to different layers, experimenting as she went along. She applied items from the Effects menu including **Surface Control: Dye Concentration**; **Tonal Control: Adjust Colors: raise Saturation**; and **Focus: Glass Distortion using Image Luminance**.

Figure 20.4 Manipulated pipe image.

The paint brushes that Judith used on the various floaters included the Liquid's **Distorto**; the Water's **Just Add Water** with **Method Category: Buildup** chosen; and the Airbrush's **Feather Tip** and **Thin Stroke**. Then she combined the effects by cloning one floater into another. She did so by clicking on a floater with the Floaters tool, choosing either the Cloners' **Straight Cloner** or **Soft Cloner** variant, pressing **Control**, Mac; **Shift**, Windows, and clicking on the selected floater, clicking on another floater with the Floaters tool, and then painting in the newly selected floater. The clicked area in the first floater appears in the second floater.

When she was done manipulating the pipe photo floaters, Judith chose **Objects: F. List: Drop All** to merge the floaters into the background.

"The fish are from a fish rubbing I did last spring at the Pacific Northwest College of Art in Portland, Oregon," Judith says (see Figures 20.5, 20.6, and 20.7).

Figure 20.5 Front half of scanned fish rubbing.

Figure 20.6 Back half of scanned fish rubbing.

Figure 20.7 Whole fish.

Judith then selected the fish with the lasso, floated it by clicking on it with the Floaters tool, and made copies by pressing **Option**, Mac; **Alt**, Windows and clicking and dragging out copies. Judith painted the fish with the same brushes as previously mentioned. She applied **Effects: Surface Controls: Apply Surface Texture** using Image Luminance to create the three-dimensional surface. She used other Effects menu items including **Tonal Control: Brightness/Contrast**; **Surface Control: Dye Concentration**; and **Tonal Control: Adjust Colors**: adjust Hue Shift and raise Saturation. She also used the **Eraser** to highlight the fish where needed (see Figure 20.8).

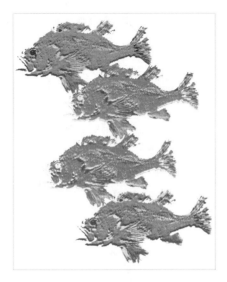

Figure 20.8 Fish copied and colorized.

She then copied and pasted the floaters into the pipe image. She used the Soft and Straight Cloners to mix the background and the floaters (**Control**+click, Mac; **Shift**+click, Windows in the background and paint in the floater). Last, Judith dropped the floaters into the background with **Objects: F. List: Drop All** and "used the Liquid's **Distorto** to meld and paint the images together."

SUMMARY

You can see that even though Painter isn't technically considered a photo-enhancement tool, it does contain some handy features for colorizing photographs. The next chapter shows ways in which artists use Painter's tools to add special effects to photographs.

21

Special Effects Image Editing

CHAPTER HIGHLIGHTS

- ✤ Special effects image editing using the brushes
- ✤ Special effects image editing using the Effects menu
- ✤ Special effects image editing using the brushes and the Effects menu

Turning photographs into paintings is one of Painter's strengths, and there are as many techniques for doing so as there are artists. Most of the examples in this chapter are clones of a photograph. In some cases you don't have to clone an image to manipulate it, it's just the way things worked out in this chapter. But manipulating a clone is a good way to work because you always have the original to fall back on if you mess up in the clone. If you don't like the changes you make in a clone, you can bring back the original by selecting **Effects: Fill**, clicking next to **Clone Source** in the Fill dialog box, and clicking **OK**. This works on image pieces, too. If you want to redo a spot, select it and fill it with the clone source, and it returns to its original state. Or paint with the Cloners' **Straight Cloner** variant.

USING THE BRUSHES TO EDIT PHOTOGRAPHS

As you've seen in previous chapters, one thing you'll never run out of in Painter are unique and varied brushes.

The following sections show some of the ways in which artists and photographers create special effects with Painter's brushes. Later in this chapter are examples of how the brushes can be used in combination with the Effects menu to produce other special effects.

Mosaics

The biggest new painting tool in Painter 4 is the mosaic feature, and artist David Scott Leibowitz uses it to alter his photographs (see Figures 21.1 and 21.2).

Figure 21.1 Photograph by David Scott Leibowitz.

Figure 21.2 *City Mosaic* by David Scott Leibowitz.

David has exhibited his altered photographs and produced images for commercial clients since 1980. He used dental tools to alter Polaroids until 1990, when he began to manipulate images digitally. With his photograph of New York open, David chose **File: Clone** to create a cloned image and **Canvas: Make Mosaic** and painted a mosaic in the clone. Check **Art Materials: Color palette: Use Clone Color** to pick up the original colors in the clone and check **Use Tracing Paper** in the Make Mosaic dialog box to reveal the original image within the clone. He then clicked the **Grout** square and selected **gray**, making the grout gray. Next David chose **Effects: Surface Control: Apply Surface Texture using Image Luminance**. He checked **Inverted**, which made the tiles appear recessed. Finally, David chose **Effects: Tonal Control: Adjust Colors** and increased Saturation to **15%**. For step-by-step details for creating mosaics, check the Painter manual.

PORTRAIT PAINTING

Nomi Wagner has been a professional photographer for 17 years, specializing in portraits of children and families. "Combining the study of rational art with the capabilities of Painter, I am now able to provide my clients with photographic portraits taken to new dimensions," she says (see Figures 21.3 and 21.4).

Figure 21.3 Photograph by Nomi Wagner.

Figure 21.4 *Catherine and Jacqueline* by Nomi Wagner.

The following steps show how Nomi transformed a photograph into a photographic portrait. First you'll make some changes to the image to make it easier to view through Tracing Paper.

1. Scan a photograph and open it in Painter.

2. Crop to the desired composition by selecting with the middle **rectangle** in the Tools palette. Choose **Edit: Copy**, then **Edit: Paste: Into New Image**. The selected area is now the new image.

3. Desaturate the photo using **Effects: Tonal Control: Adjust Colors**: Saturation slider moved to the left to make the photo into grayscale. Click **OK**.

4. Increase contrast (**Effects: Tonal Control: Brightness/Contrast**) so that highlights and shadows will be easier to see through the Tracing Paper later.

5. Sharpen with **Effects: Focus: Sharpen**. This also makes it easier to view through Tracing Paper.

Next you'll clone the image and turn on Tracing Paper.

1. Clone the image (**File: Clone**). A clone of the image appears.

2. Choose a "**peachy skin color**" in the Color palette, Nomi says. This will be the background color in the clone.

3. Choose **Canvas: Set Paper Color**.

4. Choose **Edit: Select All** (**Command+A**, Mac; **Ctrl+A**, Windows). Press **delete**, Mac; **Backspace**, Windows. The original image is deleted and is replaced by a "peachy keen sheet of paper that you can erase back to," says Nomi.

5. Choose **Canvas: Tracing Paper** (**Command+T**, Mac; **Ctrl+T**, Windows). The original appears through the Tracing Paper.

Nomi picked some brown tones and sketched in the proportions and outlines with the Crayons' **Default** variant, which she customized by adjusting the Brushes palette: Controls: Sliders palette so that all the sliders were set to **None** except for the Size slider, which was set to **Pressure**. And she moved up the Brushes palette: Controls: Size: ±Size slider. This way, when she drew, the stylus created narrow and wide strokes based on stylus pressure.

Nomi then turned off Tracing Paper and finished the piece by keeping the clone source visible next to her drawing and using the **Crayons**, **Eraser**, and Water's **Just Add Water** variant for "shading, highlighting, and a painterly look."

Nomi's favorite tool is the magnifying glass, which she accesses with keyboard shortcuts (discussed in Chapter 6). "The ability to zoom in on the tiniest detail of both the clone source and drawing gives me the vision that is impossible with the normal human eye," Nomi says.

PAINTING PHOTO-REALISTIC IMAGES

Many artists use Painter to clone photographs into "paintings," but David Scott Leibowitz has a unique style where he brings back some of the photograph, giving the image an unusual, photo-realistic quality, as in *Girl & Bike* (see Figures 21.5 and 21.6).

Figure 21.5 Photograph by David Scott Leibowitz.

Figure 21.6 *Girl & Bike* by David Scott Leibowitz.

USING PAINTER'S CLONERS FOR "FINE ART" PHOTOGRAPHY

David began *Girl &Bike* by cloning a photograph he took in New York City's Central Park.

1. Open an image in Painter. Choose **Effects: Focus: Sharpen** to heighten the photo-realistic effect when you bring back parts of the original later.

2. Select **File: Clone**. A clone appears. Choose **Select All** (**Command+A** on the Mac; **Ctrl+A** in Windows) and press **Delete** on the Mac or **Backspace** in Windows. The image clears. Choose **Canvas: Tracing Paper**. A 50% ghost of the original appears.

David toggles **Tracing Paper** on and off as he paints, turning it on to see where things are and turning it off to continue painting. Toggle Tracing Paper on and off by pressing **Command+T** on the Mac or **Ctrl+T** in Windows.

David next used the **Chalk** to bring in the original photograph. He then smeared with the **Water** to simulate oil painting, a method used by many Painter artists.

1. Select the Chalk's **Artist Pastel Chalk** variant.

2. Select **Window: Art Materials palette: Color palette**. Click next to **Use Clone Color** in the bottom of the palette. The selected tool will pick up the colors from the original and place them in the clone. Uncheck **Use Clone Color** and you can draw with any color you want. If you don't see Use Clone Color, click in the upper-right-hand corner of the Color palette to expand it.

3. In Window: Brush Controls: Size palette, move the Size slider to the left and draw to give the appearance of a chalk drawing. Move it to the right to blur the image for an impressionistic effect.

"What is of interest is that the Chalk carried different textures depending on the area I was working on," David notes. "Brush strokes made with textures like circles, culture, wriggle, and scratchy in the More Wild Textures library, Mac; MOREWILD.PAP, Windows look great for foliage when they are overlapped." Click the **Art Materials: Paper palette: Library** button to access the More Wild Textures library.

David also changed the Brushes palette: Method Subcategory to **Soft Cover**, removing grain from the stroke. "By changing the Method Subcategory to **Soft Cover**, you allow the chalk to lay flat, without texture for the concrete bench," David notes.

"The ground is crushed with the Brushes palette: Controls: Size slider set to **100** (at 300 ppi), with the Method Subcategory turned back to **Grainy Hard Cover**. I mixed up Big Canvas, Halftone and Diagonal textures in the More Paper Textures library, Mac; MORETEXT.PAP library, for ground texture."

Next, for his special touch, David "feathered back in some original detail using a medium sized Soft Cloning brush at a low opacity."

1. Select the Cloners' **Soft Cloner** variant.
2. Adjust the Brushes palette: Controls: Size slider. Move the Controls palette: Opacity slider to the left.
3. Paint in the image. The original comes back in the clone. Turn on **Tracing Paper** to identify areas that you want to bring in, then turn it off to paint.

"The people were worked with small, soft cover chalk brushes. Then I decided I wanted to lose the two people on the right to create what I believe is a stronger composition. Using the **rectangle** in the middle of the Tools palette, I selected a rectangular section right next to each person, copied it, and then pasted it over each person. I dropped both rectangular selections (**Objects: F. List: Drop All**), and finally, using the Water's **Just Add Water**, I feathered the edges of the pasted selections to blend them with the background."

USING PAINTER'S EFFECTS MENU

Besides its brushes, Painter has features in the Effects menu that you can use to manipulate photographs. You can experiment on your own by opening a photograph and applying all the Effects menu items and seeing what you come up with.

One Effects menu item whose usefulness might not be so obvious is **Effects: Surface Control: Apply Screen** which reduces the number of colors in an image. Rod Underhill has found a great use for it (see Figures 21.7 and 21.8).

Rod Underhill is a fine artist/photographer who lives in San Diego, California, and cites his greatest influence as being the late Andy Warhol. "OK, you find yourself staring at your computer screen with a deadline looming in front of you," says Rod. "The clock is moving toward the early hours of the morning, and your bed is plaintively calling your name, hoping that you'll drop by, and drop in, sometime before the sun rises. A cold wind blows bitterly through the deserted cities of your imagination, but you're not going to give up because you have a friend. The book you have in your hand. If you have a photo ready to use (such as one you've taken or perhaps a royalty-free photo) and a color scheme in mind, you're only minutes away from coming up with something fantastic."

Figure 21.7 Photograph by Rod Underhill.

Figure 21.8 *House* by Rod Underhill.

The following exercise shows how Rod created *House*.

Using Apply Screen

1. Open a photo.
2. Select **File: Clone**. A clone of the original appears.
3. Select **Effects: Surface Control: Apply Screen**. The Apply Screen dialog box appears.
4. Choose **Original Luminance** in the Using menu.
5. To change the colors, click on a square, choose a color in the dialog box, and click **OK**. Rod made the first square **red**, the middle one **blue**, and the last one **white**. The sliders affect how much of the colors in the squares will appear in the image. If you move a slider one way, you'll get more of one color and less of another. Move the sliders around and you'll see the result in the Preview window. For *House*, Rod set the Threshold 1 slider at **124%** and the Threshold 2 slider at **79%**. Click **OK**.

Next Rod added texture.

1. Select **Effects: Surface Control: Apply Surface Texture**. The Apply Surface Texture dialog box appears.
2. Choose **Original Luminance** in the Using pop-up menu.
3. Click on the **1 o'clock** position going around the sun and move up the Shine slider. Click **OK**.

Rod added some Image Hose clouds and the image was done. "A perfect image for a Fourth of July feature, perhaps, or an article about Victorian homes. And so easy!" says Rod.

Combining the Brushes and Effects Menu

As you've seen, you can either use the brushes or the Effects menu to edit photographs. Next you'll see how to use both for photo-editing.

Adding Surface Texture

One of the easiest and coolest effects for which Painter is known is its ability to add a three-dimensional surface to an image. But it's up to the artist to create something great with it. David Leibowitz used this effect in his image *Central Park Outing* (see Figures 21.9 and 21.10).

Figure 21.9 Photograph by David Scott Leibowitz.

Figure 21.10 *Central Park Outing* by David Scott Leibowitz.

The following exercise shows what David did in Painter to produce *Central Park Outing*. David started *Central Park Outing* by opening a photograph, cloning it, and "painting" in it with the **Chalk**.

1. Open a photograph.

2. Choose **File: Clone**. A cloned copy of the original appears. Choose **Select All** (**Command+A** on the Mac; **Ctrl+A** in Windows) and press **Delete** on the Mac or **Backspace** in Windows.

3. Choose the Cloners' **Chalk Cloner** variant. "Paint" in the image to bring in the photograph. David used various Brushes palette: Controls: Size slider settings.

David then brought in details from the original to restore some of the image's photographic quality using the **Soft Cloner** brush. He adjusted the Controls palette: Opacity slider to vary how much of the original was brought back.

Next David added the surface texture.

1. Select **Effects: Surface Control: Apply Surface Texture**. The Apply Surface Texture dialog box appears.

2. Choose **Original Luminance** in the Using menu. David notes that he clicks on each button going around the sun even though the differences between some of the buttons are subtle, because some of the buttons can result in really startling differences, "making certain details more prominent than others," David says. Click **OK**. Next choose **File: Clone**. You now have this version of the image available in case you want to bring it into a future version.

David then applied surface texture using original luminance several more times, varying the light source each time "to give me the right feel for any given area of the image," David notes. Finally, David painted with the Airbrush "to finish some rough edges."

SUMMARY

There you have some examples of how artists use Painter's tools to add special effects to photographs using the brushes and Effects menu. The next two chapters show photo-manipulation techniques using floaters.

22
Photo Compositing

CHAPTER HIGHLIGHTS

- ✤ Composite with floaters
- ✤ Add Effects features

This chapter shows some of the photo-compositing wizardry that two working artists—Dorothy Simpson Krause and Bonny Lhotka—are creating with Painter.

Dorothy Simpson Krause is a Massachusetts-based artist and computer graphics professor whose digital art has been exhibited nationwide. Dorothy uses Painter to juxtapose and enhance photographs and video stills for provocative, mystical, images.

Hanged Man (see Figure 22.1) was done in collaboration with Lisa Padovano for a set of interactive Tarot cards. It is a montage of a tree from the Painter 3 CD (see Figure 22.2), a cross from a photograph taken by Lisa (see Figure 22.3), and a man from Planet Art, a CD of stock images on Leonardo daVinci (see Figure 22.4).

Figure 22.1 *Hanged Man* by Dorothy Simpson Krause.

Figure 22.2 Tree from Painter 3 CD © 1995 PhotoDisc.

Figure 22.3 Photograph by Lisa Padovano.

Figure 22.4 Man from Planet Art CD.

Dorothy began *Hanged Man* by stretching the Tree image using **Effects: Orientation: Scale**. She then changed the color with **Effects: Tonal Control: Adjust Colors** (see Figure 22.5).

Figure 22.5 Tree stretched and color-adjusted.

Dorothy made a clone of the tree (**File: Clone**), filled with **KPT Gradient Designer/ Metallic/ Gentle Gold** and embossed by selecting **Effects: Surface Control: Apply Surface Texture using Original Luminance**. She changed the Light Color to pale pink to warm up the gold, Dorothy notes.

Then she chose **Edit: Select All** (**Command+A**, Mac; **Ctrl+A**, Windows) and **Edit: Copy**, chose **Window**: original tree image, and **Edit: Paste: Normal** to bring in the new tree as a floater. She chose **Controls: Composite Method: Normal** and **100%** Opacity. She brought in the cross as a floater in the same manner, with the Controls: Composite Method: set to **Darken** and Opacity at **80%**.

Dorothy used the same process that she used to emboss the tree to emboss the Leonardo daVinci drawing from the Planet Art CD. It, too, was brought in as a floater, with **Controls: Composite Method: Normal** and **100%** Opacity.

Using the Cloners' **Straight Cloner** variant, Dorothy removed the emboss from the tree within the lines of the Leonardo drawing. The **Soft Cloner** was used around the branches of the tree to bring some of the sky through the gold.

Finally, the red circle was added, floating selections were dropped (**Objects: F. List: Drop All**), and "the relationship between the cross and the trunk of the tree was evened up by cloning. " Last, Dorothy selected the outer edge and created a darker border using **Effects: Tonal Control: Adjust Colors**.

Chariot (Figure 22.6), *Hermit* (Figure 22.7), and *Temperance* (Figure 22.8) were created the same way for the series.

Figure 22.6 *Chariot.*

Figure 22.7 *Hermit.*

Figure 22.8 *Temperance.*

Another artist working with floaters and photographic images in Painter is Bonny Lhotka (see Figure 22.9).

Figure 22.9 *Winter Solstice* by Bonny Lhotka.

Bonny Lhotka is an experimental artist whose work is a blend of painting, print-making, and digital imaging, drawn from more than two decades as a professional artist. Bonny's work has also been exhibited nationally. First Bonny scanned in a pile of painted acrylic scraps (see Figure 22.10).

Figure 22.10 Scanned acrylic scraps pile.

Next Bonny scanned the front and back of an old pocket watch that has been in the family for several generations (see Figures 22.11 and 22.12).

Figure 22.11 Front of scanned watch.

Figure 22.12 Back of scanned watch.

Next, Bonny "borrowed a dead butterfly from a friend and laid it carefully on the scanner" (see Figure 22.13).

Figure 22.13 Scanned butterfly.

"Much more detail is captured from the real object as opposed to using a photo. I also make use of the natural shadows that happen during the scan. You can see that if you look carefully at the watch and butterfly edges in the final image," Bonny notes.

In Photoshop, Bonny applied unsharp mask to all four scans. She used the magic wand to select and clear the background and used the setting for the selection tool that left the shadows intact. She inverted the selection and saved it so it could be used in Painter.

In Painter, Bonny composited the acrylic scraps, watches, and butterfly. Then she chose **File: Clone**, and then she cleared the image (**Edit: Select All** [**Command+A**, Mac; **Ctrl+A**, Windows]; press **delete**, Mac; **Backspace**, Windows). Then she filled the area with KPT gradient metallic gold. "KPT gradient, I have learned from experience, will print very olive green even if it looks right on screen," so she used **Effects: Tonal Control: Adjust Colors** to make the gradient very warm toned (see Figure 22.14).

Figure 22.14 Composited image with KPT gradient after Adjust Colors.

Next Bonny created the embossed foil image (see Figure 22.15).

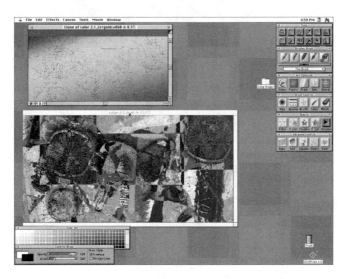

Figure 22.15 Creating foil embossed image (above) with the composited image (below) as the clone source.

Bonny chose **File: Clone** and she made the original composited image the clone source with **File: Clone Source: Composited image**. Then she chose **Effects: Surface Control: Apply Surface Texture using Original Luminance** with the Light Color on **white** and the other settings as follows:

Amount	**200%**
Picture	**94%**
Shine	**0%**
Reflection	**0%**
Brightness	**1.08**
Conc	**5.00**
Exposure	**1.41**

Then Bonny selected the composited image (**Edit: Select All** [**Command+A**, Mac; **Ctrl+A**, Windows] and copied and pasted it into the embossed image, which turned the composited image into a floater. She then chose the left-pointing hand in the Tools palette and **Controls palette: Composite Method: Overlay** (see Figure 22.16).

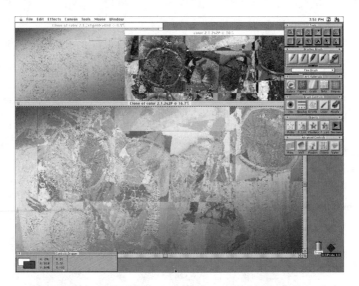

Figure 22.16 Composited image as a floater with **Overlay** chosen as the Composite Method.

Bonny pasted again, getting another floater copy and set the Controls palette: Composite Method to **Difference** (see Figure 22.17).

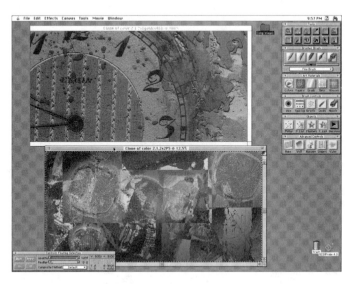

Figure 22.17 Another floater copy brought in.

Bonny pasted about 10 more times until the image was finished. She varied the Controls palette: Opacity slider to alter the transparency levels in the various floaters.

SUMMARY

From the photo compositions in this chapter, you can see that Painter is a powerful tool for combining photographs and photographic elements. The next chapter shows Painter's photographic special effects.

23

Special Effects

Chapter Highlights

- ❖ Compositing using Mask Edit Mode
- ❖ Compositing using the background mask

You can get some quick and different special effects using floaters with the background mask. This chapter shows you a couple of them.

None of the artists in this book used the background mask for the images they submitted, so I was going to explain and illustrate working with the background mask myself.

I felt bad doing so, since I'm not a working artist and therefore couldn't impart "real-world" examples of how I used this feature in my daily work. But I do know Painter, so I turned to John Derry, Vice President, Creative Design at Fractal Design, who is an artist, and asked him to be my Art Director for this chapter. What follows are John's ideas for how you would use Painter's background mask, illustrated and explained by me.

Using Mask Edit Mode

Working in the mask is another way to select in Painter, in addition to shapes, paths, and floaters. What each does is the same, that is, isolate an area of your image. Once an area is isolated, you can do things to it. These things include painting in it, moving it, or adding an effect to it. It's that simple.

The mask in Painter 4 comes in two flavors, red and white. The red flavor, which has been in every version of Painter, lets you view the mask and your image. The white flavor, introduced in Painter 4, doesn't. However, in the white mask layer, you can add effects to the mask from the Effects menu and paint with all the brushes. Very cool.

You access the red mask by clicking **Objects: P. List**: middle **Visibility** button (next to the eye) and third **Drawing** button (next to the pencil). You show the white mask by clicking the **circle** in the image window's upper-right-hand corner.

Fractal calls this view of the image *Mask Edit Mode*. One example of using Mask Edit Mode is if you want to show an object reflected in water (see Figure 23.1).

Figure 23.1 Logo Channel reflected in water.

John notes that you can turn down the Controls: Opacity slider for the reflection and get a fairly good result, but that real reflections tend to fade out the further the reflection gets from the object. Therefore, to get a more true-to-life result, add a gradient to the mask layer.

The following steps show how to make the Logo Channel reflection. By the way, Chapter 26 tells you how John created Logo Channel.

1. Open an image with water. I used the **Villa.jpg** image © 1996 PhotoDisc in the **Goodies: Photos: Urban** folder on the Painter 4 CD. I added the sky by adding **300** pixels at the top of the image in Canvas: Canvas size, selecting the area using the middle **rectangle** in the Tools palette, and then filling with a gradation using **Effects: Fill**.

2. Select **Objects: F. List: Floaters**. The Floaters palette appears. Open the Floaters palette drawer and click and drag on the **Logo Channel floater** and place it in the image.

3. Hold **Option**, Mac; **Alt**, Windows and click and drag on the floater with the left-pointing hand in the Tools palette to create a copy (see Figure 23.2).

Figure 23.2 Logo Channel copy.

4. Select **Effects: Orientation: Flip Vertical** to turn the copy upside down.

5. Click the circle in the image window's upper-right corner to show the mask (see Figure 23.3).

Figure 23.3 The floater's mask.

Next you'll set up a black-to-white gradation and fill the mask layer with it.

1. Click **Art Materials: Grad**. The Grad palette appears. Click on the **overlapping rectangles** icon in the Grad palette. It may be within the Grad palette's drawer. Close the drawer.

2. Click and drag on the **Color** icon and separate out the Color palette from the Art Materials palette.

3. Choose **black** in the Color palette. Click the **rear rectangle** in the Color palette and choose **white** if it isn't already selected. Click back on the **front rectangle**. The Grad Preview window shows a black-to-white blend.

4. Click and drag on the **red circle** next to the Grad preview until white is at the top.

5. Select **Effects: Fill**. Click next to **Gradation** and click **OK**. The Logo Channel mask fills with the gradation (see Figure 23.4).

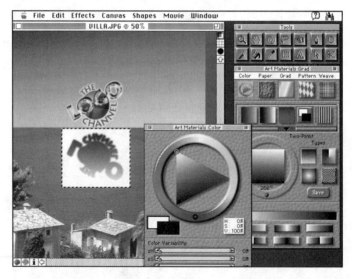

Figure 23.4 Mask filled with the gradation.

6. Click on the image window's **upper-right circle** again and the reflection appears to diminish. I turned down the Controls: Opacity slider a bit to get the final result in Figure 23.1.

COMPOSITING FLOATERS WITH THE MASK

Many artists paint in the floater's mask layer to alter its transparency, but sometimes it's wiser to edit the background mask instead.

I did the following using the **Bottles.jpg** and **Wine.jpg** images © 1996 PhotoDisc located in Goodies: Photos: Objects on the Painter 4 CD. You might want to open both so you can follow along with the upcoming steps. If you wanted to make something look like it was behind something else, you would probably paint in the floater's mask as in Figure 23.6, where the bottle appears to be behind the glasses because I painted in its mask.

Figure 23.5 Image without bottle.

Figure 23.6 Bottle placed behind glasses by painting in floater's mask.

I painted in the floater's mask with the Masking brush's **Masking Pen** and **white** selected in the Color palette.

I got the bottle floater by selecting a bottle from the **Bottles.jpg** image with the lasso (see Figure 23.7) and clicking on the selected bottle with the left-pointing hand in the Tools palette.

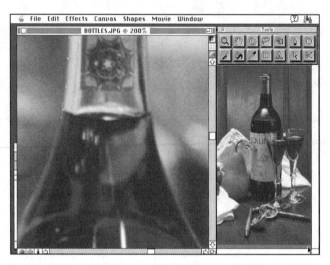

Figure 23.7 Bottle being selected with the lasso.

I then saved the floater in the Floaters palette. Choose **Objects: F. List: Floaters**. The Floaters palette appears. With the left-pointing hand, hold **Option**, Mac; **Alt**, Windows and then click and drag the floater to the Floaters palette front panel. The floater turns into a little square. Let go. The Save Floater dialog box appears. Type in a name for the floater. Click **OK**.

All is well, except what if you decide to rearrange the composition and move the bottle? You have a hole in it and now you have to choose **black** and paint in the floater to restore the image. You're too busy for that (see Figure 23.8).

Figure 23.8 Bottle, when moved, with holes.

The solution would be to paint in the glass in the background mask instead. Here's how.

1. With the **Wine.jpg** image as the current image, lose the bottle floater for now (if you made one) by clicking on it with the left-pointing hand and pressing **delete**, Mac; **Backspace**, Windows.

2. Click the **Objects: P. List**: second **Visibility** button (the one next to the eye) and the third **Drawing** button (next to the pencil). The red mask layer appears.

3. Check **Objects: P. List: Transparent Mask**. The mask becomes transparent, revealing the image (see Figure 23.9).

Figure 23.9 Transparent mask.

4. Choose the Masking brush's **Masking Pen** variant, select **black** in the Color palette, and paint in the mask above the glasses (see Figure 23.10).

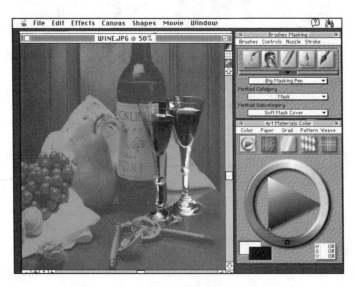

Figure 23.10 Glasses painted into mask.

I zoomed in and out to get the best view as I painted. To zoom in, press **Command+Spacebar** and click, Mac; **Ctrl+Spacebar** and click, Windows. Or, press **Command+Plus Sign**, Mac; **Ctrl+Plus Sign**, Windows, which increases magnification. To zoom out, press **Option+Command+Spacebar**, Mac; **Alt+Ctrl+Spacebar**, Windows and click in the image. Or, press **Command+Hyphen** on the Mac or **Ctrl+Hyphen** in Windows.

5. Then I hid the mask by clicking **Objects: P. List**: first **Visibility** button (next to the eye).

Next you'll bring in the bottle floater and composite it with the background mask.

1. Click and drag the bottle out of the Objects: F. List: Floaters palette and place it in the image behind the glasses.

2. Click the **Objects: F. List**: second button in the bottom row. The bottle goes behind the glasses (see Figure 23.11).

Figure 23.11 Bottle composited with the background mask.

It's the same result as before, when you painted in the bottle's mask, but this time, you can move the bottle into a different position and it's in tact (see Figure 23.12).

Figure 23.12 Bottle moved to a different position in tact.

SUMMARY

You can see from these two examples that the background mask can be a handy tool when compositing photographic images. Of course, using the background mask is also helpful when using Painter's drawing and painting tools, as you'll see in Chapter 28, which discusses how to use the background mask when cartooning.

24

Using the Image Hose

CHAPTER HIGHLIGHTS

- ❖ Create an Image Hose nozzle from floaters
- ❖ Create an Image Hose nozzle with drop shadows

As you saw in Chapter 11, "Special Effects Brushes," and Chapter 18, "Working with the Image Hose," the Image Hose sprays images and is ideal for creating repeating patterns, textures, and crowds of things like clouds, gardens, and forests. You've seen how you can paint Image Hose elements. This chapter shows how to create Image Hose nozzles from photographic elements.

I opened an image, *Autumn*, on the Fractal Design CD in Goodies: Photos: Scenic (see Figure 24.1).

Figure 24.1 The original *Autumn* image ©1996 PhotoDisc.

Then I selected some of the leaves and floated them. I used **Effects: Orientation: Flip Horizontal**, **Vertical**, **Rotate**, and **Free Transform** and **Effects: Tonal Control: Adjust Colors** to mix them up a bit. I gave them drop shadows and grouped them. Then I created an Image Hose nozzle out of them. Finally, I painted with them in an image, **Road2.jpg** on the Painter 4 CD in Goodies: Photos: Scenic © 1996 PhotoDisc (see Figure 24.2).

Figure 24.2 Autumn Leaves.

The following exercise shows how to float image elements, put them into a nozzle, and then paint with them in an image.

CREATING AN IMAGE HOSE NOZZLE WITH FLOATERS

You're going to select the leaves, turn them into floaters, and then make them into an Image Hose nozzle.

The first thing to do is to select a leaf (see Figure 24.3).

Figure 24.3 Selected leaf.

1. Open the **Autumn.jpg** image in the **Goodies: Photos: Scenic** folder on the Painter 4 CD.

2. Select the Tools palette's **lasso**.

3. Zoom up on the image by holding down **Command+Spacebar** on the Mac or **Ctrl+Spacebar** in Windows and clicking on the part of the image that you want to zoom up on.

4. Locate a leaf and click and drag around it. Using the lasso, you can let up on the stylus or mouse, which turns the selection into a shape, and then click on your most recent point and continue to the beginning of the shape. Press the **Spacebar** and click and drag in the image to move around the image to get to each part of the leaf.

5. When you've clicked around the whole leaf, click on your starting point. The path should turn into marching ants. If is doesn't, press **Return** or **Enter** on the Mac or **Enter** in Windows to complete the selection.

6. Zoom back down on the image by holding down **Option+Command+ Spacebar** on the Mac or **Alt+Ctrl+Spacebar** in Windows and clicking in the image.

Next you'll float the leaf.

1. Click on the **Floaters** tool (the left-pointing hand) in the Tools palette.
2. Hold down **Option** on the Mac or **Alt** in Windows and click on the leaf. You now have a floater copy of the leaf.
3. Click **Objects: F.List palette: Trim** to reduce the rectangle surrounding the floater.

Next you'll save the leaf in the Floaters palette.

1. Select **Objects: F. List: Floaters**. The Floaters palette appears.
2. With the **Floaters** tool still selected in the Tools palette, click on the leaf and drag it to the Floaters palette front panel. The floater turns into a little square. Let go. The Save Floater dialog box appears. Type in a name for the leaf. Click **OK**.

Proceed to select, float, and save a few more leaves. You don't need that many because you can vary a few to make it appear there are many more. Once you have four leaf floaters in the Floaters palette, close the leaf image. Next you'll gather the leaves in a new image (see Figure 24.4).

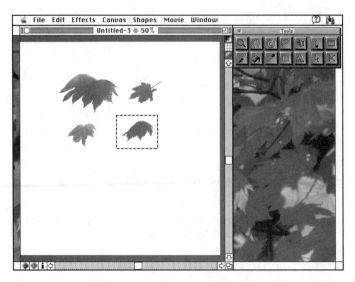

Figure 24.4 The floated leaves.

If you were going to print out an image that you painted with the Image Hose, then you would have to make your nozzle 300 ppi; but things slow down at that resolution, so you will create a nozzle at 75 ppi while you're experimenting.

1. Select **File: New**. Type in **300** pixels for Width and Height and **75** next to Resolution. Click **OK**. A new image appears.

2. Click and hold on the first leaf in the Objects: Floaters palette and drag it into the new image.

Drag out the other three leaves. I wound up with nine leaves all together but you can have any number you want. Once I had my four leaves I made copies for the other five. I copied a leaf floater that was already in the image by holding down **Option** on the Mac or **Alt** in Windows and clicking and dragging on it, continuing till I had nine floaters. Next I resized, rotated, flipped, and colored leaves to vary them (see Figure 24.5).

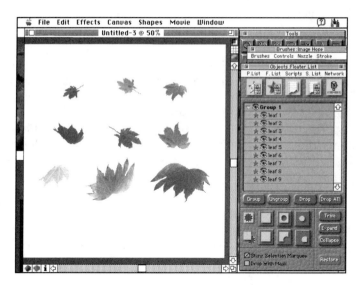

Figure 24.5 The leaves mixed up.

A couple of Effects menu items in Painter 4 make this process really easy.

1. Click on a floater with the left-pointing hand to select it.

2. Select **Effects: Orientation: Free Transform**, which converts the floater into a low-resolution reference floater. You can now edit the floater with keyboard commands.

To resize proportionally, press **Shift** and click and drag on a corner handle. To rotate, press **Command**, Mac; **Ctrl**, Windows and click and drag on a corner handle. To skew, press **Command**, Mac; **Ctrl**, Windows and click and drag on the top-middle handle. In addition to resizing and rotating, I also used **Effects: Orientation: Flip Horizontal**, **Flip Vertical**, and **Distort**.

Once you've done these operations, choose **Effects: Orientation: Commit Transform**. This restores the floater to its original state.

Next, I used **Effects: Tonal Control: Adjust Colors** and moved the Hue Shift slider to vary the colors.

After you've altered your leaves, make sure that the leaves are in the correct order in the Floater List palette. As you saw in Chapter 18, in a 1-Rank Image Hose nozzle, elements are selected from left to right in the nozzle image as you paint with the Image Hose nozzle.

1. Select **Objects: F. List**. The Floater List palette appears.

2. Click on the first leaf in the upper-left-hand corner of the image. Its name is highlighted in the Floater List palette. It should also be at the top of the list. If it isn't, click and drag on the name in the Floater List palette and move it to the top of the list. If you'd like, you can name the floater at this time. With the floater highlighted in the Floater List palette, press **Return**, Mac; **Enter**, Windows. Type a name and click **OK**.

3. Continue to click on leaves in the image from left to right in the first row and then from left to right in subsequent rows, and make sure that their names appear in order in the Floater List palette. If the name is in the wrong order in the list, click and drag the name in the Floater List palette to the correct position.

Next you'll group the floaters.

1. With the left-pointing hand selected, choose **Edit: Select All** (**Command+A**, Mac; **Ctrl+A**, Windows). All the floaters are selected. This is a nice, new Painter 4 shortcut.

2. Click **Objects: Floater List palette: Group**. The floaters are now grouped. Click **Objects: Floater List palette: Trim**. Now the floaters' rectangles are trimmed.

The next step is to create the Image Hose nozzle.

1. Select **Brushes palette: Nozzle: Make Nozzle From Group**. A new document appears with the floaters.
2. Save this new image as a **RIFF** on the Mac or a **.RIF** in Windows and name it **leaves**.

Close this document and the one you used to create the leaves. Save both.

Next you'll paint with your new nozzle.

1. Either select **File: New** and click **OK** or open an existing photograph.
2. Select the **Image Hose** in the Brushes palette.
3. Choose **Brushes palette: Nozzle: Load nozzle**. Locate the leaves nozzle. Click **Open**. Paint in the image. See Chapter 18 for information about adjusting the way the Image Hose sprays the nozzle elements. Chapter 18 also explains how to create 1-, 2-, and 3-Rank Image Hose nozzles.

IMAGE HOSE NOZZLES WITH DROP SHADOWS

These leaves are nice but one-dimensional. The next exercise shows how to give the leaves drop shadows.

Creating Nozzles with Drop Shadows

1. Open the image containing the grouped leaf floaters.
2. Highlight the group by clicking on it in Objects: Floater List palette if it isn't already selected.
3. Another nice Painter 4 shortcut is being able to apply the **Drop Shadow** command to each floater in a group at once. Choose **Effects: Objects: Create Drop Shadow**. The Drop Shadow dialog box appears. Use the default settings and click **OK**. All the floaters now have drop shadows (see Figure 24.6).

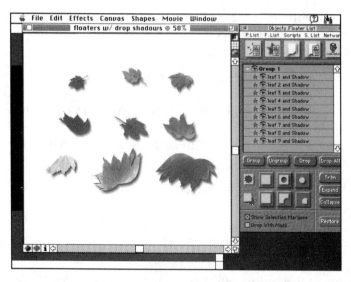

Figure 24.6 The floaters with drop shadows.

Next you have to collapse each leaf and its shadow into one floater. This you still have to do one at a time.

1. Click the **triangle** next to the group. The group opens.

2. Click on the first **floater/shadow group**. Click **Objects: Floater List palette: Collapse**. The leaf and shadow combine into one floater.

3. Proceed to collapse each leaf and its shadow into one group.

4. Once you've collapsed all the floater/shadow groups, click the **triangle** next to the group to close it again.

5. Select **Brushes palette: Nozzle: Make Nozzle From Group**. A new nozzle appears with the floaters (see Figure 24.7).

Save this new image as a **RIFF** on the Mac or a **.RIF**, Windows. Next load the Image Hose as described earlier and paint away. Now you have leaves with depth.

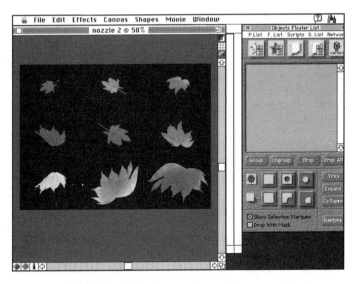

Figure 24.7 The leaves Image Hose nozzle.

SUMMARY

Image Hose nozzles can be as simple or as complex as you'd like them to be. And no matter how you set them up, you'll have a lot of fun with them.

Part VI

Special Effects for 3D, Photography, Multimedia, Slide Presentations, Video, and CD-ROM

25

Working with Type

CHAPTER HIGHLIGHTS

- ❖ Create type shapes
- ❖ Edit type shapes
- ❖ Make type shapes into floaters

Using type in Painter is both easy and tantalizing. It's easy because type comes in as a shape so you can edit it—no muss, no fuss. It's tantalizing because you can use it with any combination of Painter's brushes and special effects to create unusual type effects for illustrations, photography, multimedia, slide presentations, video, and Internet Web pages. This chapter shows the basics of working with type, that is, creating, and editing type shapes and making them into floaters.

Chapter 26, "Type Special Effects," has examples of type special effects that you can create in Painter. If the information in this chapter sounds familiar, that's a good sign. Since type is a shape, you work with it as you would work with any shape in Painter. Sometimes the fact that type is just another shape isn't always obvious, which is why I gave type shapes their own chapter. The reverse is true, too. Anything that you find out about shapes and floaters in this chapter is true for any shape or floater.

TYPE BASICS

This section is about bringing in type as a shape and editing it.

A *shape* is a vector object that floats above Painter's image layer. As a vector object, a shape is easily edited. Also, objects like type can be brought in from vector programs like Illustrator and Freehand as shapes.

Once you've edited a shape you turn it into a bitmap image by either floating it or dropping it into the background.

Working with type is completely different in Painter 4 from previous versions, and in many ways, a lot easier.

341

The manual thoroughly describes how to edit shapes, and you should go over the information there to find out all the shape-editing details. However, the manual doesn't spell out how these details relate to type. This chapter goes over the more common type-related editing maneuvers. Again, anything discussed in the manual relating to shapes can be used with type.

Creating Type

1. Select **File: New** and click **OK**. A new image appears.
2. Click on the letter **A** in the Tools palette.
3. Select a typeface from the Font pop-up menu in the Controls palette. Set the Point Size slider on the desired type size. Set the Tracking slider on the desired setting. The further you move the slider to the right, the more space there will be between letters. The more you move it to the left, the closer together the letters will be.
4. Move the cursor over the image. The cursor becomes an I-beam.
5. Click once in the image. It doesn't matter where because you can move the type around easily after it's created. A blinking insertion point appears.
6. Type the letter **K**. A K now appears as a shape in the image and is listed in the Objects: F. List palette (see Figure 25.1).

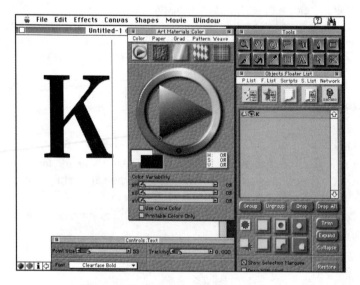

Figure 25.1 The letter *K* is a shape.

Unlike previous versions of Painter, in Painter 4 the type is automatically filled with the selected color in the Color palette.

Editing Type Shapes

You can turn the type shape into a floater at this point by choosing **Shapes: Convert to Floater**, but keep it a shape for a little while because its form is more easily edited as a shape. Please note that applying one of the Effects menu features or painting on a shape also turns the shape into a floater.

Changing Color

I usually start editing type by changing its color. You change type color while it's a shape in the following way:

1. With the K you just typed still in the image, click on the **Floaters** tool (the left-pointing hand) in the Tools palette. The letter's handles appear.

2. Press **Return**, Mac; **Enter**, Windows. The Set Shape Attributes dialog box appears.

3. Select a color in the Color palette. The shape turns that color.

To give the type an outline, click next to **Stroke**. To make it hollow, deselect **Fill**. Keep the shape filled for these exercises. Click **OK**.

Resizing and Moving

Next I usually resize and move type around.

You do these kinds of maneuvers using the **Floaters** tool (the left-pointing hand) in the Tools palette.

The following steps show the more typical type moves.

1. Click on the **Floaters** tool (the left-pointing hand) in the Tools palette if it isn't already selected. Handles appear around the K. If they don't, click on the **K** to bring up the handles.

2. Click within the **K** and drag to the right. That's how you move a shape.

3. Hold down **Shift** and click and drag diagonally on a corner of the K. The K is resized proportionally. You can also resize the letter in any direction without holding **Shift** by clicking and dragging on any of its handles.

4. Hold down **Command** on the Mac or **Ctrl** in Windows and click and drag on a corner point. The shape rotates.

5. Press **delete** on the Mac or **Backspace** in Windows. The type disappears.

6. Click back on the **A** in the Tools palette, type another **K**, then click back on the left-pointing hand.

7. Hold down **Option** on the Mac or **Alt** in Windows and click and drag on the type. You now have a duplicate of your type.

8. Hold down **Command** on the Mac or **Ctrl** in Windows and click and drag the top-middle control point down and to the right. The type is skewed. Make it black by pressing **Return**, Mac; **Enter**, Windows, choosing **black** in the Color palette, and clicking **OK**.

Painter 4's shapes can be manipulated in floater-like ways. Once you skew the second letter, you can click **Controls palette: Back** to send it behind the first letter and then move the Controls palette: Opacity setting to the left and suddenly you have a nice shadow that was easy to create (see Figure 25.2).

Figure 25.2 The second *K* is skewed, turned black, sent to back, and given a lower opacity.

At this point you'd probably start adding Painter effects, turning the shape into a floater. You can do so by choosing **Shapes: Convert To Floater**, by painting in the shape, or by choosing an Effects menu item. Some Effects items are unavailable with shapes and therefore dimmed out. Just choose **Shapes: Convert To Floater** and these items become available.

MANAGING TYPE

Now that you know how to work with a letter in Painter, it's time to graduate to words.

1. Select the **A** in the Tools palette and type **yippee**.
2. Select the **Floaters** tool (the left-pointing hand) in the Tools palette. The shapes handles appear (see Figure 25.3).

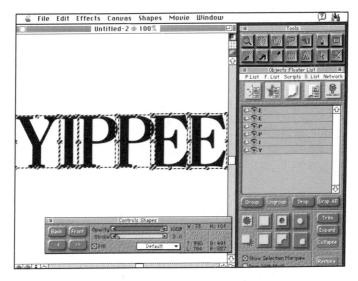

Figure 25.3 Selected letter shapes.

Now you can do all the maneuvers you've done so far, namely, move, resize, copy, rotate, and skew the letters. If you wish to edit one letter alone, click outside of the letters with the Floaters tool to deselect them. Then click on the letter you wish to edit to select it. To reselect all the letters, choose **Edit: Select All** (**Command+A**, Mac; **Ctrl+A**, Windows) or click and drag a marquee surrounding the letters.

Converting Grouped Shapes to a Floater

Now that you have a word you'd probably paint it or add an effect to it. You have to turn it into a floater first. You can't edit it in its current state.

1. Make sure all the letters are selected.
2. Click **Objects: F. List: Group**. The shapes are now grouped.

3. Click **Objects: F. List: Collapse**. The shapes now combine into one and turn into a floater, ready to be painted or edited with the Effects menu.

4. Click **Objects: F. List: Trim** to slim down the rectangle surrounding the letters.

SUMMARY

You now have the basics for working with type in Painter. The next chapter will show you some of Painter's cool type special effects.

26

Type Special Effects

CHAPTER HIGHLIGHTS

- ❧ Create three-dimensional type effects
- ❧ Create embossed type
- ❧ Create chrome type

Now that you've seen how to work with type in Painter, it's time to create special effects using type. This chapter assumes that you read Chapter 25, "Working with Type," which explains how to work with type shapes. If you didn't read it, do so and then come back here. This chapter shows only a sampling of the type effects you can create with Painter. Don't be afraid to experiment with your own designs using all the brushes and effects discussed in this book.

THREE-DIMENSIONAL TYPE

About the quickest and most interesting type trick in Painter is *three-dimensional type*. In Painter 4 the technique has been improved with the Reflection slider, as you'll see later in this chapter. You can combine a three-dimensional look with every Painter drawing and painting tool and every special effect to create countless type variations (see Figure 26.1).

Figure 26.1 Three-dimensional type effect created by Karen Sperling.

The next exercise shows how to create three-dimensional type.

1.   Select **File: New** and click **OK**. A new image appears.

2.   With the **A** selected in the Tools palette, type a **W**. A type shape appears in the image.

3.   Select a gradation in Art Materials: Grad palette.

4.   Select **Effects: Fill**, click next to **Gradation**, and click **OK**. The gradation now fills the type.

5.   Choose **Effects: Surface Control: Apply Surface Texture**. The Apply Surface Texture dialog box appears. Choose **Mask** in the Using pop-up menu. Move up the Softness slider. The Preview window shows how the Softness slider adjustments affect the height of the letter. Click **OK**. Your letter is now three-dimensional.

Three-Dimensional Floaters

You can also Apply Surface Texture using Mask to a floater. The following exercise shows how I created the *Artistry* logo (see Figure 26.2) and all of *Artistry*, the newsletter's department heads. I hand-painted the type, floated it, and then used **Apply Surface Texture using Mask**. To see how the logo appears in the newsletter, take a look at the digital samples of *Artistry* on the CD with this book.

Figure 26.2 *Artistry* logo by Karen Sperling.

Painting Three-Dimensional Type

1. I painted the sky in the background by cloning a photograph from the Painter 4 CD. The February *Artistry* on the CD with this book explains the process.

2. I started a new image and painted the *Artistry* letters with the Pens' **Flat Color** variant. Move the Size slider in Window: Brush Controls: Size palette to the left to taper the strokes.

3. With the Tools palette's middle **rectangle** selected, drag a selection marquee around the letters.

4. Select **Edit: Magic Wand**. The Magic Wand dialog box appears. Click once on a letter. A red mask covers all the letters. Click **Apply.** The mask turns into marching ants.

5. With the Tools palette's **Floaters** tool (the left-pointing hand) selected, click on the type to float it.

You may find when you float the letters that parts are left behind, causing the letters to get jagged. Painter 4 has an easy fix for this as described by John Derry, Vice President, Creative Design at Fractal Design.

1. With the floater selected, click on the **circle** in the image window's upper-right-hand corner. The floater's mask is revealed. You can reveal the image mask (if there is one) this way as well.

2. Select **Effects: Focus: Soften**. You can use the defaults and click **OK**. The jaggies look softer.

3. Select **Effects: Tonal Control: Brightness/Contrast**. Looking at the letters in the Preview, adjust the sliders until you see the jaggies soften more. Click **Apply.** The letters are smoother.

4. Click the **circle** in the image window corner to bring back the color layer.

Next you'll add the three-dimensional look. Select **Effects: Surface Control: Apply Surface Texture**. Set the Using menu to **Mask**. Adjust the Softness slider to taste as described previously. Click **OK**.

Now you'll make the shadow. You can use **Effects: Objects: Create Drop Shadow**, but I prefer to create the shadows "manually."

1. Press **Option** on the Mac or **Alt** in Windows and click on the letters with the **Floaters** tool. You now have a copy.

2. Select **black** in the Color palette and select **Effects: Fill**. Click next to **Current Color** and click **OK**. The copy fills with black. Click **Back** in the Controls palette. The shadow is now behind the first floater. Use the keyboard's directional arrows to position the shadow to taste.

Last, with the **Floaters** tool selected, choose **Edit: Select All** (**Command+A**, Mac; **Ctrl+A**, Windows). Both floaters are selected. Click **Objects: F. List: Group** to group the floater and its shadow, click **Collapse** to combine them, and click **Trim** to trim the new floater. Then copy and paste into the sky document.

EMBOSSED TYPE

Embossed type has become a pretty common type effect. It's very easy to do in Painter. The next exercise shows how to emboss type in Painter.

1. Select **File: New** and click **OK**. A new image appears.

2. Select a color in the Color palette, click on the **A** in the Tools palette, and type a letter.

You could emboss the type at this stage, but let's get a little fancy and add a three-dimensional look first as you did before.

1. Click on the **Floaters** tool in the Tools palette. Choose **Shapes: Convert To Floater**. The letter is now a floater. Click **Objects: F. List: Trim** to trim the box around the floater.

2. Select **Effects: Surface Control: Apply Surface Texture**. The Apply Surface Texture dialog box appears. Choose **Mask** in the Using pop-up menu. Move up the Softness slider. Click **OK**. Your letter is three-dimensional (see Figure 26.3).

Figure 26.3 Three-dimensional letters.

Now you'll emboss the letter.

1. Click **Objects: F. List: Drop** to incorporate the floater into the background.
2. Select **File: Clone**. A clone of the original appears.
3. Select a color in the Color palette. I used a **reddish brown** for a nice chocolatey effect.
4. Select **Effects: Fill**, click next to **Current Color**, and click **OK**. The image is now brown.
5. Select **Effects: Surface Control: Apply Surface Texture**. The Apply Surface Texture dialog box appears. Choose **Original Luminance** in the Using pop-up menu.

Turn up the Softness and Amount sliders. (Check **Inverted** for a recessed-type effect.) Click **OK**. Your type is now embossed (see Figure 26.4).

Figure 26.4 Embossed type.

CHROME TYPE

John Derry created *Logo Channel* (see Figure 26.5) as the opening graphic for the Fractal Television movie on the Painter 4 CD. Click **CD Central: About Us** to see the movie.

Figure 26.5 *Logo Channel* by John Derry.

The following steps show how John created *Logo Channel*. John started by creating a red sphere. "I created a gradation with a bias toward red," John says (see Figure 26.6).

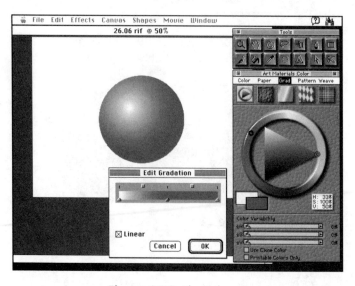

Figure 26.6 The sphere.

Here's how he created the sphere:

1. Select **File: New** and click **OK**. A new image appears.

2. Click and hold on the **rectangle** in the middle of the Tools palette to access the circle, then press the **Shift** key to constrain the selection and click and drag in the image to create a circle selection.

3. Select **Art Materials: Grad: Edit Gradation**. The Edit Gradation dialog box appears. Click on the right-hand **triangle** and select **red** in the Color palette. Click to create another triangle and choose the same color red (see Figure 26.6 to see how John set up the Gradation Editor). Click **OK**.

4. Click on the **Grad palette: Types: Sunburst** icon.

5. Click on the **Tools palette: Paint Bucket**.

6. Click in the upper-left corner of the circle. The circle fills with the red gradation with the highlight in the upper left.

7. Click on the **sphere** with the left-pointing hand to float it.

"This shading technique demonstrates the way an artist will sometimes 'cheat' to achieve an effect, in this case, a 3D sphere using 2D techniques," John notes.

John used the Airbrush's **Fat Stroke** "to create a bit of shadow to offset the highlight" (see Figure 26.7).

Figure 26.7 Shadow airbrushed beneath highlight.

John designed the logo in Adobe Illustrator "because it has the ability to put text on a curve," he says. He then brought it into Painter as a shape using **File: Acquire** (see Figure 26.8).

Figure 26.8 The Adobe Illustrator logo design brought into Painter as a shape.

Using the Floaters tool, John clicked and dragged the "Logo" portion into position over the sphere (see Figure 26.9). He rotated by pressing **Command**, Mac; **Ctrl**, Windows and clicking and dragging on a corner with the Floaters tool.

Figure 26.9 Logo placed over the sphere.

"I needed to create a specialized shadow that creates the illusion of the word Logo casting a shadow on the sphere," John says (see Figure 26.10).

Figure 26.10 The specialized shadow.

First John hid the other floaters by clicking the eyes next to them in the Objects: F. List palette, closing the eyes and hiding the floaters. Then he clicked on the Logo floater and selected **Edit: Drop** to drop the "Logo" floater. Then he applied **Effects: Focus: Motion Blur** to it "so that it would look shadow-like." Next John used **Effects: Surface Control: Quick Warp** "to give the effect of the shadow wrapping around the sphere as it would with a real shadow cast onto a sphere," says John. "Quick Warp always creates its effect in the center of an image, so I moved the word toward the upper-left corner so the effect would properly warp the word," John notes.

Next John selected **Edit: Mask: Auto Mask using Image Luminance**. He clicked on the **Objects: P. List**, clicked the third **Visibility** button to bring up the marching ants, then clicked on the **shadow** with the Floaters tool to float it.

Then John clicked the **eye** next to the sphere floater to reveal the floater and brought in another copy of the word Logo as a floater. He filled it with gold and placed it above the sphere and shadow "to test the 3D illusion" (see Figure 26.11).

355

Figure 26.11 The logo so far.

Next John clicked the **eye** next to the logo floater in the Objects: Floater List palette to hide the gold logo and work with the sphere and shadow (see Figure 26.12).

Figure 26.12 The logo hidden.

John selected **Edit: Drop** for the shadow and then for the sphere. He then selected the **sphere** with the circle selection tool. Then he clicked on the circle selection to float the sphere and the shadow (see Figure 26.13).

John clicked outside of the floater with the **Floaters** tool to deselect it. He chose the **brush** in the Tools palette and deleted what was left in the background by choosing **Edit: Select All** (**Command+A**, Mac; **Ctrl+A**, Windows) and pressing **delete**, Mac; **Backspace**, Windows.

Figure 26.13 The composited version floated as a single entity.

Next John revealed the gold text again by clicking on the floater's **eye** in the Objects: F. List palette to open it and chose **Effects: Surface Control: Apply Surface texture using Mask**, moving both the Softness and the Reflection sliders up (see Figure 26.14).

Figure 26.14 Surface Texture applied.

New in Painter 4, the Reflection slider picks up the pattern chosen in the Art Materials: Pattern palette. John used a pattern from the Painter CD. To access the one he used, click on the **Library** button within the Pattern palette. In the dialog box that appears, locate **Painter CD: Goodies: Patterns: Maps.ptl library**. Click **Open**. In the pop-up menu within the Pattern palette, choose **forest**. Try clicking on all the patterns while inside the Apply Surface Texture dialog box for various chrome effects. Choose **golden shine** for gold letters. Look at the other libraries as well. There are a lot of interesting type effects awaiting you here if you take the time to experiment.

John revealed the other text shapes by opening their eyes in the Objects: F. List palette (see Figure 26.15).

Figure 26.15 The remaining text revealed.

With a type shape selected he chose **Shapes: Convert To Floater**, then used **Apply Surface Texture with Mask** and the Reflection slider as described above with **wavy metallic** chosen in the Art Materials: Pattern library (see Figure 26.16).

Figure 26.16 Apply Surface Texture added to remaining text.

Last, John created the sky in the background.

1. Click outside the floaters with the Floaters tool to deselect them.

2. Choose a **royal blue** in the Color palette. Click on the rear **rectangle** in the Color palette, choose a **turquoise blue**, and click back on the front **rectangle** in the Color palette.

3. Click and drag the **Grad** icon to tear off the palette. Click on the **overlapping rectangles** icon in the Grad palette (it may be inside the drawer). Close the drawer and drag on the red dot on the front panel until the royal blue is at the top of the Grad Preview.

4. Select **Effects: Fill**, click next to **Gradation**, and click **OK**. You now have a sky.

John painted the clouds with the **Cumulus Clouds** Image Hose nozzle found in the default Nozzle palette library.

SUMMARY

As cool as the type effects are in this chapter, they are just the tip of the digital iceberg. Every Painter tool and feature is usable with type. Enjoy!

27

Special Effects Backgrounds

CHAPTER HIGHLIGHTS

- ❖ Paper textures as web page backgrounds
- ❖ Using the brushes and Effects menu for backgrounds

Look at a screen from a multimedia presentation, slide show, CD-ROM title, a television news show, or a web page, and you see textures, lighting, and patterns. You can create these backgrounds with Painter's brushes and special effects, and this chapter gives you some pointers for doing so. Keep in mind, though, that you can use any brush or effect—anything that's been shown in this book so far—to embellish backgrounds. This chapter shows some effects that haven't been covered elsewhere.

PAPER TEXTURES

Paper texture is Painter's primary contribution to digital images. Painter's paper textures can be found in everything from print ads and magazine illustrations to television news screens and commercials, CD-ROMs and slides, video presentations and web sites.

Peter Gruhn added the wriggle paper texture in the More Wild Textures library, Mac; MOREWILD.PAP, Windows to a web page design using **Effects: Surface Control: Apply Surface Texture** (see Figure 27.1).

Figure 27.1 Web page designed by Peter Gruhn.

The Painter manual shows how to create and use Paper textures. Paper is discussed in this book in Chapter 16, "Working with Paper," and Chapter 30, "Web Graphics."

REPEATING PATTERNS

Repeating patterns are everywhere, from abstract backgrounds in print ads to floor tiles in multimedia cyber offices to web page image maps. You can conjure up an endless array of repeating patterns with Painter's brushes and special effects. The manual details all of Painter's pattern-creation and editing tools, including the new Art Materials: Pattern palette.

Tucson-based artist John Stebbins used both Painter's brushes and special effects to create both the patterned background and foreground figures in *Dissolution, Disillusion* (Figure 27.2).

362

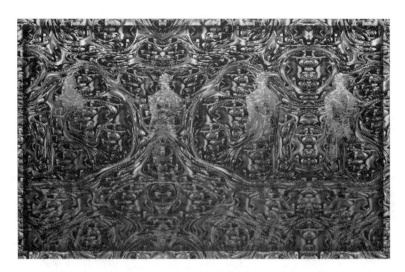

Figure 27.2 *Dissolution, Disillusion* by John Stebbins.

The following tutorial discusses the tools John used.

John started out by creating the background. First he painted with the Brush's **Smaller Wash Brush** variant. "It was just swabbing of paint on a canvas using reds, blues, and greens," John says. "It was just a bunch of color, no theme." Then he used the Liquid's **Coarse Smeary Bristles** "to smear the color around even more." Next John chose **Effects: Esoterica: Apply Marbling** using the default settings.

John took a Quickcam photo of his wife, scanned it in, and selected **Edit: Select All** then **Edit: Copy**. Then he chose the first image in the window menu and chose **Effects: Esoterica: Blobs**. He chose **Paste Buffer** in the Fill Blobs With pop-up menu. This fills the blobs with what has been copied in the image. He changed the number of blobs to **30** and the subsample to **1**.

He chose **Edit: Select All** (**Command+A**, Mac; **Ctrl+A**, Windows), **Edit: Copy**, then started a new, bigger image (**File: New**, click **OK**) and **Edit: Paste: Normal**. He chose **Effects: Orientation: Distort** and stretched out the image to fit the page. He then chose **Edit: Drop** to incorporate it back into the background.

"After the image was stretched over the new canvas, I applied marbling again, this time increasing the spacing and wavelength (the settings did not matter—I just experimented until I liked it) and the direction from top to bottom," John says. And he applied blobs again.

The next step was to choose **orange** in the Color palette and to use **Effects: Surface Control: Color Overlay** "at a spontaneous value that I liked at the moment," John says. He chose **Uniform Color** in the Using menu and clicked next to **Dye Concentration** and Opacity at **100%** "to make the image have an orange tint," John says.

"At this point, the image started to have a metallic look that appealed to me, so to help bring this out, I applied **Effects: Tonal Control: Adjust Colors**, moving the Saturation slider to the right until the image became copper/gold colored metal," John says.

Once he had his background, John focused on the figures. "Since I had my handy acupuncture doll beside me, I photographed it in many positions using my Quickcam," John says. "I could have used Poser, but I did not have it at the time," John adds. "I chose a position with his back to the viewer. I felt this expressed a sad/lonely state of the figure."

John opened the Quickcam pict in Painter and used the Masking Brush's **Masking Pen** variant to make a mask containing the figure. To do so, click the **Objects: P. List**: middle **Visibility** button (next to the eye) and the third **Drawing** button (next to the pencil). Check **Objects: P. List: Transparent Mask**, which lets you see the image through the mask layer. Then choose **black** in the Color palette and paint in the mask. Then choose the **Objects: P. List**: third **Visibility** button (next to the eye), which turns the area in the mask into marching ants. John then selected **Edit: Copy**, selected **File: New**, clicked **OK** to start a new image, and then selected **Edit: Paste**. The figure came in as a floater. John chose a **beige** in the Color palette and **Effects: Surface Control: Color Overlay using Image Luminance** and **Dye Concentration** with Opacity at **75%**.

Next John went back to the background image and selected an interesting section using the middle **rectangle** in the Tools palette and captured it as a paper texture using **Art Materials: Paper: Capture Texture**. Then he selected the image with the figure from the Window menu and applied the new texture to the figure with **Effects: Surface Control: Apply Surface Texture using Paper Grain**. "This produced an interesting effect and would help in dissolving the figure into the background," John notes.

John chose **Edit: Copy**, then selected the background image from the Window menu and pasted the textured figure onto the background as a floater. He pasted another time, chose **Effects: Orientation: Flip Vertical** and set Controls palette: Opacity at approximately **30%** and feathered 3 pixels using **Edit: Mask: Feather Mask** to soften it. Pressing **Option** on the Mac (**Alt** on Windows), he clicked and dragged out three copies of this vertical floater for a total of four reflections (look closely at the image's bottom and you can see the reflections).

Going back to the single upright figure, John chose **Effects: Surface Control: Apply Lighting** using "a reddish light coming from the top so it is cast on his head and shoulders." He clicked **OK**, then chose **Effects: Tonal Control: Adjust Colors** and "redded him up more." Pressing **Option** on the Mac (**Alt** on Windows), he clicked and dragged out three copies of this floater and spaced them out with the reflection under each. He then adjusted the Controls: Opacity to **70%** on each floater to make it semi-transparent.

When everything was positioned satisfactorily, John selected the lower third of the image with the middle **rectangle** in the Tools palette to make a "ground plane," by applying **KPT Gaussian Electrify** with a setting of **3**.

To finish the image, John used the Brushes palette's **Dodge** and **Burn** tools extensively to darken and lighten selected areas of the background. "This helped bring out a dimensionality to the background in addition to giving it that final metallic look," John says. He also lightened the areas around the figures' heads and shoulders to bring them out more.

John made the frame around the edge by selecting a smaller area of the image with the middle **rectangle** in the Tools palette and copying and pasting it. He chose **Effects: Tonal Control: Adjust Colors** to get a silver, metallic look. Then he pasted on the background and lined it up to match. He used **Burn** to darken the area around the frame to make the frame stand out. John chose **Objects: F. List: Drop All** to drop the floaters and he applied **KPT Sharpen Intensity** at level **2**.

SUMMARY

That's just one artist's technique for creating backgrounds in Painter. Combine the Effects menu items with the brushes and order some pizza. You're going to be at your computer for a while!

Part VII

Cartooning and Animation

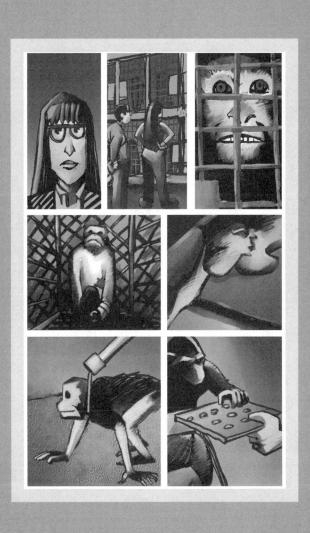

28

Cartoons

CHAPTER HIGHLIGHTS

- ❖ Cartoon Cel
- ❖ Colorizing using floaters
- ❖ Putting line art in the mask layer
- ❖ Traditional painting techniques

Cartoonists use Painter's extensive masking tools with Cartoon Cel to create their illustrations. This chapter shows how four working cartoonists—Mark Badger, Jason Fruchter, David Jacobson, and Jose Marzan—use the Painter tools of the cartoon trade.

USING FLOATERS AND CARTOON CEL FILL

Oakland, California–based comic book illustrator Mark Badger uses Painter in unique ways to create his comic book art. Figure 28.1 is from a book *Animal Rights Comics*, which Mark is doing for the People for Ethical Treatment of Animals about its founding.

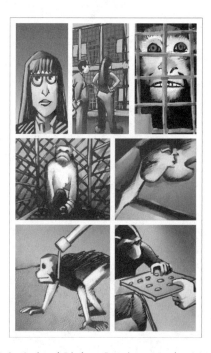

Figure 28.1 *Animal Rights Comics* page by Mark Badger.

Mark first does a base drawing using his own Tracing Paper technique, then he applies color, as described in the following section.

When Mark first got Painter, he would scan in the line art he drew in real time. He would then turn on Tracing Paper (**File: Clone**, **Edit: Select All**, **delete**, Mac; **Backspace**, Windows; **Canvas: Tracing Paper**) so that he could rework the lines, paint them black, and then add color. But he found it difficult to work with Tracing Paper because with it turned on, lines come in at 50%. "Tracing Paper was too confusing," Mark says. "I couldn't clearly tell what lines were in the Tracing Paper and what lines I was drawing. I tried using a different color in the original and black in the clone, but that didn't work because I still didn't like drawing with the lines at 50% in the clone."

Then one day while doing some corrections, he floated just a figure's head and realized, "I could do a whole page like this. The nice thing about doing comics is that I have six panels to experiment with, so I can play around a lot, unless I have a deadline and I'm just cranking things out." So Mark came up with a process in which he uses a floater as tracing paper and draws his lines in the floater if not at 100%, then very close to 100%.

The following exercise shows Mark's tracing paper technique. Mark starts by drawing a first sketch off-screen, which he then brings into Painter. He then adds ink lines and color. Mark notes that drawing a sketch and then adding ink and color to it later is a traditional comic book illustration technique. "When you're doing complicated drawings, to just sit down and draw in black ink is hard," Mark says. "In the first sketch you're working out the structure and composition. Later, when you do the ink lines, you're thinking about crosshatching and line width. You can control the way you put ink lines down based on the underlying structural drawing."

Once the initial drawing is complete, Mark scans it in and opens it in Painter using **File: Open**. Next, Mark says, "I rework the drawing some more, drawing with black, getting the shapes and composition solid."

Then he floats the image to use it as tracing paper, described in the following steps.

First you will generate a mask for the line art and then float the image.

1. With the scanned line art image open, select **Edit: Mask: Auto Mask**. The Auto Mask dialog box appears. Choose **Using: Image Luminance**. Click **OK**.

2. Choose **Edit: Select All** (**Command+A**, Mac; **Ctrl+A**, Windows.) With the **Floaters** tool (the left-pointing hand) selected in the Tools palette, click on the image. The image floats.

Next you'll fill this floater with color and then set it up so that the color fills the black lines.

1. Select a "brown, Renaissance terra cotta color," as Mark puts it, in the Color palette.

2. Select **Effects: Fill**, click next to **Current Color**, then click **OK**. The brown fills the floater.

3. Select **Window: Objects: F. List**. The Floater List palette appears.

4. Click on the last two icons in the palette's bottom portion. The black lines fill with brown.

5. Select **Edit: Drop**. The floater becomes incorporated into the background image.

Mark uses this process each time he has another page to ink and color. "My projects are 12 to 100 pages long, with about 100 to 200 pages of comics a year, and it helps to do them all the same way." To automate the process, he set it up as a *script* (*session* in previous versions) before doing the above steps, from creating the mask to dropping the floater. To create a script, click the Objects: Scripts palette **red button**, which begins the recording. Go through the steps, and when you're done, click the **black square**. The Name the Script dialog box appears. Type in a name for the new script and click **OK**. Now you can apply the script the next time you open scanned line art in Painter by choosing the script in the Objects: Scripts palette and then clicking **Objects: Scripts palette: right-pointing triangle**.

Next you'll float the image again and turn it into tracing paper Mark Badger's way.

1. Select **Edit: Select All** (**Command+A**, Mac; **Ctrl+A**, Windows).

2. Hold **Option**, Mac; **Alt**, Windows.

3. With the **Floaters** tool (the left-pointing hand) selected in the Tools palette, click on the image. A copy of the image now floats while the image stays in the background as well.

4. Select **white** in the Color palette. Select **Effects: Fill** (**Command+F**, Mac; **Ctrl+F**, Windows), click next to **Current Color**, and click **OK**. The floater fills with white.

5. With the **Floaters** tool still selected, set the Controls palette: Opacity slider at **90%**. The underlying line art appears.

6. Select **black** in the Color palette and with the Pens' **Scratchboard** Tool variant, apply your ink lines.(see Figure 28.2).

Drawing in the floater is also useful because Mark can deselect the floater and fix lines in the underlying image if they aren't clear. To deselect, with the **Floaters** tool selected, choose **Edit: Deselect** (**Command+D**, Mac; **Ctrl+D**, Windows). Choose a brush and paint in the lines where necessary in the background. Click on the floater with the Floaters tool again to resume drawing in the floater.

Once the ink lines are complete in the floater, Mark sets the Controls palette: Opacity slider at **100%** and then chooses **Edit: Drop** to incorporate the floater into the background.

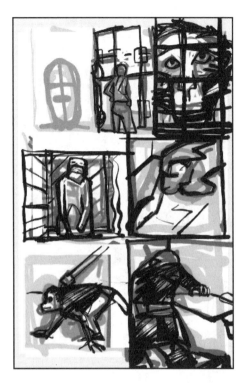

Figure 28.2 The underlying brown lines and the inked black lines in the floater (check the CD to see these color differences).

Next Mark puts the black lines in the mask layer and applies grays with Cartoon Cel fill, "working out all the compositions in terms of values." (See Figure 28.3.)

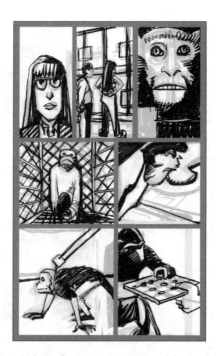

Figure 28.3 Mark Badger's composition blocked out in grays.

Here's how to put the lines in the mask layer:

1. With a line art image open, select **Edit: Mask: Auto Mask**. The Auto Mask dialog box appears. Choose **Image Luminance** in the Using menu. Click **OK**. A mask now covers the line work even though you can't see the mask.

2. Choose **Edit: Select All** (**Command+A** on the Mac; **Ctrl+A** in Windows) and press **delete** on the Mac or **Backspace** in Windows. The image is now blank but the line art is saved in the mask.

3. Select **Objects: P. List**. The Path List palette appears. Click on the middle **Visibility** button (the one next to the eye). The mask appears and you see the line art in red.

4. Next Mark turns the mask black so it resembles line work. Click **Objects: Path List palette: Mask Color**. A color picker appears. Choose **black** and click **OK**. The background mask is now black and looks like line art. This is just the mask. Click on the **Path List palette**: first **Visibility** button (next to the eye) and the lines disappear. Bring them back again by clicking on the second **Visibility** button.

Then it's time to begin to colorize, first with grays, then with colors (see Figure 28.4).

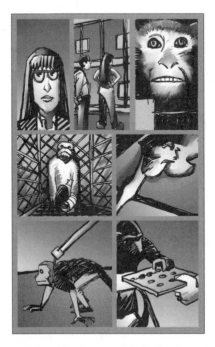

Figure 28.4 The image a little further along.

Mark uses Cartoon Cel fill. He notes, though, that he can't count on Cartoon Cel exclusively because it requires that all the line work be closed off, and that doesn't always happen, especially if someone else does the line work and isn't paying attention, or doesn't know that Mark will be filling in the color in Painter. The next section shows how Cartoon Cel works.

1. Click on the **Paint Bucket** in the Tools palette.
2. Click **Controls palette: What to Fill: Cartoon Cel**. This tells Painter to fill in areas contained within masked-off areas. Click **Fill With: Current Color** to fill with the color in the Color palette or **Gradation** to fill with a gradation in the Grad palette.
3. Choose a color in the Color palette. Click within an area that isn't masked. If the mask extends properly around the area, then the fill will just go inside the mask. If, however, adjacent areas or the whole image fill with color, then the mask is open somewhere. Choose **Edit: Undo** (**Command+Z** on the Mac; **Ctrl+Z** in Windows) to undo the fill. In this

case, you can do one of a couple of things. You can do what Mark does, which is to use the Pens' **Scratchboard** Tool to paint in color by hand. Or you can choose the Masking's **Masking Pen** variant and touch up the mask by painting in it with black. Of course, this defeats the purpose of setting up the line work as the mask, which is to avoid altering the line work.

Another situation that arises is where the mask appears to be closed off, but when you click with the **Paint Bucket**, the color goes beyond the mask anyway. In this case, double-click on the **Paint Bucket** in the Tools palette. In the dialog box that appears is a slider called Mask Threshold. You can think of moving this slider to the right as increasing the density of the mask, fortifying masked areas that aren't solid. (my interpretation, not the official programming explanation). Click **OK**. Then click in an area. It might fill properly; then again it might not. You may still have to paint in the area by hand. You'll have to experiment in each case to see what works best.

Once he has filled in as much as he can using **Cartoon Cel**, Mark paints in the rest of the color with the Pens' **Scratchboard** tool variant.

Next Mark creates floaters and fills them with color using either Painter's **Art Materials: Grad: Express in Image** or KPT map to grayscale. These tools apply color based on image luminance, or gray values. "I color one floater with a warm gradation for the face, for instance, and the other floater with a cool gradation, and layer them." Then he'll use the Brushes palette: Masking brushes to paint in one floater to reveal what's in the underlying floater (see Figure 28.5).

You're going to select an area, float it, create a mask for it, fill it, and drop it. If you want to, you can do all this in a clone to protect the original image. However, when you clone the image, the mask doesn't automatically appear in the clone.

Figure 28.5 Areas filled in using floaters.

The first thing to do, then, is to clone the image and bring the mask in from the original.

1. Select **File: Clone**. A clone of the image appears.
2. Select **Edit: Mask: Auto Mask**. Choose **Original Mask** in the Using pop-up menu and click **OK**. Now the clone has the same mask as the original. Click on the **Objects: Path List palette**: second **Visibility** button (next to the eye). The mask appears.

Next you'll float the section that you want to fill with the gradation.

1. Click on the middle **rectangle** in the Tools palette.
2. Click and drag a selection marquee in the image around the area you want to fill.
3. Click on the **Floaters** tool (the left-pointing hand) in the Tools palette to select it.
4. Hold down **Option** on the Mac or **Alt** in Windows and click on the selected area. You have copied the area as a floater.

Next you're going to generate a mask so you can fill the floater's background with a gradation.

1. Press **Command** on the Mac or **Ctrl** in Windows and click on the area that you want to fill to pick up its color. Now you can use the Edit menu to mask everything in the floater but this color.
2. Select **Edit: Mask: Auto Mask**. The Auto Mask dialog box appears. Choose **Current Color** in the Using menu. Click **Invert**. You want to mask the area *outside* the color, not the color itself. Click **OK**. A mask now covers the elements that are not the color that you chose.

Next you're going to fill the selected area with a gradation.

1. Click **Art Materials: Grad**. The Grad palette appears. Choose a gradation or create one using **Art Materials: Grad: Edit Gradation**.
2. Select **Art Materials: Grad: Express in Image**. Adjust the Bias slider and click **OK**. The gradation fills the floater's unmasked area.

Next Mark makes a second floater and fills it with another gradation.

1. With the **Floaters** tool (the left-pointing hand) still selected in the Tools palette, hold down **Option** on the Mac or **Alt** in Windows and click in the floater's filled area. A copy of the floater now floats above the original floater.
2. Select another grad in the Art Materials: Grad palette, the choose **Art Materials: Grad: Express in Image**. Adjust the Bias slider and click **OK**.
3. With the **Floaters** tool (the left-pointing hand) still selected in the Tools palette, move the Controls palette: Opacity slider to the left. The top floater is now transparent and the colors of the two floaters blend

together. Mark will also paint with the Brushes palette: Masking brushes in the top floater to reveal the underlying floater.

Mark also will "play with the Controls palette's composite modes and sometimes use the **Color** one or **Hard Light**, depending on the effect I'm looking for."

Next you'll drop these floaters into the image.

1. Make sure **Objects: Floater List palette: Drop With Mask** is deselected.

2. Click **Objects: Floater List palette: Drop All**. The floaters become incorporated into the image.

3. Click **Objects: P. List**: second **Visibility** button (next to the eye). The black lines reappear and your new fill stays where it belongs.

Next Mark does touch up, using the **Chalk** with the Brushes palette: Method Category set to **Drip** to paint details and add highlights. He'll also use **Effects: Surface Control: Apply Lighting**, "which I use in the final touches to force a little bit of focus into the panels. I usually do that on a floater and then vary the opacity to get the perfect touch and drop them."

USING FLOATERS FOR COMIC BOOK PAGE FRAMES

Mark uses one floater to frame individual panels on a page (see the previous figures).

The next section explains how Mark creates his page frame floater.

First you're going to create the frame areas by selecting with the rectangle and filling with a color. Mark uses blue. Later you will float the whole image, create a mask for the areas that aren't blue, then make the blue areas white. It sounds more complex than it is; if you follow the steps, you'll see how cool Mark's method for creating comic book frames is.

Using a Floater as a Comic Book Frame

The first step is to select areas and fill them with a color.

1. Draw a layout using a pencil. Mark's Painter image is 6 3/4" by 10 1/2", the traditional comic book page size. Draw in the areas for the frame.

2. Scan in the layout and open it in Painter.

3. Click on the middle **rectangle** in the Tools palette.

379

4. Click and drag a marquee to select a border going along the top of the image.

5. Select a color in the Color palette. Mark chooses a **nonreproducing blue**, a color used in printing that doesn't reproduce in the final printed piece. You can use any color you'd like.

6. Choose **Effects: Fill**, click next to **Current Color**, and click **OK**. The border that you selected is now blue or whatever color you chose.

7. Click outside the border to deselect it.

8. Continue to select pieces of what will eventually be the frame, including the horizontal and vertical sections within the image and the areas going along the sides and bottom of the image, and fill them with color.

9. Once all the sections have been filled in, click outside the most recently selected area to deselect it.

Next you'll float the image.

1. Select **Edit: Select All** (**Command+A** on the Mac; **Ctrl+A** in Windows).

2. Click on the **Floaters** tool (the left-pointing hand) in the Tools palette.

3. Hold down **Option** on the Mac or **Alt** in Windows and click once on the image. You now have a copy of the image floating above the original.

Next you're going to generate a mask and fill the colored areas with white.

You should still have the color selected in the Color palette that you just used to fill all the frame areas. If not, you can always get it back by pressing **Command** on the Mac or **Ctrl** in Windows and clicking on the color in the image.

1. Select **Edit: Mask: Auto Mask**. The Auto Mask dialog box appears. Choose **Current Color** in the Using menu. Click next to **Invert** to deselect it if it's selected from before. Click **OK**.

2. Click **Objects: F. List**: the last icon in the top row of icons, if it isn't already selected. The blue areas are available for editing.

Next you're going to make the frame white.

1. Select **white** in the Color palette.

2. Select **Effects: Fill**, click next to **Current Color**, and click **OK**. The frame turns white.

3. Select **Edit: Deselect** (**Command+D** on the Mac; **Ctrl+D** in Windows). The floater is deselected.

4. Select the Pens' **Scratchboard** Tool variant and a color in the Color palette and paint in the image. The strokes go behind the frame floater so you don't have to worry about messing up the frame as you paint.

As you paint each panel in the image layer behind the frame floater, you might decide that you want to move a panel from one place to another. Here's how.

1. Make sure the floater is still deselected.

2. Click on the middle **rectangle** in the Tools palette.

3. Click and drag around the panel that you want to move. The selection marquee goes beneath the frame floater and selects in the image layer.

4. Click and drag on the selection. The selection turns into a floater. Place it where you'd like it and let go.

5. Click on the **Floaters** tool (the left-pointing hand) in the Tools palette.

6. Click **Controls palette: Back**. The selection goes behind the frame floater.

7. Click **Objects: F. List: Drop** if you're happy with the floater's new position. Or leave it floating if you think you'll need to move it again. Just remember to click on it with the **Floaters** tool to select it to paint on it, or your strokes will go behind it into the underlying image area.

ANOTHER WAY TO CARTOON WITH PAINTER

New York City–based 2-D animator and Macintosh artist Jason Fruchter has another approach to doing cartoons in Painter. Jason's freelance work includes *The Head* animated television series for MTV, various commercials, and multimedia presentations, as well as CD-ROM animation and interface design.

Jason adds shadows in Painter using **Effects: Surface Control: Color Overlay**, as you can see in his cartoon character *Poker Cat* (see Figure 28.6).

Figure 28.6 *Poker Cat* by Jason Fruchter.

Jason, like many artists using Painter, starts off drawing his characters off-screen with a pencil. Unlike other artists, he then takes the line drawing (see Figure 28.7), places it on a light box, places a piece of paper over it, and draws the shapes for the shadows (see Figure 28.8), which he later reverses (see Figure 28.9).

Figure 28.7 Line drawing.

Figure 28.8 Shadow shapes.

Figure 28.9 Shadow shapes reversed out.

After scanning the line art and shadows into Painter, Jason creates a mask for the character and fills it in with **Cartoon Cel** (see Figure 28.10).

Figure 28.10 Areas filled with **Cartoon Cel**.

383

Then Jason uses **Dodge** and **Burn** in the Brushes palette to bring out the form (see Figure 28.11).

Figure 28.11 Areas painted with **Dodge** and **Burn**.

Finally, Jason combines this image with the reversed out shadows and then pastes the character into a background image. The following exercise shows how Jason uses Painter for cartooning.

Cartooning with Shadows

The first step is to draw the character with a pencil and then to draw the shadows.

1. Draw your character off-screen.
2. Next draw the shapes for the shadows on another piece of paper. Draw open areas for the shadows. In a little while, you will fill these areas with black in Painter.
3. Scan in both drawings and open the line art in Painter.

Now you'll create a mask for the line art and fill it with Cartoon Cel.

1. Choose **Edit: Mask: Auto Mask**. The Auto Mask dialog box appears.
2. Choose **Image Luminance** in the Using menu. Click **OK**. A mask now covers the lines.

3. To see the mask, click **Objects: P. List**: second **Visibility** button (next to the eye). If you made the mask black when following the exercise earlier in this chapter, turn it red now so that you can see the lines. To do so click **Objects: P.List: Mask Color**, choose **red**, and click **OK**. Click the first **Visibility** button to hide the mask again.

Next you're going to fill the areas with color using Cartoon Cel.

1. Choose a color in the Color palette.
2. Click on the **Paint Bucket** in the Tools palette.
3. Select **Controls palette: What to Fill: Cartoon Cel**. Click **Controls palette: Fill With: Current Color**. Click in an area in the image to fill it. The area now contains color. Check earlier in this chapter for possible remedies if the fill goes past your masked lines.

After the image is filled with color, the next step is to use the **Brushes palette: Dodge** and **Burn** tools to paint highlights and shadows, keeping in mind the shadow image that is about to be combined with the main image. Take a look at Figure 28.6 and you'll see where the shadows fall.

Figure 28.9 shows the finished shadow image. It is a negative of the original shadow image (Figure 28.8).

It will become clear why you have to reverse the image when you apply it later. The next few steps show how to create the shadow image.

1. Open the shadow image that you scanned in earlier.
2. Select **black** in the Color palette.
3. Click on the **Paint Bucket** in the Tools palette.
4. Click **Controls palette: What to Fill: Image**. Click **Controls palette: Fill With: Current Color**.
5. Click in the shadow shapes to fill them with black. Jason will touch up areas where necessary with the **Airbrush** and **Charcoal**.
6. Select **Effects: Tonal Control: Negative**. The image is now reversed.

Jason then softens the image to blur the shadow edges, making the character look rounder.

1. Select **Effects: Focus: Soften**. The Soften dialog box appears.
2. Move the slider to **1.00** and click **OK**.

The next step is to bring the shadow into the main image.

1. Select **Window**: the main image.

2. Select **File: Clone Source**: the shadow image.

3. Choose **black** in the Color palette if it isn't already selected.

4. Choose **Effects: Surface Control: Color Overlay**. The Color Overlay dialog box appears. Choose **Original Luminance** in the Using menu. You had to make the shadow image a negative so that it would come in as a positive when you use **Color Overlay**.

5. Click next to **Dye Concentration**. Adjust the Opacity slider to taste, using the Preview window as your guide. The higher the Opacity slider, the more contrast there will be between the shadow and the rest of the image, the lower the Opacity slider, the flatter the image will appear. Click **OK**. The image now has a shadow.

WATERCOLOR CARTOONS

David Jacobson, a staff cartoonist at New York–based Gannett Suburban Newspapers, creates cartoons for the Gannett daily newspapers in Painter. David puts the line art in one image (see Figure 28.12) and the color in another (see Figure 28.13) and combines them in QuarkXPress (see Figure 28.14).

Figure 28.12 Line art.

Figure 28.13 Color.

'I realize that all you really need to know you learned in
kindergarten, but we're not hiring right now.'

Figure 28.14 Combined image. Cartoon © 1996 Gannett Suburban
Newspapers by David Jacobson.

David draws the line art with India ink and brush. "I use a brush with India ink because digitized tablets still don't give me the subtleties that a brush can give me."

Then he scans the line art in at 300 dpi in Photoshop, cleans it up, and converts it to the size of his cartoon, which is 23.5 picas square. Then he opens the line art in Painter, clones it (**File: Clone**), turns on Tracing Paper (choose **Edit: Select All** [**Command+A**, Mac; **Ctrl+A**, Windows] press **delete**, Mac; **Backspace**, Windows; choose **Canvas: Tracing Paper** [**Command+T**, Mac; **Ctrl+T**, Windows]). Then he fills the color in by selecting sections with the Tools palette: path tools and filling with **Effects: Surface Control: Color Overlay**, turning the Opacity down to **60%** "so I can add color over color and not have the end result be too saturated," David says. "I put many overlays over each other to shade and give the cartoon depth." Then he uses the Chalk's **Artist Pastel Chalk** variant "to add texture, lines, and depth to the drawing. I also use the Brush's **Big Loaded Oils** variant to give more concentrated color in areas." Then David uses the Water's **Just Add Water** variant and the Brush's **Sable Chisel Tip Water** "to push the color around and to get a watercolor effect." Then David will "go back with the **Eraser**, lighten areas up, and go back with the tools I just mentioned until I get the effects I want. I want the end result to have a watercolor effect to it." David adds, "Sometimes I add texture with different papers and **Effects: Surface Control: Apply Surface Texture**. Sometimes I'll also add **Effects: Surface Control: Apply Lighting**."

"Once the color is done," David notes, "I bring the Painter file and the Photoshop file into Quark. I place one on top of the other, add the cutline, and output to our Linotronic-like system."

David adds, "I print out through Quark so I can get a pure black line. Printing through Painter, I get an RGB black, which is not as pure as in Quark. The black line is very important to my work, so I don't want to sacrifice the quality."

PAINTING CARTOONS IN OILS

Jose Marzan is a New York–based freelance comic artist working in traditional pen and ink for DC Comics on *The Flash* and *The Adventures of Superman*. He uses Painter to create custom-made "zip a tone" sheets and special effects difficult to create with pen and ink (clouds, science-fiction type effects, etc.).

Jose painted Superman™ ©1996 DC Comics using Painter's tools to create a "natural" result (see Figure 28.15).

Figure 28.15 Superman™ ©1996 DC Comics painted by Jose Marzan.

"My basic approach is to attempt to create works that look and feel like traditional painting media," Jose says. "However, I will use any tool in Painter, Photoshop, or any plug-in filter in the creation of the painting. I do like the ability the computer gives me to incorporate the final work with preliminary sketches in the same piece. Perhaps the reason I don't use too many filters and other things is my lack of RAM (16 megs total) and hard disk space (230 megs total), so I don't have much room to go crazy. I pretty much always begin working on an image at about 100–150 dpi (sometimes 200). I take the painting as far as I think it will go, then if need be, I resize it up (**Canvas: Resize**) and execute some sharpening (painting by hand) and final touchups (whether by hand or filter). That's pretty much it. Not much to it, really."

In the following steps, Jose shows how he painted Superman.

1. He blocked in the figure and background with the Charcoal's **Gritty Charcoal**, the **Airbrush**, and the Pens' **Scratchboard** Tool, all of various sizes (**Brushes palette: Controls: Size**). He changed brushes from Buildup to **Cover** (**Brushes palette: Method Category**), depending on need.

2. He used the same tools as in step 1 to build up detail, adjusting tool sizes for the task at hand.

3. He developed the face with **Water Color**, **Airbrush**, and Pens' **Scratchboard Rake**. He chose **Canvas: Dry** at times to dry the Water Color strokes to achieve a layering effect, as with real watercolors.

4. He used **Pencils** and **Charcoal** on the background.

5. He applied paper texture (**Effects: Surface Control: Apply Surface Texture**).

6. He created a frisket (mask) with **Tools palette: lasso** tool for the "S" shield. He painted the shield with the same tools used on the rest of the figure. The mask allowed him to paint naturally and not be concerned with the shield's edges and neatness.

SUMMARY

There you have tips from four working illustrators for using Painter to create cartoons. Cartoonists have really taken to Painter's tools. I have a feeling we're going to see more and more cartoons created in Painter in the years to come.

29

Animation

CHAPTER HIGHLIGHTS

- ❖ Using floaters in animations
- ❖ Applying effects using sessions

Jeffery Roth, Digital Production Designer and head of the Mac 3D Division at San Francisco–based Colossal Pictures, uses Painter's animation capabilities during preliminary client meetings. Colossal Pictures is a well-known film production house for commercials, games, and television.

"The directors will say 'here's an idea,'" Jeffery says, "and I draw it in Painter as they say it—it's a moving storyboard. Putting together the idea this way saves time, confusion, and a lot of money," Jeffery adds, because the "moving storyboard" more closely resembles the final product than a still image ever did. "A combination of programs is needed to achieve the desired results," Jeffery says. "Painter offers very few limitations to the creation of digital painting, so it has become a trusted ally on our productions. We use Painter and Photoshop and then take the animation into a program with professional animation functions like AfterEffects."

"After we create the storyboard, we hand it off to the SGI department to do the final," says Jeffery.

"*Totec Fire God* demonstrates some of the uses I have found for Painter's frame stacks in the production environment," says Jeffery (see Figure 29.1).

In *Totec Fire God*, the statue is stationary and the flames move.

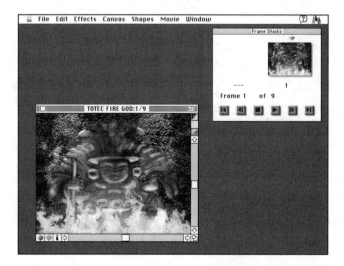

Figure 29.1 Frame from *Totec Fire God* by Jeffery Roth.

The following section shows how Jeffery created *Totec Fire God*.

ANIMATING IN PAINTER

The animation began with a **.PICT** image that Jeffery painted called *Totec god.pict* (see Figure 29.2).

Figure 29.2 The original Totec God picture.

Here's how Jeffery painted *Totec God*. First, set up your canvas.

1. Select **File: New**, then click **OK**. A new image appears.
2. Select **gray** in the Color palette and **Basic Paper** in the Paper Palette.
3. Select **Effects: Surface Control: Color Overlay**. Choose **Using menu: Paper Grain**, set Opacity at **45%**, click next to **Hiding Power**, and click **OK**. You now have a gray-toned image with a paper texture.

Next you'll paint the image.

1. Sketch the composition with the Pencils' **2B Pencil** variant.
2. Using the 2B Pencil, "lay in values" with crosshatch strokes.
3. With the Airbrush variants and the 2B Pencil, fill in areas, scaling the brush (Brushes palette: Controls: Size slider) depending on the area to be filled.
4. Fill in details with the **2B Pencil**, the Water Drop's **Grainy Water**, and the Airbrush's **Feather Tip** and **Thin Stroke** variants.
5. As the finishing touch, select **Effects: Surface Control: Apply Lighting**. The Apply Lighting dialog box appears. Set up the lighting so that the statue is lit from below. Click **OK**.

The next thing to do is to start a new frame stack.

1. Select **File: New**. The New Picture dialog box appears. Click next to **Picture Type: Movie** and enter **9** next to frames. Change the Width and Height pop-up menus to **pixels** and type **320** for height and **240** for width, and type **72** next to Resolution. Click **OK**. Painter creates a new frame stack, which is its native movie format.
2. A dialog box appears asking you to name the movie. Type **Totec Fire God** on the Mac or **TOTECFIR.FRM** in Windows and click **OK**.
3. The New Frame Stack dialog box appears.

   Jeffery chooses **2** layers of onion skin, although "3 is good, too." Jeffery notes that you can get confused with more layers. "We have 2 or 3 guys who are traditional animators at Colossal," says Jeffery. "An animator works at a circular lit table that swivels. He draws his first cel, lays a paper on top of it, sees the drawing beneath it, and uses it to draw the next cel. But if he puts too many pages on the table, he'd start to see too many layers beneath the one that he's working on; so they only work with one layer beneath the main layer at a time."
4. Click **OK**. A new image appears with nine frames in the Frame Stacks palette.

The next step is to apply a texture to the whole movie. You'll do this as a *script*, known as a session in previous versions of Painter.

1. Click on the button all the way to the left in the Frame Stacks palette to go back to the first frame.

2. Select a paper texture in the Paper palette. Click the **Objects: Scripts** icon. The Scripts palette appears. Click the red **recording** button to start recording the script.

3. Select **black** in the Color palette and select **Effects: Surface Control: Color Overlay**. The Color Overlay dialog box appears. Choose **Paper Grain** in the Using menu, click next to **Hiding Power**, and set Opacity at **100%**. Click **OK**. A paper texture appears in the first frame.

4. Click the **square** in the Scripts palette to stop recording the script. The Name the Script dialog box appears. Type **paper** in the dialog box and click **OK**. Choose **Edit: Undo** to delete the paper texture in the first frame.

5. Select **Movie: Apply Script To Movie**. The Recorded Scripts dialog box appears. Click on **paper** and click **Playback**. The texture is applied to the movie.

Next Jeffery applies a second layer of paper to customize the texture effect.

1. Click on the button all the way to the left in the Frame Stacks palette to go back to the first frame again if you aren't already there.

2. Move up the Scale slider in the Paper palette.

3. Click the **Objects: Scripts:** red **recording** button to start recording the script.

4. Select **Effects: Surface Control: Apply Surface Texture**. The Apply Surface Texture dialog box appears. Choose **Paper Grain** in the Using menu, and click **OK**. A paper texture appears in the first frame, wiping out the underlying paper.

5. Choose **Edit: Fade**. The Fade dialog box appears. Set the Undo Amount slider to **50%**. Click **OK**. The effect is faded back and now the two paper applications combine in the image.

6. Click the **square** in the Scripts palette to stop recording the script. The Name the Script dialog box appears. Type **paper2** in the dialog box and click **OK**. Choose **Edit: Undo** to delete the second paper texture in the first frame.

7. Select **Movie: Apply Script To Movie**. The Recorded Scripts dialog box appears. Click on **paper2** and click **Playback**. The texture is applied to the movie.

Next, Jeffery applied lighting to the movie in the same manner. But first he created the lighting effect so that he would have it for later.

1. Click on the button all the way to the left in the Frame Stacks palette to go back to the first frame again if you aren't already there.

2. Select **Effects: Surface Control: Apply Lighting**. The Apply Lighting dialog box appears. Set up your lighting. Notice in Figure 29.2 that Jeffery created the background light to appear to spray up and out to the sides. Once you set up the light, save the lighting effect by clicking **Save** in the Apply Lighting dialog box. The Save Lighting dialog box appears. Type in a name—call it **light**, and click **OK**. The new light now appears in the scrolling palette in the dialog box's bottom portion. Click **OK**. The lighting appears in the first frame.

3. Select **Edit: Undo** to undo the lighting effect in the first frame.

Next you'll apply the light to the whole frame stack.

1. Click the **Objects: Scripts:** red **recording** button to start recording the script.

2. Select **Effects: Surface Control: Apply Lighting**. The Apply Lighting dialog box appears.

3. Choose the light you just created. Click **OK**.

4. Click the **square** in the Scripts palette to stop recording the script. The Name the Script dialog box appears. Type **light** in the dialog box and click **OK**. Choose **Edit: Undo** to delete the light in the first frame.

5. Select **Movie: Apply Script To Movie**. The Recorded Scripts dialog box appears. Click on **light** and click **Playback**. The light is applied to the movie.

Next you'll bring in the statue twice and apply this new lighting to it to make it look three-dimensional.

1. With the lasso, select the statue's outline. When you're done, you should see marching ants. If not, press **Return**, Mac; **Enter**, Windows, and they should appear.

2. Select **Edit: Copy**.

3. Choose **Window**: the frame stack you were just working on, then choose **Edit: Paste: Normal**. The statue appears as a floater.

4. Select **Effects: Surface Control: Apply Lighting**. The Apply Lighting dialog box appears.

5. Choose the light you just created. Click **OK**.

6. Hold **Option**, Mac; **Alt**, Windows and click and drag with the left-pointing hand to create a copy of the floater. Use the left-pointing hand or press the arrow keys on the keyboard to nudge one floater just behind the other to give the statue a three-dimensional appearance.

7. With the left-pointing hand still selected, choose **Edit: Select All** (**Command+A**, Mac; **Ctrl+A**, Windows). Both floaters are selected.

8. Click **Objects: F. List: Group**. The floaters are grouped together.

9. Click **Objects: F. List: Collapse**. The floaters combine into one floater.

Next you'll paste this new floater in each frame. In Painter 4, floaters are automatically dropped when you advance to the next frame. This can be a problem if that's not what you want to happen, but in this case, it makes putting the same floater in each frame easy.

1. Click on the second button from the right in the Frame Stacks palette to advance to the next frame.

2. Continue to advance frames until you reach frame number nine. The floater is dropped in each frame as you go.

   If you keep clicking on the button advancing you to the next frame, Painter will keep adding frames, so just click to the ninth frame. If you add a frame by mistake, click the button all the way to the left in the Frame Stacks palette, then select **Movie: Delete Frames**. The Delete Frames dialog box appears. Type in the range of frames you want to delete and click **OK**. You can't delete a frame if it's the one that's currently showing.

3. Click the button all the way to the left to return to the first frame. Press **Delete**, Mac; **Backspace**, Windows. The floater is deleted but remains in the image layer.

At this point you should have the same statue in nine frames. Next Jeffery brought in the fire.

Jeffery used three picts of fire taken from some practical film ("in the film industry, *practical* means it's more practical to just film something," notes Jeffery). He copied, pasted, and dropped fire in each frame, alternating among the three pict files and using **Effects: Orientation: Flip Horizontal** on some to mix things up a bit.

Before dropping, he chose **Controls: Composite Method: Color**. The fire had a black background. Color drops out the black and reveals the image behind the floater. He also moved the Controls: Opacity slider to **40%**. "Fire flickering in front of objects creates light facets on objects, like when you're in front of a campfire," Jeffery notes, so the next step was to paint lighting in each frame with the Airbrush, the Pencil and the Water Color. Last, Jeffery painted the smoke with the Brushes palette's **Dodge** and **Burn** tools "and voila! you have an AZTEC fire god."

SUMMARY

That's how an artist uses Painter's animation tools in a work situation. Artists agree that Painter's animation tools have a way to go before Painter will be useful as a full-blown animation tool, but it does have its important uses.

30

Web Graphics

CHAPTER HIGHLIGHTS

- ✤ Creating fine art Web pages
- ✤ Creating corporate Web pages

The World Wide Web is the hot growth area for everyone these days, especially artists and designers who can put together attractive Web sites. Painter 4 provides Web graphics capabilities in the form of textures and type that, when turned into floaters, can be clickable image maps that send you to designated areas on Web pages.

Two artists using Painter extensively for their Web sites are Pennsylvania-based Dennis Orlando and Georgia-based Graham Hedrick. In this chapter are examples of their Web graphics and information about how they created them.

CREATING A FINE ART WEB SITE

Dennis Orlando is president and co-founder of SmallWorld Media Group, a full-service marketing communications company. His company's Web site can be seen at http://www.180079world.com.

Dennis, a long-time Painter artist, also has a gallery Web site for his own fine art at http://www.voicenet.com/~dorlando/.

Before creating art for the Web, Dennis recommends having "at least a basic understanding of the HTML language. Knowledge of Web browsers and Web server related issues would help enormously." Dennis used Painter 4 to design his site, create the art, and construct the image maps (see Figure 30.1).

Figure 30.1 Dennis Orlando's fine art gallery Web site.

According to Dennis, creating Web art includes three phases, namely planning, creating, and producing.

The planning phase is "the most important in the successful outcome of your site," Dennis notes, and "it is where you ask yourself questions and, based on the answers, determine how you will proceed with the next phase."

Here are the questions Dennis says to ask yourself:

❖ What is the purpose, objective, and style of your site going to communicate?

❖ What content and material do you already have available to use on the pages?

❖ What new material will you need to create to meet the content and navigational requirements of your site?

❖ How do you want the viewer to interact with this material?

❖ Will you lead the viewer through the pages in a logical path or do you want an interactive interface that lets the viewer determine the path to take?

Dennis suggests that you gather a list of available material (assets) together, make a list of art and material to be created, and outline and design a branching diagram or site map. This site map determines what links will be required to navigate from one page to another and from one area of your site to another site. Assemble a list of WWW URLs, and create names for your pages to be used in your HTML files and referenced in your clickable image map and button artwork.

❖ Before creating image maps and button bars in Painter, find out if NCSA or CERN is the map file format required by the particular web server your files will reside on. Ask your Webmaster or server administrator.

"Based on the decisions made in the above planning process," Dennis notes, "you will be able to determine how much creative work is required in the next phase and how you will save your artwork in the production phase."

For example, with the subject matter being fine art at Dennis' gallery site, he decided at the planning stage to use 24-bit JPEG files to "showcase the work at the highest quality the Web allows."

Next is the creation phase. In this phase, "all aesthetic decisions are made and artwork created and assembled," says Dennis. The following steps show how Dennis created his pages.

1. Determine the background color for your Web pages in your HTML document, be it white, black, www gray, or a repeating tile as a background pattern or texture. "The reason for this will become obvious when you see the art you're about to create placed on top of the page color that you assign in your HTML files. If you consider this now, you'll be much happier later," Dennis says. As you can see in Figure 30.1, Dennis selected black for his background for both the page and images. Using black "creates the illusion that the page is all one element," Dennis notes, "rather than several pieces all slapped together, and allows the artwork and images to merge into the page without any edges showing."

2. Establish the pixel width of your page. This is the width at which your main image maps and button bars will be created. This way, you control how wide the viewer will need to open the browser window to see your entire page. Also, determining pixel width can be used to lock your page design into place, making the rest of the page layout process go more smoothly, sort of like working with templates in Quark or PageMaker. "My pages were set up to be 468 pixels wide and will open at the default

page width of my browser's viewing area," Dennis says. "If the impact of your initial presentation and control over how the viewer sees your pages are important, don't forget this step. Also keep in mind that the average monitor size visitors will be using to view your site is probably 14 or 15 inches, and large pages require a lot of annoying scrolling. Image resolution does not need to be more than 72 ppi. The more resolution, the larger the file size; the larger the file size, the longer it will take to build on the page. People want to see pages that build fast."

3. Import materials. Dennis opened his digital paintings and resized (**Canvas: Resize**) to fit the pages. Then he turned the resized images into floaters (**Edit: Select All** |**Command+A**, Mac; **Ctrl+A**, Windows], click with the left-pointing hand in the Tools palette), named them (press **Return**, Mac; **Enter**, Windows, type a name in the dialog box, click **OK**), and placed them into a portfolio library (choose **Objects: F. List: Floaters**. The Floaters palette appears. With the left-pointing hand, hold **Option**, Mac; **Alt**, Windows and then click and drag the floater to the Floaters palette front panel. The floater turns into a little square. Let go. The Save Floater dialog box appears. Type in a name for the floater. Click **OK**).

4. Create a new image (**File: New**) with a paper color of black (click on the **Paper Color rectangle** in the New Picture dialog box, choose **black**, click **OK**) and a pixel dimension of **468** wide by whatever height, say **350** pixels. This new image is the surface where you will arrange your image maps (floaters).

5. Click and drag floaters out of the Floaters palette and arrange them in the image. You can now set and place type (use the **A** in the Tools palette) as headers, labels, or descriptive copy. With text and images in place, create a button bar for navigational control. Dennis painted his buttons. He selected an area with the rectangle in the middle of the Tools palette and painted a highlight bezel inside to represent the top and 2 sides of a raised button that's being edge-lit (see Figure 30.2).

    A shortcut would be to create a shape with the rectangle in the top-right corner of the Tools palette, choose **Effects: Surface Control: Apply Surface Texture**, choose **Mask** in the Using menu, and move up the Softness and Brightness sliders. Click **OK**. You now have a three-dimensional button. Click **Objects: F. List: Trim** to reduce the box surrounding the floater.

Figure 30.2 Dennis Orlando painted the buttons on his Web site by hand.

Then, copy and paste the button (**Edit: Copy**, **Edit: Paste: Normal**) or click and drag out copies (hold **Option**, Mac; **Alt**, Windows, click and drag with left-pointing hand) for however many links you need. Text is created (choose the **A** in the Tools palette, type the word, click **Objects: F. List: Group** then **Objects: F. List: Collapse**. For a three-dimensional effect, choose **Effects: Surface Control: Apply Surface Texture**, choose **Mask** in the Using menu and move up the Softness slider as earlier. Click **OK**.) "Since text control within HTML documents is pretty poor and font selection and color variation are limited, to say the least," says Dennis, "Painter is a great tool for creating special type treatments and placing type saved as JPEG or GIF files as image elements to dress up a page."

With the left-pointing hand, click and drag the floaters into position over each of the buttons.

6. Using the site map and page outline created in the planning phase as a guide, you're now ready to create clickable image links. Click on a rectangular floater button. Click **Objects: F. List: Trim** to trim each floater's border if you haven't already done so. Press **Return**, Mac; **Enter**, Windows. In the dialog box that appears, name the button "something clear and descriptive," Dennis recommends, then click next to **WWW** to select it. In the URL text input window type either an absolute or a relative URL address (ask your Web Server Administrator which type is required). This information (*path*) is included in the map file and will be used by the Web server to point the viewer's browser to the correct HTML file (page) that this button link represents. Click **OK**. Save this image in the RIFF format to keep the floaters floating and the Web information available. Follow the above steps to make the other floaters clickable links. Anything can be made clickable (see Figure 30.3).

If something isn't already a floater, select it with the lasso, click on it with the left-pointing hand and you have a clickable button. You may also want to create the floaters in a separate image to avoid deleting the background when you float the selection.

7. Repeat the process to create as many image maps and button bars as required for each page of your site. "It gets easier as you copy and paste your base button art or a collection of buttons onto multiple pages for a consistent navigational tool bar," Dennis adds.

Last is the production phase, where you save files in *Web-readable formats*, i.e., those viewable by Web browsers such as AOL, Netscape, and Mosaic. The two most commonly used file formats are JPEG and GIF, with GIF being the most commonly supported, according to Dennis. "Make sure when naming your files to include the file format it's saved in with its name, for example: **portrait.JPG** or **portrait.GIF**," Dennis notes. He adds that both JPEG and GIF formats have advantages and disadvantages involving file-compression sizes and bit-depth issues. The JPEG format, which Dennis decided to use, saves the image as 24-bit, 16 million colors and allows for four levels of file size compression. The GIF file has options associated with it such as interlacing, transparent backgrounds, and user-selectable bit depths up to 256 colors for a maximum of 8-bit color depth. Most Web surfers are using 14,400-baud modems and viewing pages on 14- to 15-inch monitors with bit depth of 256 colors, Dennis says. "My file format selection was based solely on how I wanted the end quality of the subject matter to look," Dennis notes. "Your decision might be based on loading speed and a test comparison of file sizes and image quality. I could have chosen 8-bit GIF or even lower bit-depth GIFs but didn't. Not all the visitors to my site will have the necessary monitor video or browser capabilities to see my work at 24 bits, but those who do can appreciate the work at that level. If I was creating a loose cartoon style site and my image quality could take advantage of the lower bit depths without suffering, I would use 8-bit or less GIF files. This would save some time for the viewer when files are loading because the files size can be much smaller."

Figure 30.3 Dennis' paintings are clickable buttons.

When saving RIFF files as either JPEG or GIF, Painter lets you save the map file. You only need to save the map file for images that have more than one clickable region. If you click on the **WWW** box, you need to tell Painter which format you want the map file saved in, **NCSA** or **CERN**. The map file is a very simple text file that includes the name assigned to each floater, the shape of the clickable region, the top-left and bottom-right pixel coordinates, and the assigned URL for that clickable region. The map file will be saved as a separate file and needs to be transferred to the Web server along with the image map artwork file. Without the map file, the image map will not work.

After selecting a file format to save your images in, Dennis recommends setting up a directory of folders for RIFF files and separate JPEG or GIF folders for the converted files and a map file folder. "It doesn't take long for all of these images and files to overwhelm your hard drive," Dennis says. Dennis suggests that you keep a log with all of the file names, image descriptions, dimensions in pixels, and associated HTML files.

He also notes that HTML files are "very particular and require exact file names to find your images. If someone else is building the HTML pages for you, this is about all you need to know. If you are responsible for the entire process, I suggest that you do a lot of browsing and viewing of source code before creating your pages. Also, it's a good idea to discuss ftp paths, server directories, and file transfer issues with the Web server administrator or ISP Webmaster before building your site."

CREATING A CORPORATE WEB SITE

Graham Hedrick is the senior designer at Iterated Systems Inc., which makes still image compression and store-and-forward video-compression tools using fractal image compression. You can see Iterated's Web site at http://www.iterated.com. Here's how Graham created Iterated's Web page (see Figure 30.4).

Figure 30.4 Iterated's home page. All images are ©1996 Iterated Systems, Inc., 3525 Piedmont Road, Seven Piedmont Center, Suite 600, Atlanta, GA 30305-1530 U.S.A. All rights reserved.

First, a design was accepted by marketing (see Figure 30.5).

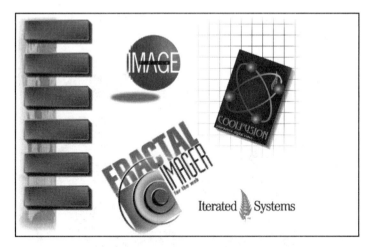

Figure 30.5 The first design.

It was decided that the entire site should have the look and feel of pages in a book (see Figure 30.6).

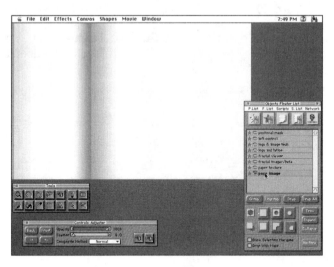

Figure 30.6 The book idea.

An outside consulting firm developed the graphic that would be used as the background for all pages.

To Graham, the page graphic seemed "flat and lacking character." Graham opened the original background image (created in Adobe Illustrator) in Painter using **File: Acquire** : desired file.

Graham wanted the pages to have "a paper page look and feel, so I applied a texture" (see Figure 30.7).

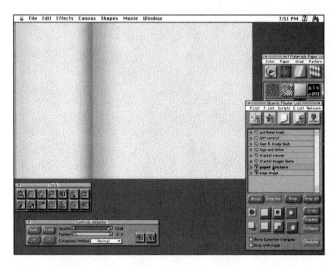

Figure 30.7 Page after paper texture was applied.

Select **Effects: Surface Control : Apply Surface Texture**. The Apply Surface Texture dialog box appears. "This dialog box is indicative of the deep control that painter provides the artist," Graham notes.

Here are the settings that Graham used to add texture to his Web page:

Paper texture:	**Basic Paper**
Using menu:	**Paper Grain**
Softness:	**0.0**
Amount:	**18%**
Picture:	**100%**
Shine:	**40%**
Reflection:	**0%**
Brightness:	**1.15**
Conc:	**4**
Exposure:	**1.41**

Click **OK.**

The background now has an organic, inviting feel to it," Graham says.

Next, "I knew that the final page would be comprised of a table," Graham says. "Consequently, I had to develop a boundary grid to indicate my safe working area" (see Figure 30.8).

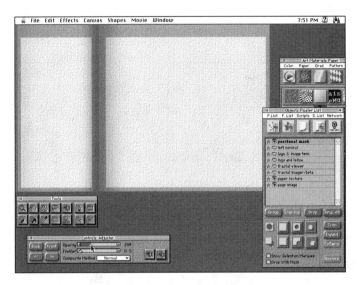

Figure 30.8 Border added to page.

Graham created the border in Illustrator and brought it into Painter using **File: Acquire**: the border file. The border appeared as a floater, which he dragged into place using the left-pointing hand. He also adjusted the opacity. To do so, either move the Controls: Opacity slider or press the keyboard or keypad numbers, i.e., the 8 key is 80% opacity, 2 is 20% opacity, etc. To return the object to 100% opaque, type **0** (zero).

Next Graham brought in the buttons and text from the composite image (see Figure 30.9).

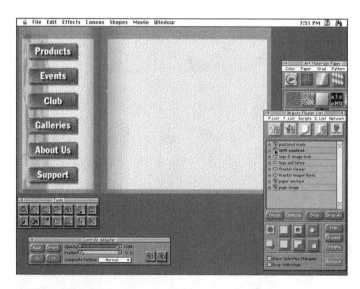

Figure 30.9 Text and buttons brought in.

Here's how Graham created the buttons:

1. In a separate document, make a selection with the rectangle in the middle of the Tools palette.

2. Choose a color or gradation and choose **Effects: Fill**. Click **OK**.

3. Choose **Effects : Surface Control: Apply Surface Texture**. The Apply Surface Texture dialog box appears. Graham used the hatching paper texture and the following settings in Apply Surface Texture:

Softness:	**0.0**
Amount:	**30%**
Picture:	**100%**
Reflection:	**0%**
Brightness:	**1.15**
Conc:	**4**
Exposure:	**1.41**

Click **OK**.

To make the selection into a floater, click on it with the left-pointing hand. To create more buttons, hold **Option**, Mac; **Alt**, Windows and click and drag on the floater to copy it. To create the drop shadow, choose **Effects: Objects: Create Drop Shadow** and click **OK**. The floater and its drop shadow are a group. Click **Objects: F. List: Collapse** to make the floater and its drop shadow into one floater.

Graham created the type as described earlier in this chapter using the **A** tool in the Tools palette and the **Group** and **Collapse** items.

The logo for ImageTech and the Iterated Systems Logo (and all other logos) were files originally created in Adobe Photoshop and brought into Painter and saved as floaters in the Objects: F. List: Floaters palette. Graham also creates floaters libraries, called *portfolios*, for various groups of floaters. Graham notes that he archives floaters and uses them over and over. "I have worked on projects where I needed an element from a previous project. I open the respective portfolio and drag out the needed floaters. The Iterated Systems home page made extensive use of floaters and multiple portfolios."

The ISI logo and the ImageTech logos were initially larger than they are in the finished piece, and Graham scaled them down using **Effects: Orientation: Scale**. After scaling the CoolFusion logo he rotated it using **Effects: Orientation: Rotate** (see Figure 30.10).

Figure 30.10 The CoolFusion logo rotated.

In the Fractal Imager logo, Graham wanted to make the phrase "Beta Version" stand out (see Figure 30.11).

Figure 30.11 Beta Version type stands out.

Graham used **Art Materials: Grad: Edit Gradation** to create a grad and filled B*eta Version* with **Effects: Fill**. He then clicked and dragged out two copies of B*eta Version* with the left-pointing hand while holding **Option**, Mac; **Alt**, Windows. He chose **white** in the Color palette and **Effects: Fill** to make one copy white. You can see the white halo at the top of the letters in Figure 30.11. He sent the copy to the back by clicking **Controls palette: Back**. He nudged the copy into place by pressing the keyboard's arrow keys. Then he filled the other floater copy with black for the shadow, sent it to the back, and nudged it down.

SUMMARY

The Internet and the Web are two of the hottest topics of conversation these days. And Painter is at the forefront of this technology, as you have seen in this chapter. All of Painter's tools and features lend themselves to web graphics and image maps, so don't be afraid to experiment.

That wraps up *Fractal Design Painter 4 Complete*. You have seen examples of how artists use Painter 4 to create and edit everything from fine art and cartoons to photographs to Web graphics. I hope you enjoyed finding out about Painter 4, and that you will use the techniques in this book to propel your own extraordinary Painter artwork.

Index